THE PARENT/CHILD GAME

THE PARENT/CHILD GAME

The Proven Key to a Happier Family

Sue Jenner

BLOOMSBURY

Published by Bloomsbury Publishing, New York and London.
Distributed to the trade by St. Martin's Press

A CIP catalogue record of this book
is available from the Library of Congress

ISBN 1-58234-091-9

Published in Great Britain 1999 Bloomsbury Publishing Plc.

First published in the U.S. by
Bloomsbury Publishing in 1999

This paperback edition published 2000

10 9 8 7 6 5 4 3 2 1

Typeset in Great Britain by Palimpsest Book Production Limited
Polmont, Stirlingshire

Printed in the United States of America by
R.R. Donnelley & Sons Company, Harrisonburg, Virginia

I should like to dedicate this book to all those with whom I worked for so many years in the Children's Department of the Maudsley Hospital, London, especially Bill Yule, Stephen Wolkind, Martin Gent, Pia Guidicelli and Stephen Scott. Their support for The Parent/Child Game made my work a positive pleasure. I particularly want to mention Rosemary Hemsley, a colleague who worked tirelessly with children and their families until her death from cancer. She is remembered with much admiration and fondness.

CONTENTS

Acknowledgements

The people who deserve first mention are the children and parents of all the families who were brave enough to trust me, and the Parent/Child Game, with their problems. I know that many felt initially apprehensive, though I am glad to say this did not prevent us from working cooperatively together towards their goal of a happier family life. My heartfelt thanks to every one of you.

I also want to acknowledge the enormously important contribution made to the thorough research and clinical basis of the Parent/Child Game by Professors Rex Forehand, Robert McMahon and Nicholas Long. Without their excellent work I would have been unable to help families in trouble, or indeed to write this book, using the Parent/Child Game.

My deepest gratitude goes to my darling children, step-children and grandchildren, for providing the most joyful experiences of my entire life. They also set me some pretty challenging parenting tasks too! I also want to thank my sister and brother, Liz and Jon, for their part in my journey through the various stages of our family's life.

And I would like to say how, without the infinite patience and talents of my cousin and personal assistant Ursula and our friend June, this book would quite simply not have seen the light of day.

Final thanks to Gil McNeil and Alan Wherry, for their inspirational enthusiasm about the Parent/Child Game; and to my partner Geoff for the innumerable cups of tea, tasty snacks and reassurances which he so generously provided throughout my attempt to bring this book to fruition.

Introduction

A Game in Which Everyone Wins

If you are a parent, this book is for you. For the first time, society is now acknowledging that we are not necessarily designed to cope efficiently with the challenges of being a parent and raising children. Alongside the revolutionary notion that parenting is not something you 'just know how to do', goes the idea that it might involve skills that can be learnt. Recognition that competent – which does not have to mean 'perfect' – parenting consists of a variety of key abilities allows a lot of important questions to be raised, for instance:

- 'Just exactly what are the special things parents have to do in order to have children who aren't destined to be "the Brat from Hell"?'

- 'There must be a secret to it all that I don't know! What is it?'

- 'Why can't I get it right even though I love them to bits and try my best?'

When no clear answer materializes, such questions can be followed all too swiftly by feelings of uselessness, overwhelming failure and hopelessness about the future of your parenting efforts.

FROM BIRTH TO THE END
OF ADOLESCENCE

Throughout this book I shall, when using the word 'child' be referring to the whole gamut of development from birth to the end of
adolescence.

Parents' responsibility for their children's behaviour is coming
increasingly under the microscope in many countries. The
British government has considered making parents pay a fine if
their children misbehave at school. In the USA the situation
varies from state to state, while in Australia and New Zealand
the situation is much as it is in the UK. Social attitudes in France
ensure that children's behaviour is clearly acknowledged as the
parents' responsibility. In the Caribbean, many men father
children by several women without settling into a parental role,
and as a result it is the mothers who are regarded as being
responsible. In parts of India, too, though the government
provides money, mothers in particular are seen to be responsible for a child's behaviour via special women's committees.

These attempts to make parents directly responsible for anti-
social behaviour on their children's part have been partially
fuelled by certain tragic events involving the murder of
children by other children. In Britain, the death of two-and-a-
half-year-old Jamie Bulger in 1992 at the hands of two older
boys proved a very bitter pill for the public to swallow. Surely,
the majority of parents exclaimed, the boys who led Jamie away
to his death must have been abnormal, perverted, sick or
corrupt.

There have been similar reactions to murders by children in
other countries: for instance in 1996 in the USA, when a
thirteen-year-old killed several of his classmates. The Caribbean
countries are reporting an increase in these shocking events. In
New Zealand, on the other hand, murders perpetrated by
children are said to be extremely rare – though there have been
four since 1970. In France it is mainly adolescents who commit
such crimes against each other. In southern India, though
children murdering others of their own age appears to be

almost unknown, they can be involved in family crimes.

So do children who commit such heinous crimes come from pathologically wicked families? No. Sadly, children who kill their peers often come from a certain kind of home which is all too common in countries around the world. I mean the kind of home where parents have little or no idea of how to raise their children to be responsible, considerate, self-confident members of society.

It is now widely accepted, across many societies, cultures, ethnic groups, religions and belief systems, that for the huge numbers of children who experience disordered conduct and emotional problems, this stage is only the beginning. Unless interrupted, the process which might start with biting, kicking and mega-tantrums at three years can in ten lead to delinquency. In twenty years another fully fledged sociopath is likely to be intimidating their partner, ruining their children's chance of happiness and adding to the worryingly high statistics in violent crime, drug and alcohol addiction, child sex crimes and child protection cases.

Perhaps the most pressing matter to consider is just how to stop this cycle from repeating itself. Until more children receive the sort of parenting that will actively encourage them to develop as assertive, sensitive, humorous and constructive members of society, the vital progress will not occur.

In Britain, information put before the 1997 Parliamentary Select Committee on Child and Adolescent Mental Health clearly shows that unless powerful parent training techniques are employed on a wide scale, the cycle will not be broken. Research and clinical practice in Britain and the rest of Europe, in the USA, Australia and New Zealand had already identified and satisfactorily tested out a specific approach. It is known as the Parent/Child Game, and its principles can be applied to every single reciprocal interaction between an adult and a child.

The traditional approach to helping troubled children was for therapist and child to spend an hour closeted together, at least once a week, often more. The parents would be given no feedback at all about the content of these sessions, which could carry on for one, two, three or more years. The Parent/Child Game is a particularly successful version of a much more modern approach where the therapist, parents and children all work together. A big measure of the Parent/Child Game's effectiveness is due to its innovative use of new technology in linking the parent and therapist by earbug and microphone, while the children interact directly with their mother and father while playing a game of their own choice. This is the 'official' form of the Parent/Child Game; but its basic ideas can be used by parents every day in the normal home environment to create a more harmonious family life for everyone.

THE FOUNDATIONS OF THE PARENT/CHILD GAME

The Parent/Child Game is solidly based in psychological theories that have stood the test of time:

● **Social Learning Theory** is all about how our behaviour and attitudes are influenced by the type of consequences we experience after having said or done something in particular – mostly praise, punishment or being ignored.

● **Child Development Theory** covers the different stages of growing up, and the sequence in which they usually appear. It is also about comparing an individual child's development with the very broad range of what would normally be expected of most children of a certain age.

● **Theories about relationships (also known as attachments)** centre on the fact that each person's uniqueness includes the way they think about themselves, others, the world and their future; also their emotional range and the way in which they behave socially. In other words, their relationship style.

The aim of this book, therefore, is to let you know the ideas behind the Parent/Child Game and the results of adopting it, so that you can reap the benefits of being a balanced, authoritative (not authoritarian) parent. Simultaneously, as a direct result of their parents taking on board the Parent/Child Game and putting its principles into action daily, your children will

THE PARENT/CHILD GAME:
THIRTY YEARS OF SUCCESS

● **USA 1965:** Professor Rex Forehand and Professor Robert McMahon were taught the technique by child psychologist Connie Kauf, who developed it while working with troubled children and their parents.

● **USA 1968:** Forehand and McMahon started research on the effectiveness of the Parent/Child Game. Their study group consisted of a hundred families with three- to eight-year-olds who showed difficult behaviour, which they compared with forty families who had no such problems.

● **USA and UK 1981:** The results were published in a book called *Helping the Non-Compliant Child*. The Parent/Child Game had shown that the parents in the study would, after treatment, manage their child's behaviour more successfully (without smacking), establish a warmer and more satisfying way of interacting as a family, and see their children in a much more positive light. The troubled children's behaviour improved. Parents were less depressed as individuals and more in tune as a couple.

● **USA and UK 1982:** The Parent/Child Game was increasingly adopted by professionals working with distressed families in the USA. I reviewed Forehand and McMahon's book, and started using the Parent/Child Game at the Maudsley Hospital in London.

● **UK 1996 USA and UK 1996:** Professor Rex Forehand and Professor Nick Long publish an update on the Parent/Child Game called *Parenting the Stong-Willed Child*.

● **UK 1997:** Government endorsement.

● **USA and UK at the millennium:** The Parent/Child Game has continued to be successfully used in helping thousands of families to live fuller and more enjoyable lives. So relax! This is no passing fad but a soundly based method with an excellent track record.

discover that pleasing their mother and father, by doing as they are told more often than not, is much more fun than being disobedient. This book carries a message of hope for all parents and children, regardless of culture, race or creed. This is at least partly because it subscribes to the optimistic and well-grounded assumption that it is never too late to change for both adults and children.

Are you still dubious about whether the Parent/Child Game is so widely applicable? For many years I worked in a large London teaching hospital, where I saw it all. Let me give you an idea of the huge diversity of families, across a wide range of cultures, religions and ethnic groups, whose quality of life and relationships were improved when we played the Parent/Child Game with them:

- Angelou, aged eight, and her mother, who were Baptists from Jamaica

- Four-year-old Reuben and his Jewish parents

- Michael, aged six, and his Nigerian father

- Five-year-old Hassan, his brother Nassim and their mother and father, from one of the Arab Emirate states. This Muslim family were originally from Pakistan, and included six little brothers and sisters

- An American father of Swedish descent and his two daughters aged nine and eleven

I have also worked with families from France, Germany, Belgium, Italy and Greece. Colleagues in Europe, the USA, Australia and New Zealand tell me that they too are using this powerful approach, with excellent results, with Dutch, Swedish, Mexican, Brazilian, Puerto Rican and Maori families.

To make the changes that can lead to showing mutual affection, love and trust within a family you need two major building blocks in place:

- The desire to progress

- Explicit information on how to do things differently and in a way that can promise positive 'results'

That is the kernel of this book: telling you what you need to do in order to achieve a balanced parenting style – a style which will truly benefit you and your children on a minute-to-minute basis as you grapple with the traumas and triumphs of daily family life.

The real secret is learning how to show your love for your child in a way that is meaningful to them. It is about being able to focus on giving your children the most precious gift of all: the firm knowledge that they are both loved and lovable.

I believe that nearly all parents love their children, or at least long to. The missing piece in many family jigsaws is not the love itself but any inkling of how it might best be shown by the kind of attention given to the children by the grown-ups. Why are so many adults unaware of the style of attention which is most likely to succeed? Basically because many of them were not treated to balanced parenting when they were children themselves, and no one has since made the secret available.

This book will let you in on that secret, telling you, in a straightforward manner that blames no one, about balanced parenting. There are no villains in this book, simply you and your children, me and mine, all trying to survive family life as best we can. I shall be talking about different styles of interacting with your children, clarifying cause-and-effect relationships by using real-life examples. As I put my message across my aim is to be accessible, upbeat and, I hope, humorous.

It will also be in some respects a personal book, as I shall include relevant details of my own experiences as a daughter, young mother and not-so-young grandmother. Some of the emotions and relationships that have crossed the generations in my own family will also be described. So I shall not be putting myself forward as an 'expert' whose own life remains excluded from the debate. I too have made mistakes and continue so to do. I may have managed to avoid major pitfalls, but that is probably because it was my good fortune to have parents who were themselves sufficiently 'balanced' – parents who, despite being noticeably less than 'perfect', were none the less wonderful at showing me that I was much loved and lovable. Having taken an unconscionable number of decades to come to terms with my lack of infallibility, I now find it a positive relief to give up any pretence to perfection. As a mother and grandmother with admitted bootees of clay, I find life much more fun. My message is this: forgive yourself for failing to achieve parental nirvana, and reward yourself for hanging on in there trying to become a more balanced mother or father.

Nevertheless, I have worked for about twenty-five years with troubled children, parents and families, so I am quite a respectable professional. I urgently want to spread the good news on balanced parenting, preferably before I reach great-grandmother status. I know too that I shall still be trying to put the Parent/Child Game ideas into practice with my great-grandchildren when they arrive.

Why am I so keen on the Parent/Child Game approach? Because its principles and practice apply across the whole life-span of a family. Because it is about meeting the emotional and psychological needs of all human beings, including you and me. Because it is about you and your children having fun. Because it is about translating the language of love into action. Because it *works*. I am not promising 'Happy Families' but I do promise 'Happ*ier* Families' – if you do the work!

JARGON – BUT DON'T BE PUT OFF!

I am, as I have already admitted, an 'expert' in the business of helping behaviourally disturbed children and their parents. As in most professions, we use a number of terms that will be unfamiliar to everyone else. In this book I have tried to avoid them where possible; but occasionally it is simpler to use the 'jargon' term, particularly for ideas and techniques that I refer to again and again. I shall explain these terms as I come to them – don't be put off, but think of them as a quick shorthand for referring to something that is (usually) aimed at making your life, and that of your children, a whole lot happier.

HOW TO USE THIS BOOK

The content of the book you will find, I hope, sensible, sensitive and reassuring. A combination of sense and sensitivity are the acme of psychological balance. The reassurance partly lies in the statement that you, as a mother or father, only need to deliver to your children the very best kind of attention for half the time. This is a research-based finding and not just the product of my fevered mind. The idea that '50 per cent will do nicely' has not, I think, been widely publicized previously. Importantly, it has not yet been made available to fathers and mothers in the front line of bickering breakfasts, loud lunches, terrible tea-times and desperate dinners!

Chapter 1 lays down some basic concepts and is the foundation for the rest of the book. Its structure is therefore slightly different from that of the other chapters, which are all divided in this way:

● **What this chapter is about,** which is a very short section that does just what it says and will enable you to select the chapter you need in a hurry! The key words for that chapter are typeset in bold.

● **An introductory section,** which includes an explanation of those key words.

● **Giving and receiving,** which focuses on the reciprocal aspects of each chapter's main theme. In highlighting what each person brings to and receives from a particular type of interaction I want to draw your attention to the reciprocity, the give and take, of all family relationships. Parenting is not something that parents 'do' to their children. It is the sum of the innumerable very complex, subtle and ever-changing interactions within a family.

● **Echoes,** in which I draw on the experiences of my own family, past and present generations. More of this kind of material is included from time to time throughout the book – wherever I think you might find it useful. And of course I have drawn on my long experience with parents and children to tell the stories of real-life cases which show how other families have successfully overcome their problems.

I hope the Echoes section will offer support, too, by showing that I am a human individual and not just a faceless 'expert'. It is rare for a clinical psychologist to open up in this way – it is normally regarded as 'professionally inappropriate'. My own view is that, by letting you know of the successes and sorrows in my own family, I will make contact with you in a much more individual sense than is normally achieved by books written by experts.

● **Setting the scene for change,** in which I shall explain some of the basic tenets of those rather formidable-sounding terms Child Development Theory and Social Learning Theory, and show you just how they fit in to handling difficult behaviour.

In my work I have often found that the most productive change occurs when the motto is: 'The best places to start are where we are now and where we would like to be.' So I shall deliberately stay away from a 'problem' focus, and concentrate instead on how to achieve progress. Homing in on difficulties means that too many books by professionals become scourges with which parents beat themselves.

● **What to do next,** which moves from principles to practicalities. There will be specific ideas for actions which will help you become the kind of parent you want to be. A lot of the ideas will be about doing things differently, though of course when you change what you do it inevitably has a powerful effect on how you feel and think about things as well.

In saying straight out what you should be doing, I am departing from the professionals' frequent reluctance to be assertive and forthright. Many of them will only 'suggest' that something 'might' work for you if you 'think it is a good idea'. But I truly believe it's time that someone stood up to be counted and told parents what to do about making positive changes in their families. I intend to be much more pushy, break with tradition, and provide specific phrases, actions, ideas and attitudes which are known to improve family relationships.

● **A quick fix,** which closes each chapter, is an at-a-glance reminder of the important messages put across in each chapter, with real-life examples and brief details of how research supports these findings.

My aim, then, is to give you firm and clear answers to that often heard cry of mothers and fathers as they struggle to cope with the latest mélange of chickenpox, chicken nuggets and the Easter chicken collage crisis: 'What shall I *do*?' I am here to tell you, no holds barred, because it is high time mothers and fathers were let in on the secrets of the language of love which can make family life so rich in rewards on even the dreariest of days.

Assertive I may be, even bossy, but far from domineering – so I *invite* you now to read on and discover for yourself how to be part of a much happier family.

1. Spare the Praise and Spoil the Child

Balanced Parenting

WHAT THIS CHAPTER IS ABOUT

The first chapter explains the basic concepts and sets up the stall
for further chapters which elaborate on these ideas. It puts the
emphasis on why you should be praising your children's sociable
behaviour, ignoring their many irritating behaviours and punishing only dangerous behaviours. You will learn, in other words,
about what is called being **Child Centred** versus **Child Directive**
when interacting with your children.

Balanced or authoritative parenting is the aim, and that entails
getting the right ratio between Child Centred and Child Directive
inputs to your child. It is all too easy to impede rather than facilitate your children's development if you don't know about this
particular secret of successful parenting.

You will also read about a concept called the Attention Rule,
and learn that you can be a good enough parent by getting the
Attention Rule right for just half the time. There is no need to
strive for an unreachable 100 per cent. A 'perfect' mother or father,
were any ever to materialize, would in all likelihood be harmful to
any child.

A Child Centred parent is good news for everyone in the family,
including yourself. Yet it is still often too difficult to put our
knowledge into practice more than occasionally. Some reasons
why this may be so will be described in Chapter 2.

CHILD CENTRED VERSUS CHILD DIRECTIVE

Some parents seem to have an enviable knack for dealing with their own children, and perhaps yours too! This knack can appear to be an impenetrable 'secret of success' unavailable to those outside the magic circle of mothers and fathers who 'get it right'. It is doubly irritating when, on asking the successful parent exactly what is their secret, they shrug and simply say: 'Oh, you know! I've always got on well with children. The house was packed with kids when I was little. Other children loved our Mum and Dad. I suppose it's in the family.' You then look around to find Sod's Law in action yet again. You see your own son or daughter in full flood being a terrible two-, frustrating three- or frightening four-year-old. Despair descends. It can still be a very difficult job to deal with your terrible ten-, frustrating thirteen- or frightening fifteen-year-old.

How can it be going so badly, this business of bringing up children, when you love them so much, give them lots of 'quality time' and have their welfare as your top priority? What do the successful parents know that you don't? Perhaps they have read the right books? You have read those same books. Perhaps they went to parenthood classes? You attended identical sessions. Perhaps they had a great childhood? You didn't, not really. Why do the grandparents in their family seem so affectionate towards and approving of their grandchildren? Yours aren't, not really, even though you wish they were. So, what is going on?

It is likely that those mothers and fathers who are the object of envy, are balanced parents. The secret of their success is the fact that they are fully aware that the time-worn phrase used in old-fashioned parenting should be stood on its head, and that when you spare the praise you spoil the child.

● **Child Centred behaviours** are the ones which meet a child's emotional needs, or actually give them something positive.

● **Child Directive behaviours** demand a response from the child, or impose a restriction on their behaviour.

Praising a child is an example of a Child Centred behaviour. But

Child Directive behaviours are not all undesirable – some are a necessary part of responsible parenting. The knack of interacting with children in a way that will result in their cooperative friendliness lies in the relative numbers of Child Centred and Child Directive inputs with which their parents provide them.

It is just this information that the majority of parents have not yet been told, even though these ideas were first researched in America as far back as the early 1970s. Until 1981, when I reviewed Forehand and McMahon's book (see p. 5), I myself, a so-called expert, had little inkling of their important work. It changed my life, both professional and personal. I was so impressed by its good sense, thorough research and novel ideas that I immediately began to use its principles both at work and at home.

My own three children were at that time, twenty, eighteen and fourteen. Perhaps, I thought, too old to respond. I was wrong. Apparently 'Child Centred' can just as easily read 'Adolescent Centred' or 'Young Adult Centred'. I tried the special balance of attention on grown-ups too, with encouraging results.

Now that this chapter's key words have been introduced, let's look at them in more detail.

CHILD CENTRED BEHAVIOURS

Attends

● Describing out loud to your child, with warmth and enthusiasm, what they are doing (so long as you approve, of course)
  ○ 'Oh! You've made a *really* tasty sandwich!'
  ○ 'You've chosen the red paints to do that *lovely* apple!'

● Commenting positively on how your child looks
  ○ 'You look *great* in that tee-shirt!'
  ○ 'Your hair looks really cool with that gel on!'

● Noticing out loud, in a positive way, your child's mood
  ○ 'You're concentrating *so* hard.'
  ○ 'You seem to have lots of energy today.'

Praises

● Clearly expressing your approval and delight towards your child
  ○ 'You're so clever!'
  ○ 'You're such fun to be with!'

● Reacting to your child's behaviour, play and conversation warmly and enthusiastically
  ○ 'Well done! That's a marvellous effort!'
  ○ 'Fabulous! What a great joke!'

Smiles

● Making eye contact with your child and smiling right into their eyes in a loving and friendly way
  ○ Giving a warm, spontaneous smile *to* your child.
  ○ Laughing or giggling *with* your child.

Imitation

● Copying your child's actions or words so that they can tell you are interested in them
  ○ 'OK, so you'd like honey on your cereal, not sugar.'
  ○ 'You're going to build a bridge,' when they say, 'I'm going to make a bridge.'

● Imitating, with genuine enthusiasm, any noises your child might make when playing
  ○ 'Vroom, vroom,' when playing cars.
  ○ 'Maaa, maaa,' when playing farms.

Ask to Play

● Asking your child what they would like you to play with them
  ○ 'What game would you like me to play with you now?'
  ○ 'You can choose what to play and then tell me what I should do.'

● Asking your child what they would like you to do
  ○ 'What would you like me to do next?'
  ○ 'Tell me what you want me to do right now.'

● Allowing your child to tell you that they would like you to sit and watch them, and complying with their wishes

● Encouraging your child to lead the activities or game

Ignore Minor Naughtiness

● Turn your head away, look bored and keep silent
  ○ Noticeably ignore your child when they are doing something that's naughty in a minor and non-dangerous way.
  ○ Make no comment but look away, half-turning your shoulder or body from them, only returning your attention when your child's behaviour is once more acceptable.

Positive Touches

● Give your child a warm, affectionate hug, kiss, pat or stroke
  ○ These must be touches which the child welcomes and enjoys.
  ○ Those hugs, kisses, squeezes and strokes which you give your child should always be appropriate to their stage of development (see p. 25)

What does being Child Centred mean?

Of the Child Centred parental behaviours listed here, I suspect you will find only two of them unfamiliar concepts: Attends and Ask to Play. Yet it is very unlikely that you haven't used both before, though in different contexts.

Attends

When your children were babies, did you ever smile right into their eyes and say things like: 'Look at you! You look beautiful in your little suit. And you're kicking your lovely strong legs and blowing bubbles all at the same time.' What seems to happen, however, is that, as babies become vocal toddlers able to talk back, we stop using this very powerful kind of attention. It is powerful because of the message such Attends give to the recipient. In using an Attend, you not only unambiguously tell your child that you have noticed in detail what they are up to, but you clearly demonstrate your approval too. Did you notice how they wriggled and gooed back at you? Roughly translated, their delighted response meant, 'That felt great. Do some more, now!'

Yet you find yourself perhaps feeling even better when you ask your toddler a question and they give a verbal reply. The reason for this switch may well be that, when busy developing their use of language as speech, young children actually need those around them to focus on this mode of expression.

The interesting thing is that even when children are clearly capable of sophisticated sentence construction their parents do not revive the Attends previously so much enjoyed by both participants. The most likely adult response to such linguistic feats as: 'I haven't seen my Barbie wedding carriage recently. Do you know where it is?' will be something like, 'No, I haven't seen it either. Why don't you play with Animal Doctor Barbie instead? I can see her from here.' An enthusiastic Attend, on the other hand, would be more like, 'You're looking for the Barbie wedding carriage because you want to play with it!'

Ask to Play
The other infrequently used Child Centred behaviour is Ask to Play. You say to your child, 'What would you like me to do now?' If the very thought sends shivers of apprehension down your spine, you will know why such phrases remain a rarity in an adult's vocabulary. Mothers and fathers are so fearful of the extortionist requests or rejecting statements their child may make that they avoid ever putting the power so blatantly into their offspring's hands. After all, lots of children need no invitation to come up with commands such as: 'Go away! You're messing up my game'; or indeed, 'Be a wolf/fairy/car, now. I want you to be a prince/lady lion/flying fish too!' Then there is the killer remark that every parent dreads: 'Go away! I don't love you 'cos you're horrid/mean/nasty.' No wonder we shun giving them what seems like *carte blanche* to misuse or abuse us.

Yet the fact is that when a mother or father sufficiently braces themselves to chance their child's potentially importunate reply, it is unlikely to be either totally impossible or dismissive. Take the risk of asking your child in an interested and genuine tone, 'What would you like me to do now?', and the response will most probably be of the order of 'You sort out all the blue pieces while I make the dragon's breakfast', or even, 'Watch me!' These are not tasks that are beyond most parents. Children accede quite graciously to the opportunity to state their immediate plans for you, especially when accompanied by lots of Attends, Praise and Smiles, all guaranteed to keep the child concentrating and persevering well with the job already in hand. Try it, and marvel at how well you and they survive!

Ignoring Minor Naughtiness

The last word, for the moment, on Child Centred behaviours must be with Ignoring Minor Naughtiness. I am intentionally using the word 'naughty'. Many professionals prefer labels such as 'unacceptable behaviours', anti-social behaviours' or 'undesirable behaviours', regarding them as less judgemental. I find that the parents and children who are the object of these endeavours are much more at home with the word 'naughty'. Its use can, of course, be criticized on the grounds that it is far too fuzzy a word to describe what in reality turns out to be a multiplicity of childhood errors, misdemeanours and perhaps even intentional mistakes. What I think is more important than the label itself is that the mother and father agree on the specific items to go on the list of minor naughties.

Clearly this is one area where single parents have the advantage: they don't have a partner with whom they have to carry out the lengthy negotiations often necessary before such an inventory can be compiled. It has been known to take weeks of hard bargaining before a final compromise can be reached! There will be more on why this should be so in Chapter 2.

The sorts of behaviours which many parents would label as a minor naughtiness are the kind that are all too often terribly annoying and yet not perceptibly dangerous. Under this heading would come such irritating activities as:

- rhythmically kicking chair or table legs

- fiddling with TV and video buttons and remote control gismos

- chewing voraciously with an open mouth

- refusing to wear hats or gloves

- nose-picking

- missing out the first syllable of a word, as in 'puter' for computer

- having a temper tantrum at the check-out in a super-store

- screaming when a third consecutive viewing of the flavour-of-the-week video is refused

- posting all their toys out of the catflap

- posting the contents of the laundry basket out of the catflap

- posting, or attempting to post, themselves out of the catflap

You name it, they do it – repeatedly. 'But why?' goes up the anguished adult's cry. The reason is that parents provide their children with masses of attention for 'being naughty'. It is so very difficult to pretend to be deaf to the child's yell for 'More, more, more' of whatever it is you wish to deny them. It is almost impossible to stay silent under the barrage of truly atrocious table manners when the meal is a special occasion. It is apparently outside a mother and father's capability to avert their eyes as their offspring energetically thrashes around on the floor of the dry cleaners. It is beyond your strength to preserve a neutral facial expression when the baby spits sieved carrots at you. In other words, giving the advice, 'Just ignore them' is infinitely more easily said than done. Yet it is readily within every parent's grasp when you learn exactly what you have to do.

Seven steps to dealing with minor naughtiness
1. Act as if you are deaf.
2. Remain absolutely silent apart from pre-planned phrases such as: 'When you are quiet/friendly/sitting still, I will take notice of you again.'
3. Unlock your gaze from theirs and stare into the middle distance.
4. Assume a neutral facial expression even if you are actually seething inside.

5. Any words you do say must be uttered in a calm, steady voice.
6. Ensure that while ignoring your child you have as little physical contact with them as possible.
7. This is the hardest one of all. Keep your stated promise to your child that you will *not* return your attention to them until they have quietened down, started to be cooperative or are physically calm.

For children under about eight years, one minute of good-quality ignoring often does the trick. It may take from five to ten minutes for older children, though you should make sure it doesn't go on any longer than that without restating your promise to the child. (It could be children if you are having the parental equivalent of a Bad Hair Day!)

Praise good behaviour
There are two other particularly important aspects to properly ignoring a minor naughtiness. One is that the moment your child starts to behave well, or at least acceptably, you must praise them for their good behaviour. But you need to be specific in your comments. For instance, had they been throwing toys around with great abandon, immediately they stop you must label their progress, not their crime. Say, 'You're leaving the toys alone now, Jack. I love being with you when you look after your toys. Well done! I think you're a very clever boy.' Avoid, as often as is humanly possible, the temptation to comment, 'About time! Who do you think is going to pick all that mess up? Not me! You'd better get it done right now before I lock them all away so you won't have any toys to chuck about and break up!'

The second aspect is to accept that for the first few days when you completely ignore your offspring's small atrocities, they will up the ante by doing whatever it is much more frequently. This is called the Extinction Burst. Don't be put off if it happens – it means you're on the way to success.

So, just when you might think ignoring an annoying habit of your child's isn't working, it really is. You just have to stick it out solidly, maybe for a week, often less. They get an unmiss-able message: 'It's not worth blowing through my straw when I've got a glass full of milk because no one is taking any notice!'

This insight on the child's part is accompanied by an associated realization, particularly welcomed by parents. It goes like this: 'I might as well stop squealing/shouting/mumbling because the only time Mum and Dad take notice is when I talk in an ordinary friendly voice!'

In other words, at this point in the procedure parent power is in the ascendant, which is exactly where children need it to be. When children push limits, their message to the grown-ups in their life is: 'Somebody stop me, please!' The sooner you nip things in the bud, the safer your child will feel, and the more they will show you how much fun it can be to spend time with them. The relationship will be improving and not spiralling down into hurtful coercion and mutual antipathy. This can happen when you let naughty behaviour go by without overt comment, until the moment when you finally snap and what could have been a brief tiff turns into a major rout.

What if you go on ignoring your errant offspring and it still isn't working? It will be because you are not getting the Attention Rule (see below) the right way round often enough. In other words, you have without realizing it been giving your child attention, and from the child's perspective criticism of minor naughty behaviour provides as much attention as does praise. Simultaneously you have been failing to provide sufficient praise, Attends, smiles and hugs for sociable behaviour. In effect your child is being taught by you, their mother or father, to be naughty in order to grab your attention.

Gaining parental attention of any emotional colour is the raison d'être of all children. It is without challenge in your child's hierarchy of 'must haves'. If you don't show them that you have noticed they are eating their cereal as opposed to splattering it across the breakfast table, they will simply come up with whatever it takes to rouse your observable interest, juice spilling, toast mashing, chair rocking, loud spoon banging. It is all well within their repertoire, and they will employ these tactics if you allow their industrious consumption of breakfast fare to go unrewarded. They cannot read your mind. Children need those VIPs, their mother and father, to speak out loud their positive thoughts.

The Attention Rule is quite easy to state, but, like properly ignoring minor naughtiness, difficult to put into practice. There will be lots more details about when, where and how to use it later in the book, more detail about different types of punishment in Chapter 3. Let's now look at the principles it embodies and the various results you can expect when you use it.

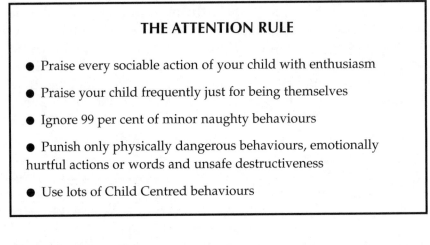

THE ATTENTION RULE

● Praise every sociable action of your child with enthusiasm

● Praise your child frequently just for being themselves

● Ignore 99 per cent of minor naughty behaviours

● Punish only physically dangerous behaviours, emotionally hurtful actions or words and unsafe destructiveness

● Use lots of Child Centred behaviours

Social Learning Theory

The principles underlying the Attention Rule are drawn from what the professionals call Social Learning Theory. Basically it states that the frequency with which we come up with particular behaviours is governed by the consequences we experience, both short- and longer-term. So, for instance, any child behaviour which is followed by adult attention, be it a smile or a shout, will be more likely to occur again in the future. That's because children find adult attention very rewarding indeed. Conversely, if when a child behaves in a certain way they have all adult attention clearly withdrawn, that particular behaviour is less likely to occur in future. But be warned for the first few days things will get much worse! This simultaneously means that your approach is working, and that your child is intent on pushing you to the limit because they desperately want the attention that they are used to following that specific behaviour.

The table on the right shows the various combinations of ways of handling bad behaviour and their effects. The more often you apply the principles of Social Learning Theory, the clearer you will become about how to increase or decrease the likelihood of a particular behaviour occurring again.

How parents' responses to naughtiness affect future behaviour

Child's attitude to parents' responses	
Liked	**Disliked**
Box 1: Positive Reward Give the child something they like immediately after a sociable behaviour Behaviour more likely	**Box 2: Punishment** Give the child something they don't like immediately after an anti-social behaviour Behaviour less likely
Box 3: Ignoring Take away your attention following an anti-social behaviour Behaviour less likely	**Box 4: Negative Reward** Take away a disliked consequence after an anti-social behaviour Behaviour more likely

Box 1

If you want your child to be less rude towards you, ignore the nastiness and bad language completely, and give them fulsome praise every time they say something sociable and friendly. That way you will be decreasing the future likelihood that they will swear at you whilst simultaneously ensuring that they are more likely to be reasonable and polite.

Box 2

Providing something which the child actively dislikes and/or finds really boring, like an instruction to clear up the pasta they have so creatively spread across the stairs, means that they will be less likely to commit this particular folly again. If you also praise them for leaving the box of spaghetti where it really belongs, the message is doubly underlined.

Box 3

Ignoring has already been introduced so I shall not comment

further at this point, though you can expect a return to this vital topic in future chapters!

Box 4

Here you can begin to see something of the complexities which face you and your children every day. An example might help to unravel the mysteries of negative 'rewards'. I myself took ages to grasp it, and that was just in theory!

The scene: the corner shop. The time: last-minute teatime shopping for you, sweetie time for your offspring. The actions: you let them have a pack of tiny mints after they have pestered for three whole minutes (that's a lot of pestering) and you can't take any more. In this situation you have negatively rewarded yourself by taking away your child's anti-social behaviour. This means that when they start whining for sweets next time, you are more likely to give in. Just what they want, and the exact opposite of your real aims! Meanwhile, you have positively rewarded your child's 'nuisance' behaviour, and so they are set to whine, whine and whine again. Hardly the outcome you desired.

What would have been the best answer? I think a combination of ignoring (Box 3) for the pestering, coupled with a small treat for a demonstration of sociable noises, would probably have done the trick.

The awesome power of praise

Before moving on to Child Directive behaviour, I want to impress upon you the awesome power of praise. Children inevitably respond to it, even if they seem to be taking no notice. Put it together with ignoring 99 per cent of their irritating little ways, and you have real parent power! They will be happier with you and themselves, and the same goes for you.

There are two major types of praise, both of which I believe every child should experience on a frequent basis – though only following pro-social behaviour. One is labelled praise. Here you would reward a specific activity, naming it in the process. For example: 'Jamie! What a lovely castle you're building! You *are* clever!'

The second is of a less focused nature and is used to show your love and affection towards, and approval of, your child as an individual person. For example: 'Sadie, my special girl! I love you so much. You're such a smashing little person.' Or the version for adolescents: 'Fiona, sweetheart, it's really great having you around. You know how much I love you!' This latter is likely to be met with a bored, 'Yeah, yeah, I *know* you love me', but don't be fooled, they need to hear it just as much at sixteen as they do at six years or six months.

I hope I have convinced you of the vital role of praise in giving your child the unequivocal message that they are both loved and lovable. Praising children following their sociable behaviour is a much more constructive use of your naturally limited energy than is shouting or smacking after naughty behaviour. I know! I tried it both ways myself, though not necessarily knowingly – more as part of blundering through each day of those early years as a young mother.

Hitting the emotional jackpot

One extra tip about making sure your child feels loved and lovable: when you put several Child Centred behaviours together, it really hits the emotional reassurance jackpot. When you say, 'That's great, Harry. Well done', in an enthusiastic manner, the impact is very constructive. If you add a genuine smile and look right into their eyes while you are doing it, the effect is quite electric. Should you stir in a hug, or squeeze of the shoulder the consequences can be cosmic. A kiss takes you into the stratosphere – unless they're eight years old, male and just coming out of school with their mates!

My eldest grandchild and I have worked out a way whereby we both enjoy our cuddles and kisses. As he is now seven I reserve my preamble for privacy at home, when I say: 'Ben, darling, I'd love you to give me a kiss. It really warms my heart up!' I wait. If he comes back with: 'Adam's got a cool new electric car that tips over and keeps going', I say: 'Sounds marvellous, darling. You sound as though you'd like one too.'

Slight pause for thought, by both parties. Then it's quite likely he will move closer, give me a quick hug and kiss and say, 'I love you, Nana.'

I'm ready with, 'That was lovely, Ben. My heart's really warm now! You know I love you a million stars.'

'And to infinity and beyond,' we both chorus.

Pause for more thought, then, 'Nana, if I saved up my pocket money, and you gave me some extra for being a helpful boy, how long do you think it would be before I had enough for the tipping car?'

I have to hand it to him, his timing is faultless!

I'm also fortunate enough to benefit from those precious moments of spontaneity when, on a warm impulse, my grand-children launch themselves at me, cling on and say, 'I love you, Nana!' Sometimes they all do it at once, four to one at present; very soon to be five to one. And counting!

So when you are getting into the swing of providing your children with Child Centred behaviours, don't hold back. Give them lashings of Attends; along with mounds of praises and smiles. Add in a few strokes, ask them what they would like you to do and also imitate their behaviour in a flattering manner. Continue this with ignoring those minor naughties, and you will be well on the way to a Family Funday. Every day.

There will be more about the emotional impact of Child Centred, and Person Centred, behaviours in Chapter 2. In fact they will be mentioned frequently throughout the book, because they are the cornerstone of loving, firm parenting.

WHAT DOES BEING CHILD DIRECTIVE MEAN?

CHILD DIRECTIVE BEHAVIOURS

Questions

- Asking your child for details of their activities
  - 'So what did you do at school today?'
  - 'What did you do round at Nicky's?'

- Asking your child to do as you tell them
  - 'Why don't you clear all that away?'
  - 'Would you like to sit up for lunch?'

- Asking your child factual questions to test their knowledge
  - 'What colour is that?'
  - 'What was the biggest dinosaur?'

Criticism

● Complaining about your child's behaviour
  ○ 'You've made a real mess of that again.'
  ○ 'You're always making such a noise!'

● Scolding your child for personality habits
  ○ 'You're such a misery!'
  ○ 'You're so mean all the time.'

● Reminding your child of their past 'failures'
  ○ 'You've always been an absolute pain in the supermarket.'
  ○ 'Oh, no! You've dropped your cup of juice again.'

Negative Face

● Giving your child a cold or disapproving look
  ○ Frowning at your child.
  ○ Closing your eyes and then looking upwards.

● Looking at your child in a bored or blank manner (unless you are purposely ignoring naughty behaviour)
  ○ Wiping all the warmth from your expression.
  ○ Yawning right in the child's face.

● Giving your child an angry or threatening look
  ○ Screwing up your whole face and thrusting your face forward.
  ○ Clamping your mouth shut, gritting your teeth and pulling your head back into your neck.

Teaching

● Giving your child advice on how to do something
  ○ Put this part there and then turn it round like this.'
  ○ 'What you should do is cut out all the small bits first.'

● Giving your child facts which they have not requested
  ○ 'That's a king penguin, not an ordinary one.'
  ○ 'Two goes into ten five times.'

Commands

● Giving your child an instruction on what to do
  ○ 'Put that down now!'
  ○ 'Get inside at once!'

- Telling your child to look at something
  - ○ 'Look! A tractor.'
  - ○ 'Look, look! The fire engine is coming.'

- Calling your child's name
  - ○ 'Tracy! Tracy!'
  - ○ 'Billy! Billy! *Billy!*'

Saying No

- Saying, 'No!' to your children as a threat
  - ○ 'No! Stop it or you'll get a smack. No!'
  - ○ 'Oh no, you don't! No!'

- Using the word 'No' as a warning
  - ○ 'No. No. Now come on.'
  - ○ 'No. Get away from there. No.'

Negative Touches

- Touching your child in a way that they don't like
  - ○ Squeezing your child's shoulder just a little too hard
  - ○ Smacking your child at any time (no matter what the provocation)

- Getting into any type of physical contact with your child which would be considered unacceptable by most people
  - ○ Pushing your child
  - ○ Shaking your child

Let me say right at the beginning that some Child Directive behaviours are a necessary part of every responsible parent's repertoire. Parents need to give commands. Parents must say, 'No.' Parents certainly have to ask questions and teach their children. Most parents do criticize at times, and pull disapproving faces – not too often, I hope, though it's easy enough to slip into the habit.

There will be more on this in Chapter 2, when I shall be talking about the fact that, as a cognitive behaviour therapist, I have seen many adults whose emotional lives have been blighted by their parents' failure to praise them. Rather, they were criticized in case they became 'big-headed', or 'too big for their boots', as their parents believed. You can avoid perpetuating such sad stories, even if you too were given a less than flying start by your mother and/or father.

In a Child Directive behaviour you yourself, the parent, are dictating what happens. Given that many parents fear not being able to control things, including their child, it is understandable that most of them use more of these 'I'm in charge' behaviours than Child Centred ones. That defeats the whole object, though at the time you don't necessarily realize what is happening.

I look back and regret many of the irrelevant commands I issued: 'Eat properly with your knife and fork!' I wish I hadn't been quite so anxious to teach my children the differences between red, orange and yellow. I doubt now whether I needed to ask all those questions: 'Well! What have you been up to?', and 'Did you do that?' I am sure I said – yelled – 'No!' much more often than was strictly necessary. I know I frowned, and looked angry or disappointed too much. I fear I was too frequently critical, and I confess that I sometimes smacked my children. *And* (not 'But') I'm pleased that I seem also to have managed enough Child Centred behaviours to offset the worst of my too directive and controlling style.

The other side of the coin

Now I want to move on to explain how each Child Directive behaviour has a preferable alternative in its Child Centred counterpart. I find it much easier to keep the balance between the two healthy when I view them as different sides of the same coin. For instance, the opposite to a Question is an Attend. That's because, while a Question demands a response from the child, the Attend gives them, gratis, something that feels good.

You could try it out for yourself. Get a friend to ask you a question about what you are doing. Then get them to tell you that the way you are mending the fuse, defleaing the cat or pruning the wisteria is really clever. Feel the difference and then swap roles.

Next time your child appears robed in an old bedcover, belted with a man's tie, wearing rubber boots and clutching a sieve upside down on their head pause before you say, full of benign adult interest, 'And who is it you're supposed to be today?' How much nicer for them, and cleverer of you, if you had said, 'Amelia, you look wonderful! I can see you've been dressing up. Would you like me to try to guess who you are?' You can then go on to get it pitifully wrong several times before you graciously give up, exclaiming, 'It's too difficult for me. Would you like to tell me or shall I keep on guessing?' Give it a go at your next opportunity – never far away in this age of dressing-up bags stuffed with every ready-made suit known to the civilized world. From Batman to Fairy Stardust, Peter Pan to Robin Hood, Pocahontas to Captain Hook, they are all available and you need do no more than join two bits of Velcro together.

The other 'opposing' Child Centred and Child Directive pairs are, I believe:

Child Centred	←——————→	Child Directive
Praise	←——————→	Criticism
Smile	←——————→	Negative Face
Ignoring a Minor Naughtiness	←——————→	Saying 'No'
Ask to Play	←——————→	Commands
Positive Touch	←——————→	Negative Touch
Imitation	←——————→	Teaching

There could be other pairings of course – you might like to see how you would link each particular Child Directive with its opposite Child Centred behaviour. Let me know your own ideas by writing to me at the address on p. 272. Think about which type you would prefer as a steady diet. I know that I would rather be in receipt of the menu headed Child Centred dishes, and I suspect you might be too.

When are commands OK?

None the less, there are times when a command should be issued, 'No' stated, questions asked and facts taught. I shall deal with criticism and with negative looks and touches in a minute. First, though, I want to talk about exactly when those times are, and how they can be recognized and best acted upon.

The usual 'getting up and out in the morning' marathon should be rich in examples. Commands are numerous, and become increasingly irate as the minutes to lift-off all too rapidly fly by.

- 'Get those pants off your head on to your bottom this minute!'

- 'Put that choc ice back in the freezer now!'

- 'Leave the cat's breakfast alone and finish your own up!'

- 'Turn that tap *off*!'

I don't even have to make up examples – they simply flood back against my wishes. Some, with my grandchildren, are more recent and therefore less forgivable. A recent champion command was, 'Stop squatting in that bidet immediately!' I can bare all only because I know that I had been giving my three-year-old grandson lots of Child Centred inputs. Not clever, though, was I? Especially as it was me who had explained, 'Well, sweetheart, a bidet is like a little bath for your willy and bum.' He had, after all, taken off all his clothes before climbing in!

The point is that grown-ups issue hundreds of redundant commands every day. They all tell children what to *stop* doing, but few clue them in on what they *could* be doing (to win adults' approval) instead. If I had said to Eoin, 'Come and wash your face now, darling', or 'Get out and do your wee in the lav, sweetheart', both he and I would have known exactly what was required.

The conclusions are that

- Many parents give far too many commands.

- These commands are often of a less than helpful, 'Stop that!' type.

- If you are giving your children lots of Child Centred attention, and getting the Attention Rule right at least half the time, you won't need to give so many commands anyway.

I think it is a good idea to make a note, over the course of one day, of all the commands you issue. Jot them down every five minutes or so. I was appalled to realize just how many totally unnecessary orders I was issuing – and that was a good day! Once again, thank heavens, I was able to comfort myself with the knowledge that I had provided several times as many Child Centred inputs, though not all Ask to Plays. On p. 40 I shall be talking about acceptable and ideal ratios of Child Centred to Child Directive behaviours.

Chapter 5 explains how to give a command that it is very difficult to refuse. So this is by no means the last you will be hearing about Child Directive behaviours. Indeed, I want to explore with you now the business of saying 'No', asking questions and teaching children.

Resentment and frustration

Imagine that there is a dominant member of your family who is ten feet tall. They are in your company a great deal. Sometimes they smile and talk with you. On occasion they swoop down and scoop you up, squeezing and kissing you. They are really good at keeping you clean, dry, rested and well fed.

The puzzling thing is that whenever you have an exciting idea and start to put it into action they stop you from enjoying yourself. At this point they always say the same thing: 'No!' They don't even listen when you try to explain your wonderful ideas or schemes. They just keep saying, 'No!'

When they leave the room, it is clearly your big chance to: explore the TV and video, have a go on the computer, rearrange the furniture and look at the magazines – all those things about which you are usually told, 'No!' You only stop when the Big One comes back and shouts, 'No! No! No!' They look angry, too, and you feel like crying because you were, after all, only investigating your surroundings. Or is that a crime nowadays, and if so, why?

Lots of one-year-olds feel just as you would – fed up, resentful and frustrated. It doesn't get any better, either – not when you're two, not when you're three and certainly not when you're four. In fact it gets worse the more mobile, independent and imaginative you become.

I recall all too vividly my own agonized shriek of, 'No! Oh

no!', as I careered down the garden to where my eight-year-old son and his buddy were busy hammering six-inch nails into the trunk of the peach tree. His explanation? 'We wanted to see what would happen if we did it.' The consequences? Goodbye large, delicious, home-grown white peaches. For ever.

Don't say no, just ignore it
The question isn't whether parents should say 'No' – clearly you must shoulder that particular burden. The issue is, how often should we be saying it? How often could you substitute your veto with simply ignoring the 'naughty' behaviour? Whatever age or size the child, half the time would be good

- 75 per cent would be better
- 90 per cent would be absolutely great

Of course, there will be times when your adult maturity allows you to see a danger that your child may not notice, and you will accompany your verbal exclamation with swift action – I don't suggest for a moment that you should ignore your child if they are at risk of physical harm, or likely to hurt others. These occasions, though, are relatively rare compared with the numerous other incidents when ignoring is not only safe but constructive too.

Naturally, it is up to the grown-ups to be Child Centred in arranging the child's physical environment, though not everyone is too sensitive at doing this. For instance, I once visited an immaculately kept home where the low coffee table was crowded with small, precious, breakable objects. The problem was that this room was the one most used by the eighteen-month-old who lived there. The result was six to eight hours per day of continuous 'No'!' by the parent as the toddler was drawn to the table and its treasures as if by a giant unseen magnet. The mother's stated aim was to start teaching this baby 'right from wrong' early in his life to ensure that he grew up as a law-abiding citizen. Incredible yet true.

ADAPTING YOUR HOME TO BE CHILD-FRIENDLY

When you are making the switch to being more Child Centred, it is helpful to remember that *you* are in charge of the home environment. Be adaptable. Only if you really want to spend masses of time saying, 'No!', 'Stop it!', 'Get away from there!' or 'Oh, my God!' should you keep your home in its pre-child state.

Being more Child Centred means parents making changes, and that includes:

● protecting children from the sharp edges of tables and worktops

● making sure you have cupboard, washing machine and fridge locks in place

● securely anchoring down bookshelves, rugs and other wobbly or slippery items

● and, of course, keeping all hot saucepan handles turned away from your children's exploring hands

It really does work!

The acid test is, of course, whether it works when you cut down the 'Nos!', bump up the ignoring of minor naughtiness and at the same time praise children for leaving the TV and video alone. The answer is yes, it does work, and numerous mothers and fathers can testify to that effect – often much to their own astonishment.

One mother of five rumbustious boys once said to me, 'Sue, I have to tell you that I didn't really believe it would work. I gave it a go, though, and it's just amazing how "going for the positives" can make such a difference. And so quickly!'

I am a very practical and down-to-earth person myself, and I would not be extolling the virtues of providing your child with more Child Centred than Child Directive behaviours had I not seen the advice transform family behaviour and relationships. Try it yourself, just for one day, and see what happens. It certainly won't do any harm, which cannot be said when too many 'Nos!' are being peppered around a child's head, whatever their age, gender or personality. In Chapter 2 I shall be talking about the emotional impact on a child of an excess of vetoes.

Asking questions and teaching children

When questions and teaching are examined, much the same story emerges. With the best of intentions adults often deluge their young charges with questions asked and facts proffered.

Many parents believe that asking their child questions and teaching them useful information is a necessary and important aspect of being a good mother or father. It seems that adults themselves find considerable satisfaction in quizzing and tutoring their children, and there is little doubt that children enjoy a certain amount of this type of parental attention.

Problems arise, however, when you give your child an abundance of Questions and Teaches at the expense of Attends and Imitations. Child Directive behaviours, when too numerous, give a child the sense that somehow they don't come up to scratch in their parents' eyes. That is not to say that their mothers and fathers intend this consequence – quite the opposite. Their aim is often to use questions to show an interest in what the child is doing, and to use teaching to help the child understand their environment with some degree of accuracy. But from the child's perspective it is likely to feel like a continuous exam setting, though one where as often as not the child receives no clear feedback about their performance.

Once more, I would like you to try biting your lip the moment you feel a question about to burst out of your mouth. Substitute an Attend. Don't ask, 'How do you like having a new baby in the family?' Say, 'You look very happy today. You seem to like being a big brother!', and watch what happens.

Remember, you are giving your child a 'no strings' message of approval when you do an Attend. Questions make a demand that children quite readily fear they may not be able to meet to your satisfaction.

I remember collecting my children from infants' school and bursting with curiosity about their day. I would say, 'So! what happened at school today?' The most common reply was an unbelievable, 'Nothing.'

What was going on here? I now see that in posing my

question I was trying to meet my own need to look and sound like an interested, intelligent and caring mother. The trouble was, at that precise point in time my children wanted tea, toys and television, not more talk. I learned to let them tell me in their own time about the wonders of the Nature Table and who shoved whom in the playground!

What they most needed from me at 3.30 p.m. was an Attend and Ask to Play, not a Question. 'You look tired/happy/cross/ hungry, darling. Would you like me to call in at the shop so you can choose a cake for tea?' went down very much better than my earnest maternal enquiries about their educational experience. That is largely because the Attend and Ask to Play was for them, while the Question was about me.

Similar circumstances surround many of our educational efforts with children. They make ideal pupils in lots of ways. They are young and impressionable; they are curious about their world and the people in it; when under five they are available for tuition from dawn to dusk. More importantly, most adults are streets ahead in the knowledge stakes.

At last! A captive audience for an exposition of our meagre information on astrophysics: 'Why is the moon in the sky, Mummy?' World religion: 'How did Jesus get borned, Daddy?' Best of all, perhaps, family relationships: 'Why can't I marry you when I'm grown-up, Mummy?' Our cogent reply to be quickly followed by yet another unanswerable poser: 'But can't girls marry each other? Aunty Julia and her friend Betty live together, just like you and Daddy. They've got a big bed too!'

No matter what their question, it is relatively easy to blind even an inquisitive five-year-old with pseudo-science, which is probably why we enjoy winning these no-contest exchanges. It feels really good to parade even flawed facts in front of a rapt audience. Mothers and fathers all enjoy showing off like this before their offspring. It cements your view of yourself as pack leader, and anyway, who else out in the big, bad world is likely to hang on to your every word with quite the same degree of uncritical adoration?

The problem is, that while you revel in strutting your stuff, frequently without waiting for any invitation from your child ('Peter! This colour is vermilion, this one crimson and this one scarlet. So now show me which is which'), their experience need not be so much fun. They would no doubt gain a more stable sense of their own value as individuals were you to say instead: 'Peter, you're doing such a lovely red picture! I'm going to do one just the same because yours is so good!' In other words, in the first little scenario Peter learns that he's a bit stupid because he got vermilion and scarlet mixed up, whereas you clearly had all the answers. In the second, Peter learns that you think he does such wonderful pictures that you wanted to copy him. So, Peter crushed or Peter confident – it's the parents' choice. In the first example the adult is leading the activity and feeling superior. In the second it is the other way round. Why sacrifice your child's sense of being both loved and lovable for the sake of puffing up your own ego?

Imitations teach the best lesson of all

Try halving the number of Teaches you do in a day, substituting verbal and non-verbal Imitations. For a child the most powerful version of an Imitation is one that has two complementary dimensions, the spoken and the gestural. When an adult copies a child it is, from their point of view, the acme of approval.

Hence, if you dropped by my house one afternoon – or at 7 a.m. for that matter – you might well see me crawling around on all fours with a colourful scarf tied in a large bow around my neck. Affixed to my knickers with a large safety pin will be my 'tail', yet another scarf. I should state at this point that, whatever the blandishments of my 'little kittens', Maeve aged six and Eoin aged three, this 'mother cat' keeps her top on! The game is their idea entirely, as are the associated activities of lapping up milk from a saucer – difficult – and eating broken biscuits from a pudding bowl – not so difficult. Let me confess. I love it! So do they. It's become a firm favourite.

When Maeve wanted to play this game while watching the *Aristocats* video, I was made to sit under a cover when my video counterpart was not on screen. Not as boring as you might think, as I sneaked a detective novel under with me. A torch is helpful if you ever find yourself in a similar situation.

Of course, the activities alter as children move through the various stages of their development. I fully expect my anticipatory joy at asking: 'Would you like me to play *Aristocats* with you?' to be callously quashed in the near future with the retort, 'Babies' stuff, Nana,' accompanied by a snort of derision at my feeble-mindedness.

Imitating is fun for grown-ups, though I'm not suggesting you spend your days crawling around in a bow-and-tail outfit – just how much milk can a grown-up lap? What I am encouraging you to do is reduce your number of Teaches. By using Imitations instead, you could be making sure that your son or daughter is learning the most important lesson in anyone's life – that you love them and think they are pretty wonderful to boot.

Chapter 2 will offer advice on some similarly powerful and perhaps potentially more damaging Child Directives: Criticism, Negative Face and Negative Touch. For the meantime, let me urge you once again to give your children twice as many Child Centred as Child Directive inputs. You have nothing lose and a lot to gain. Both you and your child can benefit – though yours, of course, is the responsibility for setting in motion the process of change, which will lead to your becoming an Authoritative Parent.

AUTHORITATIVE PARENTING IS BALANCED PARENTING

First of all, let's look at the term 'authoritative parenting' itself. Quite apart from being quite a job to get your teeth round, it can be easily confused with authoritarian styles of parenting. I have seen too many children crushed under the weight of domineering parents. Fathers like explosive sergeant majors and mothers like disapproving schoolteachers strike fear and despair into your children's hearts.

Neither does it stop there. As a therapist working with adults I see many people who, though apparently very successful, are still deep down inside craving for the father who listened instead of shouting, the mother who understood and championed instead of slowly and inexorably demolishing. All in the name of love, of course. At the end of this chapter I shall be discussing other parenting styles, including authoritarian.

Authoritative parenting is the label fairly recently applied by some professionals – researchers, theorists and clinicians – to parents who are able to be both loving and in control of their child's behaviour. It seems to have emerged in the wake of the Parent/Child Game work by Rex Forehand, Robert McMahon and their colleague Nick Long in the USA (see p. 4).

Since I started using the technique in Britain I have made some alterations, one of them being to put aside the rather pejorative 'positive' and 'negative' behaviour labels used in America. I am in touch with these authors and exchange ideas with them. Rex Forehand recently told me that he thought our work was all about 'operationalizing the language of love'. I agree. They too would, I suspect, prefer the term 'balanced parenting' to 'authoritative parenting'. The use of the word 'balanced' implies much of the essence of this style of parenting, where 'loving parents take control'.

In 1993 I wrote a booklet with that title for a documentary on BBC television. Ten thousand were sold, which reflects very clearly what mothers and fathers throughout the UK tell me. They want to be more balanced in their parenting, and are thirsting for the information which will show them the best route to follow towards their admirable goal. So, goodbye authoritative and hello balanced parenting.

Getting the balance right

Many people visualize the idea of 'balance' as a pair of equally weighted scales, like the scales of justice. Balanced parenting isn't quite like that. The way in which you can most effectively instill in your children the certain knowledge that they are precious to you *and* that you say what you mean and mean what you say is to tip the scales very decidedly in favour of a Child Centred style.

I have already made it clear that some Child Directive behaviours are a necessary and proper part of bringing up children. What I want to tell you about now is not just how to be adequately competent parents, but the precise ratio (or proportion, if you prefer) of Child Centred to Child Directive inputs needed to put you right up with the best mothers and fathers ever. The table overleaf also expresses it in percentages, which you may find easier to follow if arithmetic is not your strong point!

If you want to be a loving parent who takes control of their child's behaviour, there is every chance that you could use – indeed, perhaps you are already using – a 1:1 ratio of Child Centred behaviours to Child Directive ones (in other words, an equal number of both). Try counting your score over a ten-minute period and work out your ratio. If this amounts to two or more Child Centred for every three Child Directive you can applaud your efforts. At 1:1 you are probably being Child Centred enough to protect your children's positive self-image. They will in all likelihood not pose any serious problems. If you achieve three Child Centred to seven Child Directive you are just about getting the balance right half the time. Things are mostly all right, but there are definitely touchy areas between you and your child. Quite often bedtime and sleep routines can cause difficulties; or mealtimes; or shopping; or getting dressed and out of the front door by 8.15 a.m. A major reason for these daily sticky patches is because a 3:7 ratio leaves your child in doubt about how best to win your praise and avoid your disapproval.

HOW TO WORK OUT A RATIO

Let's say you have counted yourself over a ten-minute period saying 13 Child Centred things and 3 Child Directive things. To discover the ratio of Child Centred to Child Directive you divide the smaller figure (3) into the larger one (13), which in this example gives 4 (it's simpler to forget the bit left over). So here your ratio of Child Centred to Child Directive would be 4:1 – pretty good!

If, on the other hand, you have counted yourself making 3 Child Centreds and 13 Child Directives the basic arithmetic is still the same, but the figures are reversed and your ratio of Child Centred to Child Directive is 1:4 – not good at all!

The optimal ratio of about 6:1 Child Centred to Child Directive would give your offspring a predictable framework of behaviour for staying in your good books. Equally, they would be able to forecast those situations in which you would withdraw your attention, or indeed punish them.

Ratio of Child Centred to Child Directive behaviours

Child Centred		Child Directive	Percentage of Child Centred	Comment
1	to	10	10%	Damaging to your child. Problems frequent
1	to	3	33%	Creditable, but you should aim to do much better
1	to	1	50%	You are protecting your child's self-image and overcoming potential problems
6	to	1	85%	Excellent! The optimal ratio, giving your child a predictable frame-work for a good and developing relationship with you

Children thrive on this degree of certainty, as long as they can trust you to show your approval when they are sociable, and believe that you keep them safe when they feel afraid. These are two of the fundamental planks on which the sometimes fragile edifice of our personality rests.

The more heavily the scales are weighted in favour of you being Child Centred rather than Child Directive, the stronger your child's confidence can grow in you and in themselves. I have seen parents reverse their ratio from a destructive 1:10 to a magnificent 6:1 in under a month, and after just four parent training sessions.

● These parents experience a surge of pride in their parenting capacity and style. Their mood lifts.

- Their relationship with their child improves.

- Their partnership flourishes.

- Their children are visibly happier and make significant developmental progress.

A final perk is that the children don't just behave more compliantly, they actively want to please their parents.

Playing the Parent/Child Game

An example from my own work illustrates the point. Angela and Simon had a new baby. Angela also had four other children, and Simon one, from previous relationships. All the children were under six years of age. Angela had been brutally treated, first by her father and brothers, and then by three successive partners. Simon was a drop-out from his middle-class family in which brothers, sisters and parents all held down responsible jobs.

There were grave fears that the young couple would be totally overwhelmed by the huge challenge of bringing up six little children. I was asked to use the Parent/Child Game with them over four sessions to discover what potential they had for change. The answer was – enormous! They both found the technique very useful.

In the official version of the Parent/Child Game (the various stages of which are explained in detail on p. 271), the sessions take place in a video suite with a one-way screen equipped with an additional audio feedback loop which allows the parent to hear me via an earbug. For ten minutes the parent plays with their child, who cannot hear me as I praise, prompt and generally guide their mother or father towards a much more Child Centred style of interacting. The focus is first on inhibiting Child Directive behaviours, which is much more difficult than you might expect. Those questions, commands, teachings and Nos just keep popping out at a furious rate of knots!

After just four sessions Angela and Simon had been able to change their ratio from something like 1:12 to 4:1 or 5:1 in favour of Child Centred behaviours. This was great progress, which left everyone feeling much more optimistic than had been the case only a month previously. The family are now, a year later, able to provide all their children with balanced parenting.

Though you would be able to learn more quickly if you were to work with me in a video suite, there is no reason why, using this book and given a little more time, you cannot transform your own parenting into a more balanced style. Remember the magic numbers:

- 1:2 is just about all right

- 1:1 is good enough

- 6:1 is the show-stopper

If you combine that with getting the Attention Rule (see p. 22) right more than half the time, you should be well on the way to improved all-round family harmony, you will feel much more self-confident in your handling of your children, and they will breathe a sigh of relief that you have, lovingly, taken control.

You reap what you sow

The real magic will be experienced in the improved quality of your relationship with your child, and in your and your partner's feelings for one another. Children who are inundated with Child Directives are often surly, moody, uncooperative, angry, mean-tempered and unhappy – especially towards their mother and father, though one parent may be favoured more than the other. If a video were to be made of a child with the favoured parent, and then compared with one of the child and the less-favoured parent, it is extremely likely that the parent of choice would be using a more Child Centred style than their partner.

Children are so honest in their responses. As the most important grown-ups in their lives, moment to moment, you reap what you sow. When you next give your child an Attend, coupled with a Praise, Smile and Positive Touch, just watch them glow with emotional well-being. Set the scene so that you and your partner or a close friend give each other the adult version of the same treatment. You and they will, I predict, experience the same rewarding sense of approval.

Interestingly, when I am training psychiatrists, nursery nurses, social workers, speech and drama therapists, educational and clinical psychologists, specialist nurses, and foster and adoptive parents in the Parent/Child Game techniques, even though we are all playing roles, most of the participants report genuine and beneficial responses to receiving Child Centred attention. The same goes for the Attention Rule. Conversely, these adults report quite strong emotions of resentment, alienation and irritation when they receive a lot of Child Directive inputs.

Firmness and fondness can be combined

Many parents in the UK believe that it is impossible, not to say downright wrong, to combine fondness and firmness. They feel that if you show your love for your children by being warm and responsive it will turn them into weak and defenceless individuals, particularly the boys. In the same way, there is an ethos that you must be firm with children if they are to survive – as if bringing up children was supposed to be a family version of training for the Marines.

IT'S TIME THE STIFF UPPER LIP SOFTENED INTO A SMILE

The traditional belief in Britain is that it is only the upper classes who preserve a 'stiff upper lip' attitude to parenting – nannies in starched aprons, nursery tea, boarding school at eight and so on. Not so. Unfortunately, in my opinion, information from the USA, Australia and New Zealand, the Caribbean, France, Germany and the Netherlands confirms that this distant, cool and undemonstrative style of bringing up children is still alive and wreaking emotional havoc.

On a more cheerful note, reports from the Beijing area of China, and from Kerala in southern India, indicate that it is more common there for both fathers and mothers to be openly affectionate towards their children than to maintain a cold and disapproving attitude. I just wish stiff upper lips would disappear from every child's experience of being parented.

The Parent/Child Game makes it patently clear that this is not so. If you want your child to be happy and outgoing at school, to have lots of friends, enjoy life and be resilient, first you must give them that bubble of love which will keep them afloat in life. One of the best ways I know to achieve this aim is to be six times more Child Centred than Child Directive. Every day. All year. It's for good, not just for Christmas!

Keep your expectations within bounds

The unwelcome confrontations and troublesome relationships we experience with our children are partly related to our expectations of them. Unrealistic expectations can drive us into a more Child Directive style that actually cramps children's potential rather than encouraging it to blossom. It is relatively easy to be seduced into the 'My child's taller, brighter and altogether more wonderful than yours' competition that besets many mothers and fathers.

Of course, it is quite right for you to place yourself squarely in your child's corner. If you aren't behind them, who will be? But the temptation to engage in open, though infinitely polite, warfare with other parents regarding the relative development of your children is best firmly resisted.

As a full-time young mother of three under-sevens I spent a lot of time in the company of other mothers and their children. Over the endless cups of tea and coffee, trips to the pool, expeditions to the park and outings we would, inevitably, watch our offspring and compare their prowess. Sometimes these observations were voiced, sometimes not. Each mum openly made an effort to be charitable about the others' babies, toddlers and school age children. Each secretly hoped that their own brood was the more able and attractive – and feared that they were not.

I recall blatantly boasting how I had taught my two-and-a-half-year-old daughter to 'read' around one hundred 'flash cards' with a single word on each. But I see now that Rhiannon's early start in literacy had very little to do with her, and a lot to do with me. I was bored, living on a farm in an isolated rural community, though Rhiannon most decidedly was not. My other reason for pushing her education was even less excusable. I wanted to show that she was intellectually brighter than her contemporaries. Because of the reflected glory. Because, since she was my first child, I had unrealistic expectations of her progress.

When you set out to force the pace of your child's development – with their best interests at heart, of course – several consequences can occur. Your style of interacting with them will perforce be more Child Directive. Let's take as an example learning to read. It's teatime, and adults and children have all had a full day. Your belief is that reading ability is crucial to educational progress, and there's no doubt you are right. You have set yourself the target of a quarter of an hour's reading practice with your five-and-a-half-year-old. You have the right books. All is set for success.

Just listen to the likely dialogue, though, and you will begin to see how such academic achievement is obtained, and its emotional cost for your child.

Father or mother: 'Right. Sit down here with me and start on page 3. That's where you got up to yesterday. Not making exacting thunderous progress, are you? Now start here.'

Child: 'The dog w . . .'.

Parent: 'Come on! You could do that yesterday. Why not today?'

Child: 'Wa . . . wa . . . what!'

Parent: 'No. Not "what"! Can't you see that's an "s", like "is" and "snake"? Right, off you go again. "The dog was . . .?"'

Child: 'The dog was c . . . ca . . . I can't do that one.'

Parent: 'Of course you can! You're just not trying. Concentrate. That's what you must do – concentrate!'

The parent's ratio of Child Centred to Child Directive behaviour in this little vignette, aimed at 'helping' their child, is 1:11. The child's experience is a punishing one and likely to reduce their motivation for reading. They are also learning that their best is not good enough to please their mother and father.

The whole exercise was doomed, in fact, from the very beginning because most children of five and a half are still coming to terms with many necessary pre-reading skills and may well not get into their stride until they are around six and a half. All in all, a crushing experience for the child and one of frustration for the adult. Daily repeats of such a scene damage the child's self-esteem and the quality of their relationship with their 'helpful' parent. Or is that tutor?

Children develop step by step

It is really important, in my view, to get the developmental facts straight before beginning to teach a child anything – find out what a child may and may not be capable of at any given age before you dive in at the deep end.

This information will ensure that you are aware of your own vital role as your child's source of self-confidence, self-reliance and self-awareness. Without these basics in place, being able to read is a comparative non-starter.

Much more constructive where a five-and-a-half-year-old is concerned would be a decision to spend that same quarter of an hour reading a story to them. You can both delight in the fun as it unfolds. You will both emerge closer, more relaxed and decidedly more cheerful than you would from the reading lesson.

I know. I tried it both ways with my son, who at that age would prefer to have spent his after-school hours in the sandpit or up a tree with a sandwich clutched in one rather messy hand. The big news on the reading front is that you encourage most progress by reading your child a regular bedtime story, and not by becoming an additional teacher in their lives.

The normal stages and phases of a child's development have been extensively covered in books specifically devoted to the topic (see Further Reading on p. 269). The important point to remember about how children develop is that what is called 'normal' covers a huge range. The short table overleaf is intended to give you an idea of what could be happening to your child at particular stages in their development. If nothing else, it shows you what a lot of ground comes under the heading of 'normal progress'.

Looking for answers in the past

Questioning your own parenting skills is part of the mother and father's job description. Being able to recognize your individual areas of strength and weakness is an altogether more daunting task.

The range of normal child development

Area of development	Examples of child's behaviour	Normal age range
Language	Saying single words	9 months–2 years
	Using 4–5 word phrases	2–4 years
Intelligence	Naming colours correctly	1½–4 years
	Counting 10 objects correctly	1½–5 years
Education	Learning to read	2½–7½ years
	Sitting quietly and concentrating on listening to a story	1½–7 years
Behaviour	Controlling the impulse to hit out when frustrated	1½–10 years
	Temper tantrums	1–8 years
Sociability	Telling known from unfamiliar faces	4 months–1½ years
	Learning to say, 'Sorry'	2½–10 years
Relationships	Saying, 'I love you'	1½–3 years
	Showing sympathy for others who are hurt	1–4½ years
Emotional	Conquering fear of the dark	1½–7 years
	Labelling their own emotions	2½–6 years
Personality	Saying 'I' and knowing it means themselves	2–5 years
	Knowing with certainty that they are a girl or a boy and cannot change	2½–5 years
Psychosexual	Recognizing that boys and girls, mums and dads have different bodies	1½–4 years

	Learning to play with their genitals only in private when alone	3–8 years
Mobility and Coordination	Walking steadily alone Hopping	9 months–1½ years 1½–6 years
Physical	Being dry at night Washing and bathing themselves	1½–8 years 3–9 years

In a booklet written for a second TV documentary in spring 1994 I described, as well as the combination of Child Centred and Child Directive which we are calling balanced parenting, four other main styles:

- authoritarian

- over-involved

- inconsistent

- distant

In Chapter 2, I shall be looking at all six categories, and their likely childhood origins, in much more detail.

As I set out the major features of these parenting styles, try to see which one might most resemble your own way of bringing up your children. For example, most mothers and fathers are inconsistent to one degree or another. There will be times when your style might swing between being over-involved and distant.

I know that there were constant times of confusion for me when my children were young – and not so young, too – particularly on the Family Law and Order Ticket. Was I being too strict? Was I being too lax? Carol, up the road, seemed never to lose her temper, but then she didn't seem to smile much either. I often went from one to the other, and back again, in a matter of manic minutes. It's difficult to know where you stand. Often, looking back to the way in which your own parents interacted with you can provide quite a hefty clue! I shall be going into detail on that in a moment. I want to finish Chapter 1 with a question – often, I believe, more enlightening than a conclusion. If becoming a Balanced Parent is so clearly within your grasp, how is it that, more than occasionally, you find putting into practice the relatively simple principles of being Child Centred so difficult? Perhaps that answer too lies in thinking back to when you were the young daughter or son of your own mother and father.

Meanwhile, try the quick-fix list to see where you fit in at present, remembering that no one is ever as balanced in their parenting as they would wish. However, the distance between you and the end of the rainbow can always be shortened.

A QUICK FIX ON CHAPTER 1

1. Give enthusiastic praise every time your child does anything sociable or clearly makes an effort to get something right.

Example: Jillian, aged four and a half, gives her best friend Briony your favourite scarf. 'Jillian, sweetheart, what a kind and generous friend you are! That's my special scarf, so we'll swap it for another lovely scarf for Briony. You're such a good friend to her!'

Evidence: Research shows that children learn to be socially sensitive more quickly when they are praised for every little success rather than punished for their faux pas.

2. Ignore 99 per cent of all minor naughtiness and irritating habits.

Example: Richard, aged nearly eight, has developed an annoying habit of responding to your every remark with, 'No way, Jose.' Turn your head away, break eye contact, move away physically, stay silent and look neutral. On no account shout, 'Richard, if you say that one more time I'm going to lose my temper!'

Evidence: Studies repeatedly show that ignoring any non-dangerous behaviour consistently reduces its future frequency. Remember that the Extinction Burst, where the problem behaviour actually increases for a few days, is a signal of your success. Research advises persistence at this point.

3. Getting the Attention Rule right half the time means you are doing well.

Example: Margie, whilst singing a sweet school song, accidentally sits on the new kitten. Getting the Attention Rule right: 'Margie darling! What a beautiful song. I'll just give Mittens a little stroke and then I'd like you to sing it again. You know all the words – you're so clever!' Getting the Attention Rule wrong: 'My God, Margie! You could have killed Mittens. Can't you look what you're doing? Aah, my poor little Mittens. Margie! I've had enough of your songs for one day, thank you!'

Evidence: Repeated investigations into how to achieve control over your child's behaviour show that accurate application of the Attention Rule for 50 per cent of the time is enough to guarantee a reasonable level of compliance. Less than that leads to problems. More than 50 per cent is considered to be extremely advantageous.

2. Parents Were Children Too

Bonding Basics

WHAT THIS CHAPTER IS ABOUT

This chapter focuses on the ways in which our childhood and adolescent experiences of being parented directly impinge upon our adult behaviour and parenting style. From life in their family of origin everyone is left with an **attachment history** which includes many unresolved relationship issues. These constitute the **baggage** which all adults tote around. I shall be spelling out ways to recognize exactly where such baggage comes from. But insight must be translated into action – always a daunting task; I shall be tackling this from the parents' point of view in particular. The emphasis throughout will be on the relevance of a perspective taken across several generations in a family.

HAPPY FAMILIES?

The advertising world perpetually brings to our attention pictures of happy families. We are sated with images of healthy, youthful-looking parents, lively yet cute and cooperative children, and benignly smiling grandparents. Sometimes an engaging puppy or cuddly kitten is thrown in for good measure.

The major insult to those living in the real world is the almost obscene degree of happiness which they all exude. Yet most family photograph albums feature similar snaps. Most of us could dig out set-piece wedding pictures with everyone dolled up to the nines and smiling maniacally; or the visual record of those indistinguishable beach holidays where, apart from the children's clothes, nothing much seems to have changed over the years. Fun moments at the park, the zoo, the swimming pool. All captured for posterity and all full of families whose faces closely resemble the Cheshire Cat in *Alice in Wonderland*. He was the one with the ever-present fixed grin. Perhaps this is the way you would like to remember the past, though I believe much of the reality to have been more like the rest of *Alice*: unpredictable, confusing and plain frightening for much of the time.

Human beings have no choice as to their family of origin – the family of which they will be a lifelong member. From a child's viewpoint not only are their parents and grandparents immovable objects, every other family is assumed to be just like their own. I have often wondered how this could be, given the huge disparities between one home and another. Finally I asked an adult who had spent much of their childhood haunting the 'Happy Families' inhabited by several of their friends.

The reply was both unexpected and enlightening. 'I just presumed that those parents were putting on an act for my benefit, because that's what happened in my home. You always looked forward to visitors, as then your own parents pretended that they were happy and loved you. I knew that when the visit was over, it would all go back to normal: no proper food; no smiles; just chips and regular beatings.'

The emotional aspects of our early experiences are quite extraordinarily powerful.

ATTACHMENT HISTORIES; CHILDHOOD LEGACIES

People came before psychologists, and often all the experts are doing is to crystallize, after due investigation, ideas which have been common currency for decades if not centuries. Our childhood experience of family life heavily influences our style and competence when our own time comes to approach the many challenges of parenthood. It is now generally agreed that our early years within our family leave a deep and lasting impression. It is the sum of these, and our adolescent experiences, which are most often called attachment histories. All those who have made a study of childhood, from Sigmund Freud to Penelope Leach via John Bowlby and Benjamin Spock, are unanimous in their view that unless children receive a strong, clear message from their parents that they are loved and lovable they will not develop into self-confident, expressive, competent and caring adults.

A solid sense of self-worth resulting from being adequately parented enables a child to absorb the rapid changes of infancy and toddlerhood. The demands of emerging from the dependence of childhood; the turmoil of adolescence; the highs and lows of achieving autonomy during the journey into young adulthood – all these can be survived, sometimes even enjoyed, if your mother and father have given you the emotional buoyancy that results from each of them being enough of a balanced parent. Learning to deal with the thrills and spills of intimate relationships, and adapting to work and social environments, are also made easier if it has been long accepted that you are fully worthy of others' approval and your own satisfaction. The major challenge of the long-term commitments of being a parent is also much more likely to be within your reach.

It is my view that every human infant, whatever the circumstances of their birth, shares fundamental emotional requirements which remain constant throughout their development from newborn to the early school years. In fact I believe that these needs continue, though in varied format, throughout life. Look at the following list and see if you agree:

- Emotional warmth
- Unstinting approval
- Unshakeable security
- Positive attention
- Finely tuned stimulation

- Responsive sensitivity
- Consistent nurturing
- Appropriate physical care

Certainly, in infancy, childhood and adolescence it is your parents who supposedly supply this life-enhancing input. Looking at each item on this list in turn gives some notion of the immensity of the demands made upon parents, whether young or old, mothers or fathers, single or in partnerships, and whatever their cultural or ethnic origins.

Giving your child the best emotional start

To speak of emotional warmth is to imply that the baby receives a strong message that they are a wanted and welcome addition to the family. Observable approval from your parents, as part of your daily diet, does wonders for a child's sense of being lovable. The good news from a baby's perspective is that, in those early months especially, adults often find them irresistibly delightful. Should a young child miss out on this quite normal, and definitely desirable, adoration they can learn that even their most strenuous efforts to please are useless. Their conclusion could easily be that they must be a disappointment to their parents and worthless as individuals.

When we consider the vital role of psychological security in the early years, the link with the child's growing trust in their parents becomes clear. Luckily babies are seen as very vulnerable by grown-ups, who are usually strongly motivated to protect them emotionally as well as physically. This is just as well, because otherwise children would feel that no one properly understands how important it is for them to be able to rely on parents and other adults to be sensitive to their real needs, especially when it comes to finding safety from fear in those grown-ups' company.

Beginning the process of socialization
One of the major pluses about receiving positive parental attention when you are small is that it is a great help in the difficult journey towards being a sociable personality. The Attention Rule, when used correctly and frequently enough, plays a

central part in the process of socialization. Babies are primed, it seems, to attract attention from adults, and fortunately for them their cries are not usually regarded as naughty behaviour and thus ignored. But some infants' and young children's calls for help, comfort and stimulation do go unheeded, and they are likely to pay a heavy emotional price for this misapplication of one of the principles of balanced parenting.

The type of stimulation required throughout infancy and child-hood is closely related to human beings' voracious appetite for novelty – by which I mean not the heart-stopping shock-horror variety but that most powerfully rewarding and stimulating of events, a social and emotional interchange with other people. If young children are deprived of this kind of stimulation they may become passive, having learnt that it is pointless to thirst for something that fails to arrive. Others seek ways of stimulating themselves, sometimes through rhythmic movements.

An adult's responsive sensitivity to a baby's or child's cries is agreed to be a basic requirement of good parenting. Once more, most are fortunate in that their mother or father will persist in trying to uncover and remedy the source of their offspring's discomfort. Receiving this type of special responsiveness allows a baby to learn that they can trust their parents to answer their calls for attention. They also begin to realize some fundamentals of family relationships: when I squawk, they come running! It is bad news for some children that the major lesson taken away from these early interactions is that you need to shout very loudly to provoke any response at all. Or perhaps, if your parents are over-attentive, that there is a constant need for anxiety, though the reason for it remains obscure.

Consistent nurturing

The term 'consistent nurturing' covers a broad brief. It can include meeting a young child's psychological, behavioural, social, emotional, intellectual, language, play, personality, educational, physical, sensory, motor and psychosexual developmental needs, all on a continuous and ever-evolving daily basis. No wonder many new parents feel almost paralysed under the huge burden of their responsibilities! Luckily these needs do not usually have to be met all at the same time, though they do tend to crop up in fearsome little groups.

It is in the face of this overwhelming avalanche of demands that parents strive mightily to provide their young children with balanced parenting. It is no surprise that you are likely to slip quite regularly. At those moments, caring parents will attempt to learn some constructive lesson from their temporary failure to get the balance right. In attempting to give your child consistent nurturing, you are also enabling them to develop an awareness of others' feelings and situation. The growth of our ability to see things from someone else's point of view, is a very important aspect of human development. Should a baby or child be so badly treated as to distort or destroy their nascent capacity for empathy, in later life they are likely to experience serious problems in personal relationships and parenting.

Mothers and fathers of newborn babies, older infants, toddlers and young children know that the sheer physicality of the care they provide is unavoidable. Being able to give your offspring suitable physical nurturing is a vital first base from which their other areas of development spring. Small children and babies can die if their physical care is not up to scratch, so the responsibility for parents is enormous.

In order to give your child the best start during those early years you need to have your senses on major alert for most of the time. You will need to listen carefully, look closely, touch gently, taste experimentally and sniff bravely. If you stay in physical and sensory touch with your young children they will be learning the importance, and pleasures, of physical intimacy. This will be a lesson of great significance in terms of their later social and psychological development and their ability to communicate within varying kinds of relationships.

The psychological baggage we carry into adulthood

You can see from this brief overview of every human being's basic needs that the consequences of whether or not your parents managed to provide them for you are crucial. Much has been made in literature, the cinema and the theatre of the complex and dire consequences of parenting that misses the psychological mark – unsurprising, really, when happy, functional family relationships often make such boring entertainment. They do wonders, however, for the peace of mind of the participants. None the less, the debate still rages over whether, if Herr Mozart had been less pushy towards his prodigiously talented son, Wolfgang Amadeus' genius would have flourished as it did. My own view is that there are many more parents who thus overburden their children than there are genius child musicians!

Statistically, it seems that the majority of parents are just about good enough at meeting their children's vast array of basic developmental needs. What exactly 'good enough' entails will be discussed in Chapter 6. My point is this: such is the human condition that, however successful parents have been in supplying warmth, approval, security, attention, stimulation, sensitivity and nurture, everyone carries the baggage of unresolved relationship issues into their adulthood. Merely the size of the sack varies. But whatever its shape or contents, it becomes part of our own attempts at parenting.

BAGGAGE HANDLING

Some adults' psychological tote bags are relatively small, manoeuvrable and easily opened, while others will be struggling with enormous, unwieldy and viciously shut loads. But there is, I believe, no point in attributing blame to any of the players in the Family Game. Each generation strives, to the best of their ability, to provide what is needed by the next. Illness, wars and economic privation, as well as healthy, peaceful and affluent times, are all part of the human scene.

However, I don't consider that our fate is written in the stars. Neither do I subscribe to the view that if you want something hard enough you will get it. I lean more towards the idea that all individuals possess a mixture of strengths and weaknesses, and it is each person's responsibility to maximize the former and compensate for the latter. There is little doubt, though, that an awareness of where it all came from would be of enormous help if you are to find the motivation and stamina to tackle the contents of your psychological baggage, whatever its weight.

Ask yourself some questions

Some therapists use a questionnaire called an Adult Attachment Interview as a sensitive and informative way of getting a grown-up's view of the important relationships in their child-hood and adolescence, together with their wishes for their child in twenty years' time. Recent research into attachment theory suggests that, when adults attempt to answer questions, the manner in which they reply is perhaps a more powerful indica-tor of the type of baggage they are handling than is the actual content of their answers. For instance, if your answers are brusque and dismissive, it is likely that your family of origin was characterized by distant relationships where the bonds of love were given short shrift. Conversely, were your replies to be long, involved and emotionally chaotic, your relationship with your parents is likely to have been 'enmeshed' – in other words, over-close and confusingly contradictory.

Professionals divide the range for 'normal' people – whoever they might be – into:

- distant and dismissive relationships

- enmeshed over-involved relationships

- 'autonomous' or functional relationships

It seems that the main hallmark of the third, most desirable, group is the ability to be thoughtful about, and apply psycho-logy to the contents of our attachment history. I know I would like to be in that group, though it is more likely that I veer towards the enmeshed side of things.

Here are some examples of the type of questions used in the Adult Attachment Interview. You could tape your replies. You could take turns with a partner or friend. You could decide to give it a miss. You could also discover quite a lot about your parents and your own style of attachment, and the kind of bag-gage which is passed down the generations in your own family.

- How was your relationship with your parents when you were very little?

- What is the first memory that you have of them?

- Which five words would you choose to describe your relationship with your father, and with your mother, during the time when you were a child?

● What happened in your family when as a child you were emotionally upset?

● Were the grown-ups in your family ever rejecting towards you?

● Did you lose anyone special to you while you were a child?

● What do you think caused your parents to behave towards you as they did?

● Do you think your childhood experiences have influenced your personality?

● What is the single most important thing, learnt from your own childhood, that you would like to pass on to your children?

Some people find such an exercise enlightening, while it can produce rage, tears or a blank defensiveness in others. What is important is that you have begun to think actively about the sorts of experiences you had as a child and their possible influence on your present-day style of parenting. In the next section I am going to try to encapsulate the main varieties of parenting, so that you can ponder a little longer on the likely inter-generational links in your own family. Recognizing these links and patterns is the first step towards improving your parenting style. Remember that the distance between you and your goal can always be shortened.

GIVING AND RECEIVING

In order, starting with the most prevalent style and ending with our old favourite introduced in Chapter 1, I shall describe

● inconsistent parenting

● authoritarian parenting

● over-dependent parenting

● distant parenting

● neglectful parenting

● balanced parenting

Each of these styles is part of the 'giving and receiving' in family interactions. Ideas on how to adjust your style if, after reading what follows, you realize it is needed, will be put forward in *Setting the scene for change* (p. 72) and *What to do next* (p. 82).

Inconsistent parenting

This style of parenting makes it difficult for your child to predict the likely outcome of any interaction with you. For instance:

Gillian, aged ten, tries constantly to please her mother as she yearns for approval. When Mother says, 'Come upstairs with me,' she rushes to comply, only to be told irritably, 'Don't crowd me! Keep your distance!' Gillian, feeling rejected and disliked, obeys and files away a reminder not to 'crowd' her mother. So on the next occasion Gillian lags behind. She is hoping for approval, but is told instead, 'Don't hang back! I'm not infectious, you know!' Crushed and confused, Gillian tries to close the physical gap but her mother cries, 'No need to breathe down my neck! You're not a baby now!'

These were the painful recollections of a thirty-year-old woman who still felt that, as she could never get anything right, she was worthless as a person. This depressing and illogical belief – professionally, she was very successful – had been directly caused by her mother's unpredictable behaviour. Happily, Gillian was able to benefit from Cognitive Behaviour Therapy; has now cleared out much of her 'baggage' about this relationship; and is beginning to feel worthwhile as an individual and to trust that others find her valuable too.

High levels of consistency are quite easy to achieve over short periods, but over a day, a week or a lifetime such regularity is impossible. None the less, children thrive on a regime which they can forecast, and consistency in handling them must remain your goal, however unlikely you are to achieve it fully. From the child's perspective, inconsistent parents are both

- available and nowhere to be found
- warm and rejecting

- approving and critical

- in control and overwhelmed

In essence, they are both reliable *and* unpredictable. There seems no way of knowing with any certainty what their mother or father will do next. This is because the adults' responses have more to do with their own immediate emotional status than with their child's actual behaviour. So the children of inconsistent parents can suffer from

- low self-confidence

- insecurity and anxiety

- behaviour problems

- downright unhappiness

Why, when you so definitely don't want your children to feel insecure, does it end up like that? I think it is likely to be because your own parents were, in their turn, inconsistent with you in childhood. If you remember

- frequently lacking self-confidence

- feeling insecure and anxious

- having problems in trusting others

it could well be that your own parents, though doing their very best, somehow failed to give you the stability and predictability which you needed so much as a child. It may be that you still feel like this, at least some of the time. It is likely that in your childhood there were times when

- you were subjected to broken promises

- your best efforts were praised one minute and criticized the next

- it felt scary because you seemed to be running the show and your parents didn't know how to take charge and be firm and fond

If these sorts of memories predominate, you are probably having problems in trusting others and could be repeating your parents' pattern even as you consciously try to do the opposite. There is no doubt that, if your own parents were not sufficiently balanced in style, you may well end up hoist with their petard in your own parenting efforts.

All this does not, in my view, preclude future positive change in your style of bringing up your own children. With this, as with all less-than-perfect styles of parenting, insight is a helpful first step. Acknowledging the influences of the previous generation is an important ingredient in becoming more consistent and balanced in your parenting.

Authoritarian parenting

The main characteristics here are:

- being too directive
- being insufficiently concerned with the child's perspective
- being disapproving
- being too concerned with appearances and self-image
- passivity and over-dependence
- fear of, and antagonism towards, authority figures
- anxiety about being spontaneous
- rebelliousness
- feelings of not being worth listening to
- emotional insecurity

Overall, if your mother and father make all the decisions and their ideas cannot be challenged, you can end up believing that you are powerless and unable to contribute anything of value however hard you try. If you look back to your own childhood and have lots of memories of

- having little self-confidence
- being afraid of your parents

● having little control over even minor events

● feeling utterly powerless in your attempts to put across your own views

it is likely that your parents were too authoritarian in their parenting style. You may still, too often, experience a replay of the times when

● you were over-ruled

● you were deprived of the opportunity to show true independence

● you feared the disapproval and criticism of those in authority

Should you as an adult still choose the option of doing as you're told more often than not – or, conversely, be the only one who is allowed to make decisions, you are probably too authoritarian in style.

Over-dependent or over-involved parenting

This type is often associated with unresolved psychological issues related to loss. Parents of this kind exhibit the following characteristics:

● very over-protective

● intrusive and interfering

● too anxious

● emotionally too close to their child

From the child's perspective there is not enough 'space' for them to become an individual in their own right. It can be almost as if your mother and father are living your life for you!
Over-involved parenting can produce in the child:

● a fragile sense of their own identity

● feelings of being smothered

- fearfulness

- resentment and frustration

- problem behaviours

- emotional explosiveness

You may find that, despite your own best intentions, you are repeating your parents' over-dependent child-rearing pattern. If you can vividly remember feeling:

- smothered to the point of explosive frustration

- afraid to deal with anything unless your parents were close by

- resentful that even your feelings were not your own

it is likely that your parents were over-involved in your life as a baby, toddler, schoolchild and adolescent. You may recall:

- desperately wanting to do things for yourself and being frustrated by your parents' over-protectiveness

- trying to establish your own friendships, only to have your parents become 'one of the gang'

- setting off on a new venture only to have your pleasurably excited anticipation thoroughly undermined by your parents' anxieties for your safety

If this sounds familiar, you are likely to be wrestling with some unresolved issues to do with loss of personal space, independence and sense of individual identity – all of which could be affecting your relationship with your children.

Distant parenting

This style is often characterized by:

- finding little time for your children

- giving priority to work and other activities

- finding it difficult to show warm feelings

- saving your energy for yourself

- regarding your children simply as a responsibility

- finding parenting all duty and no fun

- leaving most of the daily interactions with your child to someone else

If this sounds like a description of mothers and fathers who work, I want to state quite categorically that pursuing paid employment does not necessarily lead to distant parenting. You have noted, I am sure, that though bringing up your children makes running a large department store look easy, the former is unpaid while the latter would keep you in financial clover! Working full-time does, however, limit the amount of time you can spend with your child, so making sure that you provide quality if not quantity means that a balanced style becomes even more important.

Many children with distant parents feel that there is almost nothing they can do to gain attention from their mother and father, except perhaps to be very naughty indeed. As the child of a distant parent you may find it difficult to attract any warmth at all, and therefore begin to wonder if your parents love you. So distant parenting is likely to cause a child to

- feel unsure of their place in their parents' affections

- believe that they are somehow a failure

- long for approval and warmth yet at the same time be afraid of emotional intimacy

- learn that in order to obtain any attention at all, even if it is critical, you have to behave badly

- experience constant anxiety about whether they are really loved

You yourself as an adult might, despite many successes in your life, be unable to shake off doubts about whether you are truly lovable and loved. Perhaps, in striving to maintain their own emotional balance, your parents were fearful about reaching out to embrace you – literally and metaphorically. Because of your memories of times when you had

- no sign from your mother and father that they approved of you

- no cuddles to express their warmth

- no chance of experiencing the glow that comes from being told, 'I love you'

you could now be using a similarly distant style with your own children.

Neglectful parenting

This term is most commonly applied to adults who are

- unable to meet even their children's basic physical needs at an adequate level

This does not mean that if your child has headlice, glue ear or ringworm you are neglecting them. Up to 50 per cent of children in an ordinary classroom will be suffering from one or more of these conditions because they are so contagious. The main hallmark of neglectful parenting in this instance is the failure to take efficient steps to get rid of the nits and eggs, worms and glue.

Children who are neglected often try to look after themselves – or an eight-year-old, for instance, will be trying to feed, clean and supervise six-year-old twin siblings. As you can imagine, neglected children are exposed to huge areas of seemingly unending uncertainty:

- Will there be any food in the house today when they get home from school?

- Will Mum or Dad be there to put them to bed tonight?

- Will they have any socks or pants to wear to school tomorrow?

- Will it be so cold indoors that they won't be able to sleep?

● Will they be, once more, sleeping in a room where the only furniture is a urine-soaked mattress on the floor?

The reasons are various, and need have nothing to do with the parents' income or social standing. There are children living in homes which run to the employment of nannies, au pairs and cleaners, but who have to exist on a diet of cornflakes and cold toast. I know. I've seen them.

Why would a parent behave like this towards their children? It might be because they themselves were so psychologically and emotionally damaged in their youth that they don't view their own behaviour as wrong in any way. Alternatively, severe mental illness, learning disabilities or having been seriously abused as a child, as well as dependence on drugs and alcohol, can each play a major role.

Were you to have, quite undeservedly, suffered such privations yourself in childhood, as a parent you might well be putting almost too much emphasis on making sure that your children are always well fed, clean and smart, and subject to a clear routine. In other words, you may have over-reacted and become a physically over-dependent parent. You may, on the other hand, have developed the attitude that a spartan lifestyle is good for growing children. One effect is more certain: that you as a grown-up find it hard to feel empathy towards others, or conversely veer strongly towards an unnecessary degree of solicitude.

Balanced parenting

Since this ideal style of parenting was the main focus of Chapter 1, and will continue to occupy centre stage throughout the rest of the book, only a few additional snippets need be mentioned at this point. If you are fortunate enough to have been provided with balanced parenting throughout the first twenty years of your life, you have a clear head start in meeting the many challenges of bringing up your own children. Your offspring may already be experiencing you as someone who can:

● lovingly take control

● be fond and firm where appropriate

- show warmth and approval

- set clear limits and stick to them

- show and tell your child that you always love *them* even though you do not approve of what they sometimes *do*

- ignore minor naughtiness

- praise at every opportunity

- be flexible and reasonable

- listen to what they have to say

- allow them choices

- only punish when their behaviour is totally out of bounds

- and, of course, naturally have 'off days' when you cannot 'keep it all together'

Every parent, however marvellous, will experience failure at some time or other. There will be days when, for a variety of reasons, you may snap, lose your cool, flop around and feel useless, and generally experience a crisis of confidence. Indeed, from your child's point of view those days when you feel pathetic as a parent are very necessary if they are to develop a realistic view of relationships. They will also learn to forgive themselves for their lapses as they watch you 'pick yourself up, dust yourself down, and start all over again!'

Other useful personal qualities that can evolve from being cared for by a balanced parent are:

- fundamental security in the knowledge that you are loved and lovable

- the knowledge that you are a reasonably self-confident and communicative person

- a healthy capacity for emotional intimacy

- creative and adventurous energy

- a resilient and stable enough personality to enable you to deal with life's inevitable disappointments

- empathy with others

- a willingness to curb the need for instant gratification

- the ability to cry without feeling shame

- the capability to deal with your own and others' angry feelings

Sounds too good to be true? In reality, of course, the perfect person or parent cannot exist. You are still *you*, and everyone has their own idiosyncratic psychological and behavioural twists and turns. But it is still important to know what you are aiming for in terms of the kind of individual and mother or father you would *like* to be.

ECHOES

Before I go on to tackle the practicalities involved in making positive parenting progress, I want you to be quite clear that you are not alone in finding it difficult to pinpoint your baggage, peer into its contents, absorb its present meaning and start to resolve some of those painful left-over issues from your childhood. I too struggle in much the same way! To encourage you, let me tell you about some of the load that I hump around with me and periodically attempt to sort out.

I was a war baby, born in 1940. That fact alone had a powerful impact on my early life, for a number of reasons. First my father, with whom I had established a strong bond, went away to serve in the Royal Navy for two and a half years. Then I and the rest of my family were evacuated to the countryside, far away from the familiarity of home in the danger zone around London. Rising five I was very ill, and spent six months in hospital without seeing any of my family – such was the unenlightened medical practice of those days. You can see that disappearing adults, separations and moves were the name of my early Family Game.

To my enormous good fortune, both my mother and father (once he returned home) managed for much of the time to be adequately balanced parents. But there was one undoubted wartime trauma in my childhood. The curtain in the doorway of the garden air-raid shelter caught light and set my baby sister's cot on fire. I did the only thing that seemed possible for a three-year-old and screamed 'Mummy!' loudly. She must have arrived from the nearby kitchen within seconds, assessed the situation, swept my sister out of the burning cot, placed her on the grass outside and immediately came back for me. In those few seconds after my mother rescued my sister, and before she came back for me, my infant reaction was to assume that only one child could be saved, and it wasn't me.

The psychological legacy? A lifetime spent very hard trying to be the one who is chosen first! What strikes me now is that such a brief, if dramatic, interlude should have had such an enduring effect. If my parents had been significantly less balanced, the impact could well have been much more destructive.

I know that I was very angry with my mother for 'abandoning' me in hospital for six months. She told me later that, despite the nightly bombing raids, she came every evening to the back of the hospital and climbed on to a rubbish bin so that she could peer over the wall into the lighted ward where my bed was. Very poignant in retrospect. At the time I was busily learning as many 'swear words' as possible for my return home. My mother hated bad language. Enough said! Neither would I speak to her on my father's return from the war, referring to her only via him and calling her 'that woman'. Causing problems? Me!

During my adolescence my parents were, in comparison with those of my best friends, very strict. This meant that, in my hectic pursuit of boyfriends, I lied to them with quiet regularity. 'Just off to play tennis with Jill!' Off to roll around on the grass with Jack, more like. It was only in my twenties, after becoming a mother myself, that I realized the value of their protectiveness and accurately translated their behaviour as another manifestation of their love for me.

I grew up, despite these alarms and excursions, with a solid set of assumptions about what mothers and fathers actually did. I learned that fathers don't ever smack you, though very occasionally mothers did, particularly if exasperated beyond all reason. I learned that mothers are at home while fathers go out to work. I learned that cuddles and kisses are a happy family's coinage of affection. I learned that hearing, and saying, 'I love you' felt grand. I learned that you could be forgiven for bad behaviour because you were loved and treasured as a person. I learned that mothers draw and cut out paper dolls and help you make clothes for them. I learned that fathers let you help with painting rooms and planting vegetable seeds. I learned that mothers praised artistic efforts and that fathers were proud when you won the Egg and Spoon Race at the school sports day or passed your exams. I learned that reading could take you anywhere, and teach you everything.

It is obvious to me that my childhood experiences, both pleasurable and difficult, have continued to exert a good deal of influence in terms of my personality and my mothering. For example, I stayed with them when they had to go to hospital, I worked hard at making my children the top priority without, however, confining myself to the kitchen sink; and I made sure that their father was thoroughly involved in enjoying their company. I have continued to struggle with the notion that, in order to be chosen first, you have to outshine the competition; and its corollary, that if you are not so chosen you may be rejected to the point of death. My nightmares have always been about leading my children to safety – all a little silly now, as they have not hesitated to point out. Particularly as they are all very much taller than me and now in their thirties!

So even clinical psychologists have baggage to handle. Indeed, some would say that in taking up my profession I was quite clearly attempting to deal with the contents of my own personal Pandora's Box. As I get older, I become increasingly aware of the powerful role which my mother and father, and their mothers and fathers, have all played in shaping the type of relationships which I have. Most importantly, they affected those relationships lived as a mother and grandmother. However, I have to agree with the sticker in the rear window of a car into which I quite gently drove a few years ago. It read, 'I just love being a grandmother – it's a pity it didn't come first!'

SETTING THE SCENE FOR CHANGE

As this chapter's emphasis is on family patterns of child-rearing across generations, I shall concentrate on the particular principle of Social Learning Theory (see p. 22) which refers to vicarious learning, or modelling as it is often called. Implicit in the Parent/Child Game is the maxim: 'Learning by imitation is an important tool in discovering the ways in which family relationships are acted out.' The relevant aspects of Child Development Theory here relate to the powerful lessons that children learn from those really significant and influential beings, their mother and father.

Like parent, like child

Vicarious learning is of course subject to the usual rules about the impact of various types of consequences on the probability of a certain behaviour being repeated (see p. 23). It is easy to observe in young children: you show them how to clap; they have a stab at it too; you smile and laugh and clap your hands some more. Ergo, there will be lots more baby clapping in future. Should you ignore their efforts, after a shortish burst of applause from your toddler, clapping will die a quick death. When this principle is applied to more complex psychological areas such as the expression of emotions, the strength of its impact on family relationship styles can readily be seen.

All humans are born with identical central nervous system capacity for experiencing, processing and expressing feelings. If a brain specialist electronically stimulates the same points in several people's brains, similar reactions of fear, anger, humour, optimism and so on can be produced. The range of such emotions is relatively limited and has not, in my view, progressed greatly since the beginning of human history. But each of the basic emotions contains an almost infinite number of shades and tones. When you stir in the complications which inevitably arise unless you live in a large sealed vacuum flask, then the subtleties of any interaction between adult partners, father and son, father and daughter, mother and daughter, and mother and son can become a huge and frightening explosion of the occasions for vicarious learning. Or it can prove fascinating. It all depends if you're having a good day or not.

Small wonder, then, that you can witness scene after scene, in any big store, park, street, school or home where children express their feelings in a style learnt directly from their parents. These parents in their turn imitated their own mothers' and fathers' manner of interacting with others.

Take the family style for showing approval, one to the other, within and across generations. The Butler family, for instance, use phrases such as, 'Hmph! Not bad, I suppose', or 'Well, it's better than last time but there's still a way to go.' Then the Fergusons: 'Can't you manage any better than that?', or 'Call that a picture/kettle holder/sandcastle/bookmark/coffee table?' While in the same street the Coxes' style goes something like this: 'Is that all you think of me? I'm insulted that you should think a box of embroidered hankies could buy my approval.' Nearby, the Haldane parents are issuing rather cool approval: 'Mm. It's OK', or 'Quite nice, really.' While the Blooms may be going to the opposite extreme: 'My darling! My precious! My love, you are very clever/talented/lucky/pretty/ athletic', or 'Oh! My God! It's fabulous, I never dreamed you'd be able to do it, and you *have*!'

Naively, I once supposed that a praise is a praise is a praise. Now I know better. I know that a praise can, according to the relationship style of the person issuing it, range from straightforward condemnation through despair and anger to cloying dependence.

Converting insight into action

There *is* a constructive way to model genuine praise, as you will see from the precise details in *What to do next* on p. 82. Anyone so motivated can put it into practice, even if it is not the model with which they grew up. Whatever interaction style you imitated as an infant, toddler, schoolchild and adolescent; whatever its effect on you, you *can* learn to be more Child Centred (indeed, more Person Centred) as long as you want to change. Even though you might remember being unsure about how to gain your parents' approval; unable to find the space and assurance to be yourself; feeling afraid that you had no right to power over your own actions; and fearing that your very best efforts were not going to bring warmth and focused attention from your parents, you *can* move on constructively.

Everyone has the capacity to make positive changes in the way in which they parent their children.

Remember, we all make mistakes. No one is a perfect parent – life is far too complex, demanding and unpredictable for that. You may be all too aware of your own shortcomings. You may be beginning to understand how your difficulties as a mother or father could be linked to your own early experiences as a child. But you may be pretty stumped when it comes to working out how to make a start in changing your parenting style.

Since it is not easy to convert insight into action, I shall make some suggestions for how you might begin. The ideas I am going to set out are intended to be a guide to your first steps after having begun to understand the link between your own and the previous generation's style of parenting.

Apart from the empowering statements below, another move which you can make is to confide in a sympathetic friend or relative about your plans to change your style of parenting. You could tell them something about your own childhood, and then listen to whatever they might want to tell you. Only say as much as is comfortable. Discuss with them the links that you have seen between your early experiences, and your intention to be a more balanced parent in future. Should moments of chaos loom, despite your best efforts, then use the appropriate emergency self-help line. Think of this phrase as a kind of extended mantra. You may find it convenient to write it down clearly on a postcard, or to stick it to the fridge door in magnetic letters. Just repeat it to yourself whenever you are losing confidence and feel in need of urgent moral support!

Getting away from inconsistent parenting
If you have identified yourself as a rather inconsistent parent – or should I say *when*, as every mother and father is inconsistent to one degree or another – you have probably realized that you need to make progress on issues of trust and control. To begin getting it right, try saying to yourself:

- I do have the skills to be a balanced parent.

- There is a lot to be gained for all the family from my taking loving control.

● My children need me to be consistent so that they can learn to trust me.

● When I am more in control, as a mother or father, then I will be more in charge of my own life.

● *I can learn to trust myself.*

EMERGENCY SELF-HELP LINE FOR INCONSISTENT PARENTS

I can be more consistent because I know my children need to trust me and learn to control their own lives.

Getting away from authoritarian parenting

You may have realized that you are too authoritarian a mother or father. If so, I expect you have discovered that there are issues relating to power and independence that need your positive attention. As a first step to getting it right, try some self-instruction along these lines:

● I have a lot to gain by giving up some of my power: my children would not be so afraid of me and we could become friends.

● My children need me to allow them some power over their own lives so that they can eventually become independent people.

● I won't lose my children by helping them towards independence, because they will want to spend time with me of their own free will.

● I know it feels risky to take more of a back seat, but I could win my children's cooperation and that is quite a prize.

● *I can allow myself not to be all-powerful.*

**EMERGENCY SELF-HELP LINE FOR
AUTHORITARIAN PARENTS**

I can give my children the power they need to become independent and it will be good for all of us.

Getting away from passive parenting

If you are the adult child of authoritarian parents you may have
gone to the other extreme by becoming passive, fearful and
submissive in your interaction style. This is more common in
mothers than in fathers. The useful self-instruction phrases for
starting to get it right are:

- I have a lot to gain by showing my children that I am the
one in control of family life: my children will respect me
and I needn't be afraid of them, so we could become
friends.

- My children need me to exert some control over their
lives so that they can learn to trust me to keep them safe
until they can be more independent.

- I won't lose my children's affections by lovingly taking
control, as they will feel more comfortable in our relationship and so will actively want to spend time with me.

- I know it feels dangerous to try to take more control, but
I could win my children's cooperation – a valuable
commodity.

- I can allow myself to take more control.

**EMERGENCY SELF-HELP LINE FOR
PASSIVE PARENTS**

I can take charge of my children's behaviour when necessary and
it will benefit us all.

Getting away from emotionally over-involved parenting
Should you believe you may be an over-involved parent, and
are aware of unresolved issues on personal space and identity
from your own childhood, you could start getting it right by
helping yourself psychologically in the ways listed below,
saying to yourself:

● I can learn a new, more balanced way of parenting.

● I am aware of the links with my early childhood experiences, and that is a very important step in the right direction.

● My children need me to give them more space to be
themselves so that they can develop their own special
identities.

● When I give more space to my children, I will be giving
more space to myself.

● *I can learn to be myself.*

**EMERGENCY SELF-HELP LINE FOR
EMOTIONALLY OVER-INVOLVED PARENTS**

I can let go and give my children the space they need to develop
their own individual identities, and then my children will love me
more.

Getting away from distant parenting
If you recognize yourself as a distant mother or father, you are
probably aware that there are some emotional loose ends to do
with approval and love from your own childhood. Keep repeating to yourself:

● There will be so much for all of us to gain by showing
my children that I really do love them.

● I can learn to say to my children, 'I love you' without the
sky falling in.

- Making links with my own childhood is a major step forward.

- My children need me to express my love for them if they are to develop into confident and communicative individuals.

- When I show approval of my children they will want to please me and being with them will be more fun.

- *I can learn to approve of myself.*

EMERGENCY SELF-HELP LINE FOR DISTANT PARENTS

I can show my children the love I feel for them and I know this will help us to be a closer family.

Getting away from spartan parenting

Should you realize that you were seriously deprived of material comforts and predictable behaviour from your parents when you were a child, you may adhere to rather spartan standards for your own offspring. It is likely that you have been left in confusion about nurturance and emotional intimacy. You can initiate progress towards a more balanced style by self-instruction using these phrases:

- I can give my children regular treats without ruining their personality development.

- My whole family will benefit when I allow my soft side to show more often.

- Allowing myself to be emotionally close to my children will help them to learn that close relationships are good.

- I can be fond *and* firm, as the children need.

- *I deserve treats too.*

EMERGENCY SELF-HELP LINE FOR
SPARTAN PARENTS

I can nurture my children and myself because everyone deserves
that type of attention.

Getting away from physically over-dependent parenting

Alternatively you may, because your own parents neglected
you, have reacted at the opposite extreme by over-indulging
your children. This too is likely to relate to unsolved problems
concerning nurturing and emotional intimacy. When you
decide that you want to move forward, start by saying over and
over again:

● My children need me to say, 'I love you' more than they
need another new pair of trainers.

● I can show my love for my children in ways other than
decorating their bedroom every six months.

● I can help my children learn that money can't buy you
love.

● *I can show my love for my children by being sensitive to their
emotional rather than physical needs.*

EMERGENCY SELF-HELP LINE FOR
PHYSICALLY OVER-DEPENDENT PARENTS

I can give my children my balanced attention, which is worth
much more than its weight in gold.

Getting to the goal: balanced parenting

When you begin to believe that you are providing balanced
parenting for your children, and have dealt fairly successfully

with any problem baggage to do with trust, loss, power, love and caring, you need to:

- congratulate yourself on a task well handled
- acknowledge that there are still a few wobbly patches in your parenting prowess
- stir up the courage to admit that there is always room for improvement in the momentous task of parenting

So, taking a deep breath, try getting it even more right by telling yourself:

- The more balanced I am in my parenting, the better it is for my children.
- When I'm getting it right for my children I'm doing myself a big favour too.
- Families are more fun when parents get the balance right.
- I know it all takes time, energy and dedication to be a balanced parent, but so too would being inconsistent, authoritarian, over-involved, distant or neglectful. Anyway, I *know* my balanced efforts are really benefiting my children.
- *I can learn to have more confidence in myself.*

Other moves you could make would include, as always, swapping ideas with other mothers and fathers about how you are trying to be even more balanced as a parent. Talk about balanced parenting and the importance of Child Centred behaviours with a trusted friend. You might try discussing your struggle to deal with the unresolved issues from your past and how, even though you are pleased with your progress, you realize it is all part of an ongoing process. Mention the links you can see between your own childhood and how you are trying to bring up your children. Always be available to reciprocate by listening to other parents.

EMERGENCY SELF-HELP LINE (EVEN BALANCED PARENTS NEED ONE!)

I am doing OK. What my children need is balanced parenting, not perfection.

Pause for reflection

So how do you feel so far? Overwhelmed by the journey ahead? Pleased with the progress you have already made? Perhaps a little of each.

You may find that the practical steps outlined below under *What to do next* are easier to deal with than the more complex and subtle psychological aspects I have been detailing. But 'talking to yourself' in the ways suggested above is proof that you are beginning to move towards your goal of being a more balanced parent, and it has proved a powerful tool for solving the problems that constitute our baggage from childhood.

Talking to others and sharing your hopes and fears is also a very positive step forward in making changes in your own behaviour and feelings about yourself. I know that it is often easier not to speak out. I too have been on occasion afraid of being ridiculed and so have kept silent. But this is wrong, because generally you will find that, once you open yourself up, others are quite eager to follow suit – to the benefit of all involved. Be brave – I tried it, and I can assure you that the rewards far outweigh the imagined risks.

In this chapter so far I have tried to show what it is that all babies, and older offspring too, need from their parents. I hope you have also gleaned that your and my parenting styles are related to early childhood experiences when, despite wanting the best for us, our parents could not quite meet our needs.

WHAT TO DO NEXT

Now I want to move on to some practical suggestions for each style of parenting that will help you sort out what to do next.

Remember it is likely that you demonstrate aspects of several parenting approaches. You will probably find it most useful to 'graze' through the menu of suggestions in *Setting the scene for change* and *What to do next*, picking and choosing those items which ring personal bells. By mixing and matching in this way you can come up with a tailor-made package which will let you off-load some of the leftover baggage from your attachment history, and take up the exciting challenge of beginning to make the changes which will bring back the fun to your family life.

If you are too inconsistent

● Give balanced attention. Praise your child for good behaviour and ignore all minor naughtiness.

● Save punishments for really awful behaviour and remember that smacking does *not* help in even the short term, never mind the long run. (There will be more on punishment in Chapter 3.)

● Give your child clear commands and praise them as soon as they start to do as they are told.

● Write out a plan of campaign, and *stick* to it.

● Reward yourself with little (or big!) treats for making any and every move towards being more consistent.

If you are over-authoritarian

● Make a list of the areas in your children's lives where you make all the decisions. Then decide those where you could safely give your offspring the chance to put their point of view across.

● Listen attentively to your child's perspective on things.

● Work out what activities your children could safely do independently of yourself, then let them go ahead, and praise their efforts even if they are not totally successful.

● Gradually extend the areas of independence of thought and action which you give your child. (Warning: this can take up to twenty years in my experience!)

● Plan ahead, and reward yourself as you meet each target.

If you aren't assertive enough

● Draw up a list of all the areas in which your children, rather than you, seem to be making the decisions. Then decide which of them you strongly feel should have you at the helm and start putting Child Centred behaviours into action.

● Be brave about putting your own ideas across to your children – mothers and fathers are often right!

● Decide which specific activities you believe should be supervised by you in person, then stick to your guns.

● Gradually work towards the situation in which you and your children are fully aware of when and where they can stretch their wings, and when and where Mum and/or Dad will be in charge.

● Work out a programme of change for yourself, and give yourself treats for every little step in the right direction.

If you are over-involved

● Work out what small and safe things your child could do alone, with a friend or another trusted adult, and positively encourage them to go ahead.

● Try learning a relaxation technique to reduce your anxieties, and use it when you are feeling panicky about letting go of your child.

● Only gradually increase the degree of independence which you allow your child, so that there are no shocks for anyone involved.

● Talk to your child and find out what they think and feel about togetherness, while making sure that you are the one who guides any changes made.

● Write out your short-term and final goals and give yourself a reward whenever you achieve any of them.

● Praise yourself heartily for each positive step you make towards giving your child the room to develop their own identity.

If you are rather distant

● Make a list of the advantages of showing your loving feelings, and then weigh it against the disadvantages of hiding them.

● Try saying, 'I love you', softly at first if that is easier, once a day to each of your children. Be ready to repeat it a little louder if they look surprised.

● Plan to spend some time alone with your child doing something you both enjoy. Even half an hour can mean a lot, though two half-hours mean much more.

● Show your children, by praising them and their efforts as often as possible, that you really are noticing and approving of them.

● Congratulate yourself on coming in from the cold and beginning to be a warm, loving and balanced parent.

If you are too spartan

● Write down all those times when you use a veto towards your children's desires for material goodies. Say to yourself, 'Just because I didn't have luxuries, there's no reason why my children shouldn't have some on occasion.'

● Plan carefully which of your child's most burning wishes you can financially afford, and when. Remember that not going to Disneyland has no known adverse effects on a child's development!

● Say to your children, 'No one gets everything they want and often you have to wait. But you have my love *all* the time, and that's worth a million jewels.'

● Treat yourself to 'a little something' each time you manage to be indulgent towards your children.

If you are over-indulgent

● For a week jot down in a diary all those times when you gave your child a toy, sweet or video when a hug, praise or 'I love you' would have been better for their soul.

● Say to your children, 'I want you to learn that money can't buy the most precious thing in the world, and that is love. Maybe you can have a mountain bike one day, but for now I want to give you a big hug 'cos you're gorgeous.'

● Work out a plan for the next six months and decide for yourself what material treats you will allow your child. Discuss with other parents what is reasonable in the line of pocket money, for instance.

● When you have given your child a cuddle instead of a Cabbage Patch doll, pamper yourself with a treat such as a long bath and lots of lovely smellies.

If you feel you are getting balanced

● Make sure you tell your children that you love them, loud, clear and often.

● Ensure that you are praising your children's efforts and activities as often as you possibly can.

● Check that you are giving them enough personal space to develop their very own sense of identity.

● Watch out in case you aren't allowing them sufficient independence or aren't listening carefully enough to their views.

● Set up treats for all the family and have fun together.

● Congratulate yourself and any partner on being good enough parents, and make sure you get some time to yourselves to be grown-ups together.

● Remember that children need parents who know how to enjoy themselves as adults when they are off duty as parents.

A QUICK FIX ON CHAPTER 2

1. You can learn to understand your attachment history by looking at the parenting styles of the different generations in your family.

Example: Philip's father worked away a great deal and was very strict when at home. When Philip himself became a father, though he worked from home, he too was a strict and distant parent, often shut in his study for twelve hours a day. Philip's sister Megan, on the other hand, became a rather submissive woman whose three sons regularly ran rings around her. Once Philip and Megan understood the cross-generation links at work in their extended families, both were able to become more Child Centred.

Evidence: Studies frequently show that mothers and fathers are likely to repeat the pattern of child-rearing used by their own parents. Alternatively, some may go to the opposite extreme as a reaction against painful childhood experiences. Self-help strategies are known to facilitate positive change.

2. Gradually unpack your own baggage. It will help you to progress as an individual. It will also benefit your children to have a mother or father who is not so weighed down by past experiences.

Example: Sonia, mother of two daughters, had never been her own mother's favourite. As a result she had spent her child-hood trying to outshine her sister Diana and believing herself to be a failure in comparison. Sonia was shocked to realize that she too had a favourite amongst her daughters. When Sonia had unpacked some of the baggage from her own early life, she recognized that, whatever her mother's attitude, she was just as valuable a person as Diana. As a result of tackling the painful aspects of her attachment history Sonia became more self-confident both as an individual and as a mother. She found herself no longer needing, in her turn, to favour one of her daughters over the other.

Evidence: Research findings persistently report that ignoring the long-term impact of emotional hurts received in childhood from one's parents is associated with continuing relationship problems. The parent/child relationship is no exception. Studies demonstrate that motivation to achieve change is a fundamental requirement of progress towards a more realistic view of one's own personality potential.

3. Whatever your present parenting style you can, if you are determined enough, learn how to be a more balanced parent.

Example: Jane and Simon both found it difficult to be consistent in their parenting. Their family life with son Tom and daughter Miriam was unpredictable in the extreme. Both parents came from similar family backgrounds. They worked hard at understanding the links between their own childhood experiences and their current parenting difficulties. They jointly decided to put the Attention Rule into operation for a week to see if it made any difference. In consequence, Tom and Miriam became more cooperative and seemed to feel more secure. Jane and Simon discovered that they too felt more relaxed and less confused.

Evidence: Scientific investigations regularly show that adults can change their style of interaction with their children. The basic requirements are quoted as being sufficient motivation, a knowledge of the Attention Rule, and Child Centred parenting principles and practice.

3. Speaking Out, Not Acting Out

Emotional Flashpoints

WHAT THIS CHAPTER IS ABOUT

Chapter 3 gives priority to the psychological price paid for bottling up strong emotions and eventually acting them out, as opposed to being able to speak about them out loud. The ways in which styles of dealing with the emotional flashpoints endemic to family life can persist across the generations will also be a focus. The wide range of differing responses which any one individual can produce in a high octane exchange, and the possible reasons behind this, provide other avenues to be explored, as does the whole issue of the potentially positive alternatives to the acting out that is such a temptation in the heat of the moment. The key words here are **challenges, reactions** and **solutions**.

HOW PEOPLE DEAL WITH EMOTIONAL OVERLOAD

Anthropologists tell us that in comparison to most of the animal kingdom, human beings as individuals are quite peace-loving and laid back. When, for instance, was the last time you saw a newspaper headline: 'Father eats five of his children because fridge was empty?' The grown men of our species no longer have to fight and vanquish every male adolescent who looks at the mother of his children. Nor, thank goodness, do women have to stalk around with a pair of scarlet knickers in full view when they feel horny. Apparently there is more good news in that, though humans often live in very close proximity to one another, killing someone simply because they put a foot over your doorstep is relatively rare.

The trouble is, that still leaves mothers and fathers, sons and daughters with a great number of overpoweringly strong feelings swirling around during the daily interactions with those who live in close proximity: the other family members. Research on the effects of overcrowding on other species shows that some 'freeze' and hope to get by unnoticed and unhurt. Others rage around biting all those they can sink their little pointy teeth into. A few try to organize a kind of cooperative living plan. And some end up trampled to death in the rush for food or mates.

There have been moments in my own family's life when emotions were so fevered that I felt like strangling anyone within reach. But the fact is that people are capable of voluntarily inhibiting even their strongest impulses – witness the lack of dead bodies in my kitchen just before Christmas lunch for fifteen.

That people have the ability to suppress their emotions, to swallow their feelings, is not in doubt. Neither is it questioned that they can just as easily let those violent forces rip. What seems less clear is why, given the destructive nature of bottling it up and acting it out, humans so seldom exercise the third option, which is to speak out about the ebbs and swells of their feelings. The emphasis here is on the use of language as a vehicle for expressing complex and powerful emotions.

In my view there are a whole host of factors which, combined at the critical flashpoint in an interaction, lead to our either firmly closing our mouths or opening them in order to sound off in angry, injured, fearful or confused tones. This latter is *not* what I mean by 'speaking out'! When you realize that everyone is in effect *taught* how to respond and behave regarding the expression of emotions, antagonistic and/or loving, then the crucial role of your experiences in your own family of origin begins to emerge. Once again, though, simply because you learned as a child to 'turn the other cheek', 'hit them where it hurts' or 'just walk away' from relationship crunch points, you don't have to perpetuate in the next generation your family's style of dealing with challenging interactions. Positive progress is open to everyone who really wants to take the sting out of family affairs and put the love back into them.

Challenges

You can tell when a family challenge is really in the offing. It is when, even though it is snowing outside and the central heating has broken down inside, your emotional temperature shoots up from 0 to 100 degrees in as many milliseconds. It may well be that, in your family, it is possible to predict quite accurately when the next flashpoint will occur. They can be caused by any number of things, though patterns tend to establish themselves, often across the generations and certainly within the confines of a particular family consisting of just parents and children.

All levels of interaction are involved: between mother and father, father and son, son and daughter, daughter and mother, father and daughter, mother and son, son and son, daughter and daughter. However, I shall be concentrating here on those interchanges which involve either a parent and child, or two parents. The mysteries of sibling hate fests and fun hours will be dealt with in Chapter 6.

Personality matches and mismatches

Let me tell you about what I see as the more common precursors to family thunderstorms. Perhaps one of the most powerful, though often unacknowledged, factors is temperament or personality. It seems you are born with a particular pattern of wiring in your nervous system, plus some individual biochemical mixtures, which can have a potent impact in terms of temperament whatever your social or emotional environment.

For example: everyone knows that John's father is a morose old devil, while his mother is a sparkling personality; everyone knows that little Cindy and her sister Jenny are like chalk and cheese; everyone knows that Tim gets on really well with his father but seems to clash with sickening regularity when it is just he and his mother at home; and so on ad infinitum. It seems quite clear then that, because of differing temperaments, there are likely to be matches and mismatches between family members.

You could also think about it in terms of the division between introverts and extroverts, especially as it is claimed that these two types of personality have differing physiological thresholds for stimulation. She wants the heating up and he dodges around the house turning down the thermostats; he finds loud music almost painful and she simply loves it when the whole house vibrates to the thudding bass of a heavy rock band; she adores parties and he is never happier than when sitting quietly alone with his newspaper and a cold beer. None of these she's or he's is right or wrong, but they are very different, and while mismatches of this magnitude can be exciting they can also lead to friction and flare-ups.

You will very probably find such mismatches of temperament or personality in your own family; I know they occur in mine. Not that it is all clashes of style. There are also likely to be family members with whom you feel especially relaxed, or of whom you are particularly fond. This is the up-side, when you get a match with a relative. But even this similarity can prove to be a source of problems: lots of parents say they feel close to the offspring who most resembles them, but that for this very reason the relationship is often strained.

Then there is the great night-owl and up-with-the-lark divide, which can cause mothers and fathers terrible fatigue. Young children love to start their day at 6 a.m., but at that time of the morning the adult body clock is shrieking, 'No, no, it's too early!' When the two adults in a family have very different waking and sleeping patterns, that too can be a flashpoint. There you are, out on your feet at 9.30 p.m., and your partner in life jauntily says, 'What about a giant pizza and then a boogie?'

If you can at least recognize these mismatches in temperament and body clocks you can pinpoint likely future trouble spots. And on the plus side, these very discrepancies may allow each partner some precious time alone. The presence or absence of harmony at home, it seems, is often more to do with how such differences are handled, rather than the fact that they occur in the first place.

Misunderstandings

A second cluster of factors which can lead to domestic explosions consists of those usually called misunderstandings. You know the kind of thing. A mother or father says to young offspring: 'Stop that or there'll be trouble.' What they really mean is, 'I want you to stop making so much noise as I have an appalling headache. You can play with the new Lego, as long as you are quiet.'

Outcome? The child, not knowing about the headache, and thoroughly enjoying playing Wrecks and Accidents with a large toy ambulance, helicopter and car, understands the communication to mean: 'You can keep on crashing the toys loudly for a while, just don't make the emergency siren noises so often.'

Result? A screaming match as the adult with the incipient migraine shouts: 'Put those bloody cars down and stop that racket', whilst wrenching the offending objects out of the child's grip. The child all the while is shouting too: 'It's not fair! It's not fair! I did what you told me!' It is this type of misunderstanding that can put everyone off their stroke for the rest of the afternoon. Both parent and child feel confused, unappreciated and resentful.

When it's adult-to-adult, misunderstandings can be especially far-reaching in that, should they not be resolved, the whole family can become embroiled in a 'mood' which lasts for days. Weeks in some cases. Half a lifetime in others. In parent-to-parent miscommunications, quite frequently one parent makes a remark in all innocence which their partner wrongly interprets as an attack on them or an accusation about something in their own life that they hope is not known to the other. Put succinctly, secrets are a killer of family fun and a direct threat to the hard-won harmony between grown-up couples.

The problems of everyday life

A final kind of challenge to the equilibrium of family relationships could be headed 'Real Life'. In this range of factors I would include the whole gamut from physical illness to losing your job; from the dog being run over to a prolonged power cut; from haemorrhoids to the car giving up the ghost on an unfamiliar back road. Neither does it always have to be bad news that acts as a challenge. Actually getting that promotion at work; setting the date for your wedding; producing that first baby; signing for a big house loan – all these officially 'good news' events also entail adjustments that can result in flashpoints.

Reactions

What about your reactions to the various scenarios painted above? I don't mean in theory, or from the comfort of an observer's armchair, but in the heat of the fray when a red mist seems to be forming in front of your eyes as the squawk goes up for the thousandth time: 'Where's my gymbag/briefcase/cheese biscuits/blue felt tip with a fine nib/emerald ring/yellow shirt?'

How about being a child on the receiving end of 'Jeanette! Christopher! If you're not down here in one minute flat I swear I'll give your breakfast to the dog!' What would your reaction be, for instance, were you to have spent an exhausting day juggling work and home commitments only to be told by your beloved: 'God, you look rough!' How do you feel when in a stormy moment your child says to you: 'I don't love you any more 'cos it's my birthday and you won't give me a toy pistol/wee-wee doll/giant teddy/complete Manchester United strip/tiara to wear to school!'

I used to react with an attempt at sweet reason, which was regularly overtaken by irritation that my children seemed convinced such goodies should be theirs for the asking. It would be impossible to cite all the variations on the theme of reactions to emotional flashpoints, so I shall leave them for now – with the promise that I shall be using numerous other examples in the rest of this chapter.

Solutions

As I shall be looking at these in detail later in this chapter in *Setting the scene for change* and *What to do next*, at this point I shall just talk about some of the 'family history' stuff that can nobble us before we even start to try to sort things out. There is also the chance, of course, that somewhere in our attachment baggage are a few examples of effective problem-solving for those incendiary moments. When you think of the primitive state of your emotions; the frail grip of logic; and the power of feelings roused by clashes of temperament, misunderstandings and the stresses and strains of real life, it is a wonder that so few family members end up being pushed out of the window! Happily, there are many other ways in which temperatures can be reduced, explosions defused and relative sanity restored.

It is none the less important to acknowledge that, were you to have grown up in a family where the sign of 'trouble' was a week-long silence, you yourself are likely either to imitate this 'solution' or swing to the opposite extreme and thoroughly enjoy a good fight. Both verbal fights and actual fisticuffs can seem to some people better than tight-lipped withdrawal. I shall be discussing this much more fully in *Giving and receiving* and *Echoes*. Conversely, of course, if you come from a family where for generations throwing cups was the order of the day, you may later find yourself drawn towards walking, or even running, away from flashpoints. Or it could be that you in your turn find slinging crockery around so satisfying that you may add in the odd bowl of cornflakes or yesterday's congealed pasta, just for kicks.

None of these 'solutions' is actually anything more than an emotional reaction, primed by the behaviour you witnessed as a child. Yet the jump from making what seems like an involuntary response to pursuing a damage-limitation tactic in an emotionally tense and psychologically dangerous face-off is huge. However, if you and your loved ones are to avoid the injuries that can result from such family fracas, you must acquire these diplomatic domestic skills.

GIVING AND RECEIVING

I wonder how you felt when your mother or father were really angry with you. You can perhaps remember feeling a whole mixed bag of emotions: fear, anxiety, stubbornness, rebellion, rejection and being unjustly accused of the crime of the day. Perhaps on these occasions you were smacked 'for your own good'.

To smack or not to smack

Smacking is still a topic which stirs up people's feelings in many parts of the world. In some countries, such as Sweden, it is illegal to administer physical punishment to your child. The change in the law there, though it took place as long ago as 1979, was not followed by one single prosecution, because as part of the legislation parents were properly educated on other methods of discipline.

In Britain a parent's right to smack their child remains enshrined on the statute book, while in the USA, Australia and New Zealand the situation seems to be much the same. Indeed, one book published recently in the USA positively advocated smacking, while well-known figures in the UK openly declare their commitment to 'a good thrashing' as a useful child management technique.

In Caribbean countries beating 'naughty' children has traditionally been seen as a duty for parents and teachers who had children's best interests at heart. In India, by contrast, only a light smack is believed to be justifiable.

In my work I have often come across parents who smack. Many explain that they only punish their children in this way 'when they've been naughty and they deserve it.' A frequent addition to this reply is, 'My parents smacked me and it didn't do me any harm.' Maybe this is the type of answer you too would provide.

When parents first said this to me I felt rather powerless in the face of their robust denial that they themselves had suffered any harm from this punishment. It was a frustrating experience because, contrary to my own impression of these adults as people who clearly had difficulties in fulfilling their role as a mother or father, they themselves were maintaining a stance of unbothered 'competence'.

My dilemma was resolved quite quickly, however. I noted that when the grown-ups said it had 'never hurt' them, my own mind filled with images of them aged three, five, eleven and fifteen. In these images the child who had yet to become the adult excusing their parents' behaviour was prey to all the fears, rejection and rebellion that beset your offspring when you smack them. It then occurred to me that I should be asking them how they had felt when they themselves were children and on the receiving end.

When I did, their responses were of another calibre altogether. Unanimously, the self-justification of their own behaviour as parents who smacked their children crumbled before my eyes. Their response this time was without exception to say, 'It was awful/horrible/terrible. I hated it.'

This point often marked a breakthrough in their willingness to examine the probity of smacking their own children, and with it the potential for accomplishing positive change in their parenting and moving towards a more balanced style. In other words they could begin to envisage an alternative way of responding to their children's naughtiness, by becoming more Child Centred and less likely to use physical punishment.

What triggers smacking?

Do you think you would respond in this way? I myself was very rarely smacked, so why did I end up smacking my own children on occasion?

Perhaps I had learnt that infrequent smacking was OK. Or I might have been examining the impact of various punishments on my children's behaviour. No such sanctimonious luck. No, the reason I smacked my children when I did was because, quite simply, I was furious with them. My triggers for smacking covered a wide range. See if any of these ring a bell with you:

- Throwing hammers through plate-glass windows

- Walking on the roof of the house in the rain (more on that one later!)

- Chucking sand at people

- Getting black oil all over a new cream coat

- Bouncing maniacally on the sofa

- Tormenting the cat

I could go on! You too, I suspect, could find many similar occasions in your memories of dealing with your children's difficult, dangerous and downright defiant behaviours.

My own personal position, as will by now be obvious, is that smacking is something all parents should do their very best to avoid, whatever the provocation. As the Swedish parents of the last twenty years have found, there are many other more effective and less emotionally damaging ways in which to socialize those lively little animals called children. I now truly regret those smacks I administered to my own children – so much so, in fact, that as a grandmother I have never, and will never, smack any of my grandchildren. Not only would it be ineffective, I simply could not bear the idea that Ben, Maeve, Eoin or Elliott would feel, even for a second, that I did not love them.

When you want to act out

What exactly do you experience at the moment of letting go? What are you thinking at the point when you begin to act out, instead of speaking out? There seems to be quite a regular little package of sensations, thoughts and feelings involved. See how many of these apply to you:

Sensations

- Increased heart and breathing rate
- Rush of blood to the head
- Prickling palms and soles of the feet
- Clenched jaws
- Knotted stomach
- Tense muscles
- Stinging eyes
- Forcefully closed lips
- Buzzing in the ears
- Hum in the brain
- Adrenalin surge
- Time either 'standing still' or whizzing by very fast
- Reduced awareness of what is happening round about
- Intense focus upon the errant child
- Pounding pulse
- Physical irritability

Thoughts

- 'Right! That's it!'
- 'I can't take this any more!'

- 'I've snapped!'
- 'Now you're in for it!'
- 'This is beyond the limit!'
- 'You little sod!'
- 'I'll get you this time!'
- 'I'm not putting up with that!'
- 'Oh, no you don't!'
- 'I'd like to strangle you!'
- 'You're not getting away with that!'
- 'I'll kill you, you little bastard!'
- 'You're driving me mad!'
- 'I've lost it!'
- 'You little shit!'
- 'I don't believe it!'

Feelings

- Unable to cope
- Out of control
- Vengeful
- Wanting to punish
- Angry
- Frustrated
- Overwhelmed
- Powerful
- Driven
- Vicious
- Despairing
- Resentful

- Determined
- Frenzied
- Aggressive
- Hopeless

The explosion

So what happens next? Next is the explosion. Next is the moment when you act out instead of speaking out. Next is when you give your child a smack, dab, tap, swipe or passing blow. And after that? How do you feel after having delivered the physical punishment? Amongst your fairly immediate reactions would probably be the following.

Sensations

- Release of physical tension
- Resolution of adrenalin surge
- Slowing of heart rate and pulse
- Stopping sweating
- Slackening jaw
- Slower breathing
- Wider focus of attention
- Physical relaxation

Thoughts

- 'Oh, God, I shouldn't have done that!
- 'What have I done?'
- 'That'll show her/him/them!'
- 'I hope nobody saw me!'
- 'I don't care if anybody saw me!'
- 'Are they hurt?'
- 'Will it show?'
- 'Anybody else would have done the same!'

Feelings

- Relieved

- Ashamed

- Triumphant

- Guilty

- Despairing

- Hopeless

- Loving

- Vindicated

What's it all about?

Sounds familiar? Probably so. In fact, if you don't recognize yourself in there somewhere, your recommendation for sainthood is assured! Apart from the process of acknowledging that, yes, there are moments when you become as one of the Furies, and also feeling relieved that you are patently not alone, what else do you notice?

Fight or flight – aggression or avoidance

The explosion point is characterized by our old favourite, an excess of adrenalin. Human beings in general – and after all, parents are only human beings tackling an enormously difficult task – respond to an adrenalin surge in a predictable and limited number of ways. It is the old triad of flight, fight and paralysing fear.

It seems to me distinctly possible that, when you smack your child, you are responding in the 'fighting' mode. Were you to choose the 'flight' option, you might actually be behaving in a much more constructive fashion. I don't recommend allowing yourself to become immobilized with panic in the face of your offspring's intransigent peccadilloes, however!

When you think about it physiologically, your states of aggression and avoidance are virtually identical. So what makes us go for one rather than the other when at flashpoint? It could well be a learnt attitude and pattern of behaviour. But remember that what can be learnt can be unlearnt. It should, therefore, be entirely within your grasp to adjust your interpretation of the psychological free radicals swirling around inside you milliseconds prior to acting out.

Don't be caught out – plan your response

You could, were you so inclined, label the adrenalin surge as a serious red alert warning that you should speedily put some physical distance between you and your child. Or you could interpret it as the sign that now is the moment to recall how devastated *you* felt when you were smacked by your loving Ma and Pa, and thus stay your hand. You might see it as a signal simply to count to ten. Yet again, you might rapidly realize that this is the opportune moment to ignore naughty behaviour.

The point I would like to put to you is this. Adrenalin surges are incredibly powerful. In the absence of a planned response to unbearably provocative behaviour by your children, you and I are more rather than less likely to act out. The trouble is that humans were originally equipped with the capacity for such potent mobilization of their resources mainly for situations of extreme danger – imminent death or destruction. Can you really equate this emergency equipment with the episode last Tuesday when you totally lost your rag? When Lauren, in a spate of 'helpfulness', picked off all the flower heads on your special house plant and then had the nerve to present them to you as a bouquet, smiling all the while? Seriously, the answer must be 'No.' Yet Lauren got a smack, and so did Henry for giggling fit to bust at what he saw as a marvellously ingenious activity.

The lesson here is that, if you are not careful in your role as mother and father, you will find yourself expending on petty occasions the high-power energy that should be kept in reserve for really dangerous times. Not only that. In the aftermath of lashing out, both you and your child suffer because you have been unable, or even unwilling, to stop and think before acting. The key word here is 'planning'. The process of planning your tactics is a necessary though not exhausting or too time-consuming task. In *What to do next* I shall enumerate the techniques you could apply and explain how to put them into practice.

How does a child feel about it?

I want now to focus on what it can be like for a child to be on the receiving end of an adult's acting out. Think back to the last emotional flashpoint you 'shared' with a fellow grown-up, especially one where you felt yourself to be in the clear while they obviously saw you as the transgressor. Try to unpick the mass (or should that be mess?) of reactions which you experienced. Then decide which items on the list below applied to you:

- Anxiety
- Confusion
- Frustration
- Resentment
- Outrage
- Uncertainty
- Rejection
- Hurt
- Anger
- Sadness
- Feeling unfairly accused
- Feeling misunderstood
- Hostility
- Vindictiveness
- Distress
- Hopelessness

Then ask yourself whether there is any reason to believe that children should react to parallel situations in a dissimilar manner.

It is, of course, fully acknowledged that children may not be able to articulate their sensations, thoughts and feelings with the level of sophistication to which adults aspire. None the less, much recent research points to the likelihood that a child who cannot accurately label a physical, psychological or emotional event is not at all incapable of having such inner experiences as those just listed. So imagine those complex and powerful feelings which you had at your last flashpoint, and then transfer them to your child at that moment when you last 'lost your cool'.

There is another dimension to add – that of comparative physical size. Supposing your opposite number in the flare-up had been two feet taller than you. The whole incident would then have taken on seriously threatening overtones.

When you let rip at your child they feel afraid of you. They believe you no longer love or like them. They are terrified because the person whom they trust to keep them safe is out of control. They expect to be abandoned. They have little idea of how to get back in your good books, and in any case they can't think straight because of the adrenalin surge that *they* are experiencing. They may be worried that they might wet themselves, or be unable to control other bodily functions. Most of all, they are desperate for you to stop. No wonder you often respond by comforting the child who was, just a few moments earlier, the object of *your* adrenalin surge. It seems as though mothers and fathers are actually aware, even in the midst of a confrontation, that they are not the only protagonist in emotional disarray.

Try, now, to go through the lists on pp. 98–100 and tick off those characteristics which apply to you. When you have done that, sit still for a moment, close your eyes and visualize how a very similar experience might be for your child. I predict that you will want to move on to find out how to adapt your past style of converting frustration to first anger and then the aggressive act of smacking. Research shows that, while feeling wound up is often associated with anger, aggression is not the inevitable consequence. If you *choose* to behave differently at the emotional flashpoints in your family, you *can*.

In *Setting the scene for change* I shall explain how you might begin to shape up for such change in terms of opting for a problem-solving approach as opposed to the cathartic (for you) approach of 'letting rip'. I hope you agree with me that, though there will undoubtedly be occasions when you will not be able to manage your adrenalin surge in a constructive fashion, it is surely better for family harmony if you are making strenuous efforts to take the less damaging route towards the resolution of emotional flashpoints.

ECHOES

Notwithstanding the fact that my own family would very probably fall into the group labelled 'normal', its history has not been without its emotional flashpoints. These were moments of such high tension that it was, at least temporarily, beyond the grasp of the protagonists to effect the 'healthy' option of 'talking it through'. There were also other moments when, despite the intense nature of the feelings involved, some version of speaking out and not acting out was just possible. Before I open this particular can of worms, let me reassure you that all the living members of my family to appear in this melodramatic feature have given their consent!

My mother Kathy's childhood around the time of the First World War contained one well-remembered series of flashpoints centred on mealtimes. As you have no doubt experienced yourself, the preparation, presentation and consumption of food within a family setting is often the emotional cauldron that makes very strong feelings bubble up.

She was one of three sisters, of whom she and the younger Maisie were both gigglers. Mealtimes were an especial trial: although the girls were, unusually for those days, allowed to talk, they were not allowed to giggle. As a result Kathy, considered by her mother Ada to be the *agent provocateur*, was regularly sent to her room with no more food for the rest of the day. This treatment clearly contributed to Kathy's view of herself as the least favoured of the three sisters.

She was rescued by the way in which her father Caleb responded to this persistent 'scapegoating'. Kathy would obediently go up to her room, apparently quite resigned to her foodless fate. Officially in secret, Caleb would leave the table a little later and make a sandwich in the kitchen. His appearance in the back garden, accompanied by a covert whistle, was the signal for Kathy to let down from her window a piece of string. Caleb would tie the string around the sandwich and she would haul up this gourmet treat to consume in her penitentiary room.

The point here is that Caleb, perhaps the more balanced of the two parents, defused much of the potentially damaging psychological impact on Kathy of her mother's favouritism.

In the 1950s I was in my adolescence; a period of development rightly acknowledged as tempestuous. A peak flashpoint occurred when I arrived home from school, aged fifteen, and told my mother I was engaged to a lad called Ken, who worked on the Thames barges and was all of sixteen himself. My mother was furious and said I was insane. I was still a child. What about my studies? Then, just for good measure, she slapped my face when I shouted that she was too old to understand! What cheek! And it was mine that stung as I raced upstairs, flung myself into my bedroom and cried bitterly because my life might just as well be over and I myself dead. *Then* they would be sorry!

The resolution to this flashpoint was a combination of a cooling off period for both mother and daughter; subdued negotiations over tea; and a compromise reached by bedtime. Needless to say, and exactly as prophesied by my mother, the affair of the heart with Ken petered out very quickly and he was replaced by yet another in my long string of boyfriends. Time was important in regard to this confrontation and, in retrospect, my mother used it as her ally after her first explosive outburst, which, though reprehensible in some ways, was understandable in others.

More recent emotional storms in my family have centred around that difficult transition phase when young adults first leave home. At nineteen my brother Jon's youngest son Matthew had been highly critical of both his parents for a couple of years. It seemed almost as though, without a grand finale fight, Matthew could not move on to full independence. Indeed, at one point before he moved out, things did in fact become rather physical between Matthew and Jon. However, once some literal and emotional distance had been established between them, their relationship steadied and is in fact now progressing well. A physical stand-off between father and son at this point in a family's development is not uncommon. Though speaking out would be preferable to acting out, for psychological reasons the latter sometimes precedes the former.

Moving down the generations, emotional flashpoints are, of course, still occurring. My granddaughter Maeve, aged five, generated an enormous explosion just before Christmas when she discovered she had left in her now locked infant school a special card for her mummy and daddy. It had been carefully crafted out of brightly coloured tissue paper over a stencil of 'Baby Jesus and the Three Kings', and her reaction to its loss was quite shockingly intense.

So was her attack on her mother, my daughter Rhiannon, as the culprit of the piece. 'You should have remembered!' wailed Maeve, tears of disappointment and frustration jetting from her eyes. My own attempts to soothe the situation by saying I had some pretty tissue paper in the car, and so another card could be manufactured, were met with outraged screams of: 'It's not the *same!*'

Rhiannon was much more successful. She quickly told Maeve that, yes, it was very sad but such an outburst was not on and so Maeve must go into the kitchen until she could calm down. When Maeve had sufficiently recovered herself she rejoined the rest of the family, at which point she was offered a big cuddle by her mother which allowed her a few more hiccoughs of an emotional kind before she settled down for a consolation squeeze. I am pleased to say that my own children, now grown-ups, quite often handle flashpoints rather better than I did myself when they were younger.

A family tree – the DIY approach

My own mother had an acute sense of family history and a year or so before her death in 1996, at a ripe old eighty-six, she presented us with a family tree going back to the 1700s. Naturally I knew none of the distant ancestors personally, but from generation of grandmothers I have first-hand experience and so could comment on their personalities. My own discussions with siblings, cousins, nephews, children, step-children and grandchildren demonstrated just how many differing perspectives can be held on any one family member. For example, my mother's older sister René was variously described as 'prissy', 'beautiful', 'uptight', 'warm and loving', 'a bit of a martinet' and 'the best mum you could ever have'.

Compiling your own family tree, drawing on information from older relatives when necessary, can be an interesting and revealing exercise. In most families patterns seem to recur. For example, adults often choose partners with the opposite personality type from themselves. So introverts and extroverts frequently pair up. A case of opposites attracting? Or could it be that, in seeking a partner, you are more likely to fix on someone who complements your temperament than on a psychological identikit?

'And', not 'but'

If you decide to draw up your own family tree put aside an hour or two, as it is not the quickie you might expect. How about using it to fill an otherwise dull rainy afternoon, and let everyone join in? The sample trees on the right show you how to do it if you aren't sure.

First get hold of a really large piece of paper (try an art supplies shop), and lay it either on a big table or on the floor so that people can twirl it around when they want to add something. Start with the names and birth dates of your parents – grandmas and grandpas to your own children – at the top of the sheet: there will be two pairs of these. Then add the next generation (your own), and so on. Try to keep each generation on the same level across the page, to avoid confusion. Add the names of husbands, wives and partners, using an equals sign (=) for marriages or partnerships and include the dates of these events.

It can be extra fun for your children if you add in some dates for historical context, such as the Second World War, or the first moonwalk. Maybe some of the older generation could be tempted to join in, and recount a few stories of the good old/bad old days!

When it comes to adding in your own children's generation they will no doubt be impossible to restrain, so let them loose with their jumbo pens to fill in their own names and those of their cousins. You could help them out with dates if necessary. By now, your tree should look something like the one here. If you want to add in brief comments on personalities, as I have started to do on the sample, feel free (I say more on introverts and extroverts on p. 135). You will probably get some widely differing viewpoints!

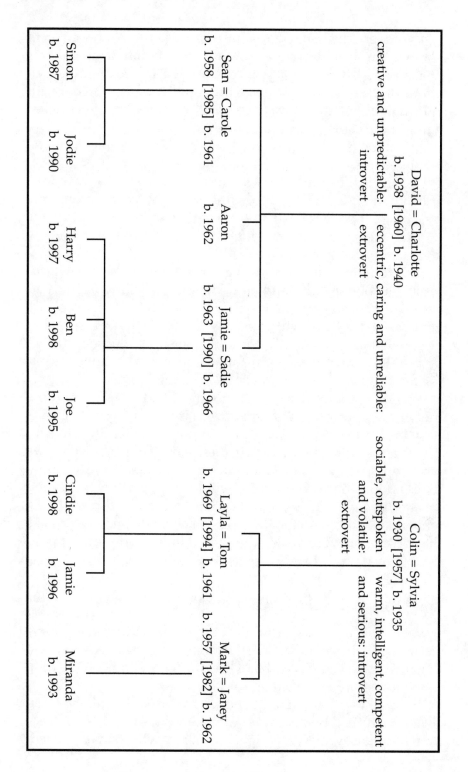

David = Charlotte
b. 1938 [1960] b. 1940

creative and unpredictable: eccentric, caring and unreliable:
introvert   extrovert

Colin = Sylvia
b. 1930 [1957] b. 1935

sociable, outspoken   warm, intelligent, competent
and volatile: and serious: introvert
extrovert

Sean = Carole
b. 1958 [1985] b. 1961

Aaron
b. 1962

Jamie = Sadie
b. 1963 [1990] b. 1966

Layla = Tom
b. 1969 [1994] b. 1961   b. 1957 [1982] b. 1962

Mark = Janey

Simon
b. 1987

Jodie
b. 1990

Harry
b. 1997

Ben
b. 1998

Joe
b. 1995

Cindie
b. 1998

Jamie
b. 1996

Miranda
b. 1993

I wonder whether your overall conclusion will be similar to the one I reached after studying my own family tree, which is that my relatives and myself are quite a mixed bunch. Each individual is often a mass of contradictions, with both admirable qualities and personality problems even when viewed through my naturally rose-tinted specs.

If you too find this, let me tell you that you can transform the emotional tenor of your view of a family member by substituting 'and' for 'but' in your description of them. For example, when I describe my grandmother Maude as 'generous *and* grasping', it suggests her idiosyncratic foibles. Were I to have written 'generous *but* grasping', the positive trait is somehow negated.

The technique of substituting 'and' for 'but' is a powerful problem-solving tool, and one known to reduce overheated family ties. When you are learning to make this change, heavily emphasize the 'and' when you say it. Saying it like that makes it possible to laugh gently about the person in question. There is certainly much less room for whipped up hostility, resentment or revenge when you use 'and' in this way.

When I drew up my own family tree I had a feeling of some rather grand project in progress, with myself as a small, transitory element of the scene. The continuity; the varying strands; the surprise alliances; the tragedies and misfortunes, the joys and hopes – all go to make up the rich tapestry of every family tree. I hope your own exercise will leave you with a refreshed perspective on your own place in the design, and perhaps an enhanced realization of the role which emotional flashbacks have played in your wider family, and indeed your own particular branch of the tree.

SETTING THE SCENE FOR CHANGE

I was out. My mother, who was supposed to be in charge, was resting. When I got back I discovered that my eight-year-old son and his seven-year-old pal had been found walking on the roof. And quite frankly, I went ape-shit!

It is all a very long time ago now, but I can still recall the scene when I returned home. I was Adrenalin Woman! I felt shocked, horrified, angry and very frightened about what had happened.

Only a tiny amount of this storm of feelings was directed at my mother. The great majority was siphoned off all over my son, the friend having been safely returned to his parents.

Catharsis versus problem-solving

How is it that I was unable to stay calm or rational, and instead became a frenzy of fear and fury? To understand that little episode, we need to look once again at the relevant aspects of Social Learning Theory, Child Development Theory and Cognitive Behaviour Therapy, and at the principles of the Parent/Child Game. That will make it easier for you to move on to adopting the tactics presented in *What to do next*.

Let's compare the two approaches: catharsis (or getting it all out of your system) and problem-solving. In Chapter 2 I introduced one of the basic planks of Social Learning Theory: when any behaviour is followed by a rewarding consequence, that behaviour is more likely to recur. I want you to think of that now in relation to handling the high levels of anger and anxiety experienced at emotional flashpoints.

So what happens when your style of dealing with emotional flashpoints is to express that anger and/or anxiety verbally and physically? One likely outcome is that, in fear of you, the other person stops doing whatever it was you went wild about. What this means is that you are being rewarded for venting your spleen and are therefore more likely to react in the same uncontrolled way in future.

In the short term this approach can seem to work, but the long-term cost in deteriorating family relationships is high. You may very well be obeyed, but in the process you may lose the affection, trust and spontaneous love of your child or partner.

Be prepared

What, though, if you were trying the problem-solving approach? Would such a strategy get rid of the anger and anxiety? Would problem-solving mean that there were no more emotional flashpoints in your life? The answer to the last two questions is an unequivocal 'No.' If only life were that simple!

However, one of the main advantages of a problem-solving

approach is that it allows for a planned response. In other words, just at that crucial moment when all reason is disappearing into the red fog of anger or the icy excitement of anxiety, you have a prepared structure and sequence to which you can cling – that is, as in life-saving. If you knew that a life-raft was available, and you had successfully used it several times before, what then? Maybe, instead of being *more* likely to lose your temper when Dean and Tracy, in a moment of inspired creativity, throw the ironing into the bathwater, you might find rescue at hand in your problem-solving strategy.

Knowing about problem-solving options means you don't need to remain a victim of your own emotional flashpoints. The family patterns can be broken. You can avoid many of the troubling and upsetting aspects of a real humdinger confrontation.

What you, and I, *can't* avoid is feeling at boiling point again some time. Acknowledging this, and saying to yourself, 'I *can* find different ways of dealing with these adrenalin surges', is the first step towards altering the whole emotional intensity level in your family. Apart from telling your children or partner that you love them, I can think of few more truly positive actions to help you and your family enjoy life together more. Make the commitment to open the door marked: 'Problems Can Be Solved', and kick shut the one labelled: 'Beware, High Explosives'. You won't regret it.

This is also the case when you look at the Parent/Child Game. Thousands of mothers and fathers have learnt that anger outbursts and anxiety highs are not the only way to react to an emotional flashpoint. They quickly realize that, when you are being Child Centred enough, the frequency of confrontations is reduced. If you are meeting your offspring's needs for fondness and firmness, family relationships become more rewarding for everyone. By increasing for just one week the number of Attends, Praises, Smiles, Imitations, Ignoring Minor Naughtiness and Positive Touches, you might well notice an improvement in getting from breakfast to bedtime without major explosions. It is all up to you. You can choose either to put your energies into the old destructive patterns of behaviour, or to channel them into a more Child Centred approach.

Improved family life involves adult relationships too

You can use exactly the same techniques in adult-to-adult confrontations in your family. And resolving these fraught moments without tears or bloodshed also has a positive knock-on effect for your children, of course. Simply convert Child Centred tactics into Adult Centred. The principles are exactly the same, but you should make different allowances for age and development. Take the issue of intent. Small children are such creatures of the moment that they rarely set out to wind up Mummy or Daddy and ruin their day; but adults are quite capable of that kind of scheming behaviour.

With an Adult Centred approach, emotional flashpoints will prove to be much less of a regular feature of family life. A good style is to talk only about your own feelings. This cuts out the damaging impact of all those 'And you *never* . . .' or 'And you *always* . . .' remarks, which are guaranteed to light a fuse. Instead, try something like this as part of your problem-solving strategy:

- 'I feel as though you are irritable with me too much of the time.'

- 'How can I help you to feel more relaxed at weekends?'

- 'I would love you and I to go out together, just us, once a month.'

- 'I'm so very, very fond of you that I would love us to spend more time together.'

- 'I find that you dropping your clothes on the floor in the bedroom and bathroom makes me feel cross with you. How can I help you keep things more tidy?'

- 'I want to save more of our money. How can I set things up so that can happen?'

- 'My feelings were very hurt when you ignored me at the party. I really need you to pay me more attention when we are out together.'

The main object is to get across the message that you want them to change their behaviour *and* that you still love them as a person.

Keep those thoughts positive

The contribution of Cognitive Behaviour Therapy lies in self-confidence-enhancing suppression of what are called Negative Automatic Thoughts and their substitution with Positive Automatic Thoughts. The former are guaranteed to depress your mood and behaviour; the latter to uplift both. Read the following list and ask yourself: 'Which way of thinking about things makes me feel better?'

Negative Automatic Thought	↔	Positive Automatic Thought
'I *can't cope* with another row.'	↔	'I *can* plan to deal with rows differently.'
'I'll go *crazy* if I don't get some peace.'	↔	'I *can* fix it so that things are calmer.'
'I'm a complete *failure* because of all the arguments.'	↔	'I *can* make trouble spots less frequent.'
'I'm *powerless* to change all the fighting.'	↔	'I *can* energize myself to produce positive changes.'
'All the problems are *my fault*.'	↔	'I *can* change my own behaviour.'
'It will *always* be like this, one flashpoint after another.'	↔	'I *can* take charge of the situation and alter it.'

It is easier to challenge the Negative Automatic Thoughts if you see them for what they really are: errors of thinking in relation to the facts. For instance, perhaps you have a tendency to over-generalize in the direction of misfortune or disaster: 'It's bound to be a fiasco because that's my kind of luck', or 'Christmas was a catastrophe because I cooked the turkey upside down' (one from my own life!). Then again, you could be making the error in thinking which makes you blame yourself for all the major and minor ills that befall you and your family: 'It's my fault he didn't pass his exams/job interview/Beaver badge in Urban Wildlife.' Or: 'I ruined her chances of getting a good secondhand car/university degree in engineering/those lovely silver earrings.'

The thing to remember when these nasty little thoughts crop up is that they are:

- always illogical

- capable of being successfully challenged

- ultimately counter-productive

Aim for the Positive Automatic Thoughts that are the mirror image of the negative ones, and your view of yourself, your world and your future will become distinctly more optimistic and accurate.

The 'So what!' response

One other helpful tactic from Cognitive Behaviour Therapy is the 'So what!' response. It is a great buffer against those doom-and-gloom predictions you may be making. Its main strength lies in the way in which it so rapidly deflates the anxiety that often accompanies Negative Automatic Thoughts.

For instance, suppose you were in the process of last-minute shopping for your son's seventh birthday celebrations. He has made it abundantly clear that unless he and every one of the nine guests can wear a plastic Batman facemask throughout, his day will be ruined. It is already 12.30 and the party starts at 3.30, by which time you have to get the food and party bags ready. Then the shock. It seems Batman masks have apparently never existed; certainly there are none to be bought in the local shops.

Dilemma time. Even slight panic time. Your thoughts? 'It will cause mayhem! Darren will be impossible. He'll have one of his tantrums and the whole party will be a wash-out. It's all my fault. I should have bought the masks last week! What can I do? Oh, God! What a fiasco it's all going to be!'

At this point on the downward spiral say forcefully to yourself, 'So *what!*' You will find that your mind clears and the adrenalin surge retreats. Instead of expending all your energy on non-productive Negative Automatic Thoughts and their consequences, feeling helpless and hopeless, you can now channel it into finding a workable solution such as:

● Buy three sets of face paints and put their Batman faces on by hand as they arrive. Make sure there is lots of black.

● Buy ready-made party food and spend your time making Batman masks by hand. (I've tried it: all you need is card, elastic, scissors and a large black felt marker!

● Buy ten small Batman figures, hide them around the living room and announce, in tones of huge enthusiasm, a Batman Treasure Hunt.

● When you announce the change of plan to Darren put it in an extremely upbeat manner, oozing confidence that he will *not* have a tantrum and there will be *no* emotional explosion in the hall when the guests arrive.

The 'So what!' self-instruction reminds us sharply that most of the problems we predict, even were they to happen, aren't the end of the world. It is a most relaxing thought to have at your beck and call, and frees you up for creative problem-solving. Give it a go – you have only your bad feelings and defeatist behaviour to lose.

WHAT TO DO NEXT

This section sets out the really practical tactics for reducing the frequency of emotional flashpoints in your family. The solutions and techniques to be used on those inevitable occasions when, despite everyone's best efforts, an explosion does occur, will be presented in the *What to do next* section of Chapter 4.

Avoid making assumptions

One tactic is not to make assumptions. This is more difficult than it sounds, because we all make so many during the course of a single day. For example, when your partner says, 'I'll be late back this evening', you might readily assume that because he is normally back by 7 p.m. he means 7.30 tonight. By not asking for further clarification but just making an assumption, you could be heading for an emotional confrontation later when the said partner finally shows at 10 p.m.

If you don't make assumptions you will be using a Cognitive Behaviour Therapy technique. You will be correcting a very common error in thinking, which is to imagine we can read someone else's mind. Work out which issues or events are associated with emotional flashpoints in your family interactions. Then make a positive decision to try very hard to avoid assumptions on these topics.

Broken Record and Active Listening techniques

You could try the Broken Record technique to discover the necessary details to ensure you both know exactly what the other means. All it involves is saying 'Why?' in an amiable way every time your child or partner holds forth on one of the potential flashpoints.

When you tie this in with Active Listening to what the other person may have to say on explosive topics, you are likely to see a reduction in the number of high-voltage explosions in your family. The key to Active Listening lies largely in the non-verbal messages you are giving to your children or partner. Follow these pointers:

- Make good eye contact with the other person.

- Turn your body so that you are facing them directly.

- Murmur noises like 'Mmm' or 'Uh-hu.'

- Give brief physical contact of a friendly kind.

- Ensure your facial expression is one of observable interest.

- Smile and/or look saddened, as appropriate to the content of their narrative.

The verbal side of Active Listening includes genuinely reflecting to the speaker some of their own phrase. For example, if Tricia, aged twelve, says to you: 'Something horrible happened at school today', you can respond, 'Something awful at school today?' Put as a question, this could help Tricia to talk about her experiences; at the same time she will be noticeably reassured by your words and attitude that you really are listening properly to what she has to say.

Reward non-flashpoint behaviour

Back to the Parent/Child Game for information on a really crucial tactic if you want to decrease the likelihood of emotional flashpoints. It concerns the rewarding of 'non-flashpoint' behaviour on a regular and consistent basis. Although this sounds quite sensible and easy to do, the first is true while the second is not. So what makes it difficult to put into practice?

Some of the reasons could be to do with baggage regarding praise or rewards for good behaviour. Perhaps you were rarely praised as a child. If you have personal sensitivities about praise and rewards, look at Chapter 2 again to help you find a way forward. Or it could be that you always intend to give credit for non-flashpoint behaviour, but forget to put theory into practice.

To help you realize the importance of enthusiastically responding to acceptable and desirable behaviour, look at Chapter 1 again and read about the Attention Rule (p. 22). Meanwhile, here are some concrete ideas for you to try out.

For young children
Give them a choice of a small piece of fruit (grapes are good), a tiny piece of chocolate or a sip from a favourite drink at fifteen-minute intervals all the time they are emotionally relaxed. After your first successful day or two, you could increase the gap to twenty minutes and so on. Deliver praise for being calm.

For older children
Draw up an interesting Star Chart, put it in a see-through envelope and hang it up somewhere in clear view. Talk through with your child what sort of reward they would like for success. Tell them they can gain a star, in their own choice of colour, for every hour or chunk of the day when they are emotionally calm. These stars can be added up once a week and exchanged, at a pre-agreed rate, for the back-up reward. Again, after a

successful week or two, increase the time periods. Deliver praise for being relaxed.

For teenagers

Sit down with them and negotiate a contract whereby both parties get a lot – though not all they want – in exchange for providing the other person with something that they find valuable. Contracts need to be signed by all concerned, and renewed every week. Should one party renege, it is part of the contract that everyone gets together as soon as is possible to renegotiate terms in the light of the transgressor's failure to keep their part of the bargain. Remember to praise your opposite number generously and frequently for the absence of emotional flashpoint behaviour.

If the 'So what!' response doesn't totally succeed

Now, back to Darren at the Batman party. Imagine that he has been only partially mollified by your admirable efforts to provide the theme as requested. Suppose he is behaving in a way which seems to threaten an emotional explosion, though without going the whole hog. How should you best respond, given that you also have the nine little pals to deal with, as well as trying to ensure that you actually have a home left when the potentially destructive festivities close?

Your best bet is to play it cool and ignore the sullen looks and mini-pizzas ground into the carpet under Darren's anarchic heel. I believe the main priorities for the grown-ups here are to ensure that the birthday boy is not sent upstairs in disgrace; does not cry in front of his friends and manages not to be sick. This may well sound obvious, and indeed there is nothing very startling about these priorities except the difficulty you can experience when putting them into practice throughout a three-hour bunfight.

Preparation is the key, believe me. Swear to yourself you will keep smiling at the guests behaving well and ignore the rest, including your own little darling! Remember that good ignoring naughty behaviour has to be consistent. There must be no observable clenched teeth or white knuckles. What you do in the privacy of your own kitchen/bedroom/garden shed is, of course, entirely up to you. You must also:

● Make your expression neutral if looking in the direction of the dervish child.

● Ensure you don't speak to them unless murder looks imminent.

● Avoid clutching their arm, yanking them to one side and saying with a venomous hiss, 'This is the last party you ever have/are invited to.'

● Maintain a calm demeanour even if you do have to visit the kitchen/bedroom/garden shed more than twice. (You will not, of course, be attempting the party without a helpmate.)

● Persistently say to yourself: 'I am ignoring Darren's hideous party behaviour and that's the right thing to do. It's Child Centred and it works. Keep going.'

● Remind yourself that, when the last guest has departed in the company of their parent and party bag, you will have earned a large glass of your tipple of choice.

Best guessing

Here is a useful tactic which can both reduce the frequency of potential emotional flashpoints and help in the aftermath of a roller-coaster row which 'got away'. When you are interacting with children, they need to know that you are at least trying to understand their varying moods and psychological shifts. Given that they cannot read your mind – though naturally they believe you can read theirs – one of the helpful ways to show you are in touch with their fluctuating emotional status is the best guess. In my work with seriously disturbed children, where often my major aim is to help them to rebuild their shattered self-confidence, best guesses are an essential tool in building up a trusting attachment between myself and the child.

Here's how to do it. One person says to another words along the lines of: 'Sometimes children/adults feel . . .' At this point you mention, in terms suited to their age and degree of under-standing, what you estimate is their main emotional problem of the moment. For instance, 'Sometimes children/adults feel . . .

- ... that it's just not fair when they are told off for something they didn't do.'

- ... very sad inside when someone precious seems not to care about them.'

- ... really angry when their special things are taken and broken up by someone else.'

- ... ever so worried that they might not be good enough for X, Y or Z.'

- ... so alone that they would rather be with horrid people than no one at all.'

- ... very fed up when no one notices how hard they have been trying.'

- ... that they want to cry when their special person has had to go away.'

- ... like hitting someone when they can't understand you properly.'

- ... afraid that they won't ever feel safe and happy ever again.'

- ... sure that they are the worst failure in the world.'

When you add, 'Tell me if I've got it right or not', the floodgates tend to crash open and you find you are talking about the *real* emotional issue as opposed to its various smokescreened presentations such as being:

- angry that both Mummy and Daddy shouted at them for breaking the coffee pot, yet determined to try and please them somehow

- miffed that the painstaking clearing up of the Lego avalanche has not been mentioned or noted

- irritated beyond endurance that their latest artistic venture is clearly a mess

You have noticed, I am sure, that a whole range of dispirited feelings convert to anger and annoyance when expressed from 'behind the screen'. When you best guess a child or adult in your family, you are in effect holding out a friendly hand and inviting them to come out into the open about their real emotions. With a 'How can I help you feel better?' tacked on the end, a best guess can be a wonderful life-saving tactic.

A QUICK FIX ON CHAPTER 3

1. Frustration and anger need not lead to shouting or smacking. Other responses will increase the security of your child's attachment to you, help their overall development and decrease the likelihood of future emotional flashpoints.

Example: Thomas, fourteen and already nearly six feet tall, arrives home at 1.30 a.m., having solemnly promised to be back by 11.30. Jane and Colin, his parents, are frustrated and angry with their son, largely because for two hours they have been terrified that he might have been involved in a road accident. Though Colin would like to give Thomas 'a bloody good hiding', what he actually does is speak out instead of acting out. He firmly insists there must be no recurrence. Jane weeps, partly from relief and partly with fury. The teenager, taking full advantage of the emotional moment, promises he will always be home on time if only he can have one 12.30 a.m. curfew each weekend. Jane and Colin agree to give his suggestion a trial run.

Evidence: The debate on whether aggression is the inevitable consequence of feeling both frustrated and angry raged for a considerable time. It was eventually decided, after some studies had shown that, whatever might happen in the animal kingdom, humans showed varied reactions to frustration and anger, aggression was not inevitable. Some humans positively choose to avoid aggression and so refrain from shouting, smacking, pushing, punching and so on at an emotional flashpoint, thus offering a healthy model for their offspring to emulate.

2. Positive Automatic Thoughts and self-instructions improve competence and self-confidence, and also reduce the frequency of emotional flashpoints.

Example: 'I just can't hack it! I'll go mad! I'll strangle someone!' yells Sebastian at his eight-year-old girl twins, who have just finished spraying the kitchen with cream from a 'squirter'. The situation deteriorates.

'I *can* sort this out! I *will* stay sane! And I shall keep my hands to myself!' Sebastian says to himself as he tells Jacqueline and Stephanie to get a roll of kitchen paper so *they* wipe up all the cream. The situation improves.

Evidence: Clinical research projects have examined the comparative efficacy of Negative and Positive Automatic Thoughts in producing healthy outcomes in emotionally charged situations. The results show that similar amounts of energy, attention and perseverance go into both. However, when a Negative Automatic Thought is successfully challenged and replaced by its positive counterpart, the outcome is significantly more balanced and involves a lift in mood plus more competent problem-solving.

3. Planning ahead to use Child Centred and Adult Centred behaviours, like praise and ignoring pre-tantrum states, will make emotional flashpoints less likely.

Example: Michelle is finding life with her three-year-old son difficult enough without her partner Paul coming home at midday and responding to his son's tantrums with indulgent laughter, as opposed to the ignoring which she had already been trying for four days. Michelle decides to continue using Child Centred ignoring with Wayne, and simultaneously to negotiate with Paul that he will try the same style for ten days.

Paul really did his best and Michelle made sure to praise him each time he succeeded in ignoring Wayne's tempers. The ten-day Child Centred plan made all the difference in defusing a potential family flashpoint.

Evidence: Research has shown that if a damaging confrontation is to be avoided, constructive suggestions, ignoring antagonistic attitudes and pre-planning of consistent tactics are likely to produce the most positive outcomes.

4. Who's in Charge?

Loving Parents Take Control

WHAT THIS CHAPTER IS ABOUT

Chapter 4 will reinforce the notion, apparently resisted by so many people, that fondness and firmness do indeed go together in parenting. Children don't need their parents to be their 'pals' – they need the grown-ups to take charge, though in a sensible and sensitive manner. I shall be providing an extensive range of **tactics** for balancing love and limits, as well as details of the small practical difficulties which can **sabotage** the best-laid parental plans to be the one taking charge. The other key term for this chapter is **parent power**.

HUGS AND KISSES NEED RULES AND REGULATIONS

In early 1993 a BBC television producer called me and said he was interested in making a documentary about the Parent/Child Game. It marked the beginning of a new phase in my work with parents and children using this technique, for what he was offering me and my colleagues in the Children's Department at London's Maudsley Hospital was the chance to show it in action with a real family who were experiencing problems.

A four-year-old boy and his family came to the clinic for six half-days over a two-week period. The boy's mother had one-to-one appointments with a social worker to help her deal with the recent death of her father; the boy and his older sister each had individual and joint play therapy, and the father, mother and boy took part in the Parent/Child Game sessions. You can imagine the scene in a busy child psychiatry department, with cameras, lights, sound equipment and lots of TV personnel – controlled chaos would be an accurate description!

Out of this mayhem evolved a programme called *The Family Game* which seemed to strike a chord with tens of thousands of parents. I was inundated with telephone calls and letters from mothers and fathers who all wished *their* family could benefit from the undoubted advantages of the 'earbug' technique. My greatest personal satisfaction lay in the solid recognition from fellow-professionals and parents alike, that the work I had plugged away at for twelve years was undoubtedly making a positive contribution to the daily lives of parents and children.

When I became an independent consultant clinical psychologist in 1994 I was able to continue using the Parent/Child Game in training other professionals, in helping individual families, and in my work as an expert witness in child protection cases being heard in the civil Family Court. I should very much like to use the Parent/Child Game's official 'earbug' approach with small groups of interested parents. A micro-tech wizard is designing a 'mobile' version of the Parent/Child Game's technical bits, so perhaps this wish will be granted sooner rather than later. I do hope so: I would love to reach an even wider audience. If you are interested, write to me at the address on p. 272.

The booklet which I wrote to accompany the TV programme was called *Loving Parents Take Control*. I chose the title with a particular aim in mind: to juxtapose two elements of bringing up children which seem, in many mothers' and fathers' minds, to have become mutually exclusive – 'love' and 'control'.

I introduced this notion in earlier chapters. My aim now is to go through, in detail, the whole business of how to combine fondness and firmness in the balanced way which can lead, believe it or not, to children who *want* to do as they are told. Children who, a good 80–90 per cent of the time, keep to ground rules. Children who are given structure *and* sensitivity. Children who feel *very* secure in the knowledge that you love them *and* that there are some behaviours which you, the grown-up in charge, will simply not tolerate. Children who understand that hugs and kisses are always balanced with rules and regulations.

As heavily hinted in Chapter 1, there are no mind-bendingly novel principles involved in the secrets of successful parenting. Using the ideas from the Parent/Child Game in a consistent fashion will, however, allow you to get across to your children loud and clear the message that they need so much to hear if they are fully to realize that love and limits go hand in hand when loving parents take control. The pure relief that I have seen on the faces of three- to thirteen-year-old 'tyrants' is not just chance. What they have experienced is the enormous lightening of the load that is theirs when you and I are demonstrably not in control of the fun and furies of family life. Imagine if, with no training or support, you or I were to be given, without asking for it, the running of the country – a country populated by confused and inconsistent giants! I for one would pray to be immediately 'beamed up' out of the chaos bound to ensue.

Even if you staunchly believe that kisses and keeping the rules don't really mix, I would urge you to tackle this chapter. My optimism that you too can lovingly take control in your family is founded not just on the theories of child psychologists but on my clinical work 'at the coalface'. It comes as a direct result of personally witnessing innumerable families' progress from a state of child terrorism to one of security once mums and dads are running the show in a sensible and sensitive manner. Many of the families I speak of were fighting enormous odds:

- lorry loads of baggage
- no one to act as a positive model of balanced parenting
- no partner to offer support
- social isolation
- depression

None the less, they managed to make progress via my voice in their ear. So the most powerful inducement I can offer is that being a loving parent taking control actually *works*.

Parent power

As already indicated in Chapter 3, an individual's temperament or personality is an important ingredient in the family stew. On the hot stove of family relationships you have probably noticed that particular couples seem to be poison to one another, while others appear to be enjoying a permanent honeymoon. Neither are all these twosomes heterosexual adults. Some can comprise, for instance, a father and son; mother and one daughter; two sisters, a brother and one sister. The importance of people's personality profiles, in terms of the delicate and complex inter-relationships within a family group, is under-rated at your peril.

In the *Giving and receiving* section of this chapter I shall be dotting 'i's' and crossing 't's' relating to childhood temperament types:

- easy

- slow-to-warm-up

- so-called difficult

That covers about 99 per cent of those children you and I both know and love. I shall also tell you how to identify the one which most closely fits the bill for your particular child.

The same goes for adult personality types. If you can roughly categorize yourself too, you can get a clearer idea of how and when your own qualities are going to ease or obstruct relationships with the other members of your gang. Knowledge of this sort, along with the accompanying insights, can endow mothers and fathers with a very necessary 'outside edge' vis-à-vis interactions with their children. Remember, too, that anything which increases your chances of being Child Centred in the way that you care for your child is very likely to increase the amount of love demonstrated in your family.

Loving feelings aren't, however, the whole story – if only they were! If you are going to take control as well, you will need not only the motivation to do so, but tried and tested tactics to put it into operation. For an introduction to these vital underpinnings of a happier family life, read on.

Tactics

The overall strategy, then, is to become a truly balanced and Child Centred parent. But a strategy without tactics is like trying to win a football match without fielding any players.

In earlier chapters I listed some tactical ploys to help you become more Child Centred and to clear out some of your own psychological baggage as a precursor to that task. In this chapter I shall be outlining tactics which can help you to:

- set clear ground rules
- give irresistibly clear commands
- release anger in a non-damaging fashion
- give attention to victims and not aggressors
- apologize and make reparation
- hone up your skills at best guessing

All these tactics are particularly useful in the wake of emotional flashpoints which reach explosion level. Despite all your best efforts you need to acknowledge that there will still be conflagrations over the cornflakes and terrible troubles at teatime. It is, quite simply, the nature of the beast; and it is no good pretending otherwise. Anyone who tells you that you can banish anger from your life would be trying to sell you the remedy for a passionless existence devoid of those surges of inexplicable joy which are the high point of family life.

One of the secrets of success is to acknowledge this very human trait without allowing yourself to be crushed into inertia. Having a bag of tricks, aka tactics, up your sleeve is a very effective method of banishing the 'Oh, no! Not *another* temper outburst' blues which can threaten everyone on occasion, however stalwart in their progress towards a more Child Centred and thus loving home life.

Sabotage

A spanner in the works is never good news. It is uncomfortable to realize that there are saboteurs in your own family

– that people you treasure, including yourself, are capable of destructive behaviour.

Sabotage has many faces, the most innocuous of which are probably the ways in which the sheer practical aspects of life appear at times to be ganging up against you. Modern reliance on machines is an apt example. Think of all those times when

- the vacuum cleaner puffed out muck instead of sucking it up

- the car wouldn't start

- the alarm failed to go off and you were late for your important meeting

- the washing machine flooded the kitchen

- the computer crashed

But some of the most dangerous acts of sabotage, capable of wrecking whole families, if only for a day, stem from human beings rather than inanimate objects. By this I mean those acts which, whether fully conscious or not – and everyone would be far more comfortable if the emphasis was on 'not' – undermine the potentially healthy functioning of your family.

In *Setting the scene for change* I shall list the kinds of behaviour which can be termed 'sabotage'. Each family member, whether nine or ninety, is at times capable of this destructive approach. I hope you will also appreciate that, when such behaviour is identified, you have to do more than point an accusing finger at someone, or even at yourself. Identified sabotage requires tact and not attack. So how to tackle it, once laid bare, will be dealt with at some length. When you think about it, unless you are able to handle this aspect of family life even the grandest strategies and the most effective tactics will fail to make the grade.

GIVING AND RECEIVING

As you read this section you may start to realize that you know much more about your child's temperament than you thought you did. First I am going to present the official version of the characteristics featured by each personality type. Please note that the categories are not rigidly watertight, and can vary across the years of childhood. Then I shall provide a question-naire which will enable you to find out your own child's personality type. There seems to be little rhyme or reason in what kind of child you have. Nervy parents have easy offspring. Calm mothers and fathers end up with a very hard-to-manage so-called difficult child, and slow-to-warm-up children arrive out of nowhere! And should your child have been a so-called difficult infant, this does not necessarily mean that the same temperament will apply at four, ten or fourteen. Children are much too complex, and too responsive to their family environments, for that to be so.

So-called difficult children

These children prove to be the most challenging to manage on a minute-to-minute basis. They often

- have negative moods
- have unpredictable bodily functions
- have changeable feeding and sleeping patterns
- find problems with a change of activity or scene
- avoid novelty, whatever its form
- avoid new social experiences
- show high levels of persistence

Slow-to-warm-up children

Though having some traits in common with the so-called-diffi-cult group, these children can, if sensitively managed, gradually move into a style more reminiscent of an easy temperament. These children:

- resist change at first
- respond to the gradual introduction of novelty

- appreciate predictable routines
- show fairly brief, though intense, negative moods
- are initially reluctant to approach new social experiences
- slowly warm to a new situation or person
- when settled, show a positive mood and approach to a degree of novelty, rather than avoiding it
- can be very persistent on occasion

Easy children

Children who come under this category are the ones that bug-eyed, sleepless and exhausted first-time parents often crave. Easy children characteristically:

- have regular biological functions (eating, sleeping etc.)
- have a consistent positive mood unless very upset, tired or ill
- approach new situations and people with enthusiasm
- are highly adaptable to changes in routine/expectation of events
- tend to be easily distractable
- embrace novelty
- enjoy high levels of stimulation

Which child is yours?

So which profile most nearly fits your Andrew, Beth, Chloe or Damian? To help you decide, here are some everyday situations where temperament tells.

	Child 1	Child 2	Child 3
Dawn	○ Wakes between 5 a.m. and 8 a.m. ○ Starts to cry, it seems as soon as their eyes open. ○ It is often quite difficult to pacify them. ○ You may have to try food, a cuddle, a drink, a toy, changing their clothes or more sleep before you hit on the right note. ○ They may be irritable whatever you do.	○ Always wakes around 7.30 a.m. ○ Stays in their cot/bed/room quite happily as long as there's something interesting to do. ○ You can hear them laughing and vocalizing quite contentedly. ○ When you go in to get them they greet you with enthusiasm. ○ They are quite willing to start the day however you choose, as long as they are not hungry.	○ Usually wakes between 6 a.m. and 7 a.m. ○ Often starts off in a grumpy mood which gradually lightens. ○ It is helpful if there is a regular routine which you follow each day. ○ If the pattern of early morning changes unexpectedly, they protest. ○ When they have eaten, they are quite ready to get on with the day as long as there are very few surprises.
Daytime	○ Easily moves from one scenario to the other, full of exploratory enthusiasm. ○ Often tires of an activity quite quickly and enjoys a day packed with incident. ○ Food is enjoyed, but cannot be given much concentrated attention. ○ You can find their ebullience quite exhausting. ○ They love surprise treats and show their enjoyment in a heart-warming fashion.	○ Only seems to enjoy their day if a well-known routine is followed. ○ Talk of novel or surprise events upsets them until they get used to the idea. ○ They may still find new situations and people difficult to deal with, however well prepared by you. ○ Given time, though, they can thoroughly enjoy themselves. ○ There may be sudden squalls over what appear to be minuscule details.	○ Approaches the day as if it were a minefield of unpleasant potential. ○ Seems unable to anticipate anything much with observable enthusiasm. ○ Shies away from things that you genuinely thought would be fun. ○ Tears seem to be constantly threatening. ○ You wonder if anything you do really pleases them.
Dusk	○ Cooperates well with the bedtime routine as long as it stays the same. ○ Indeed, they may have a tantrum if you so much as alter one tiny aspect of the usual pattern. ○ They often take a long time to wind down their last game. ○ Should you try to hurry them along you are likely to meet with sudden bursts of hostility. ○ Provided there are no unexpected incidents, they settle well and sleep soundly.	○ Never seems ready for bedtime, however many warnings you give. ○ Sometimes they are tired by 6 p.m. and at other times they are still going strong at 9 p.m. ○ They tend to greet the prospect of sleep with something like anguish. ○ On an especially good day they may drop off quite peacefully, after yet another story. ○ After one of their bad days they may find it very hard to sleep, and be fitfully awake during the night.	○ Might be reluctant to end their day but can quite easily be coaxed by promises of a special story. ○ Thoroughly enjoys a really active bathtime. ○ You may find it quite difficult to institute a regular routine, as they always seem to be thirsting for novelty. ○ Surrenders to sleep almost mid-sentence on one of their favourite topics. ○ Likely to sleep deeply and well, awaking refreshed and raring to go.

I suspect you already have a good idea of just where your child fits into the Dawn, Daytime and Dusk vignettes. But just in case you have any doubts:

	Child 1	Child 2	Child 3
Dawn	So-called difficult	Easy	Slow-to-warm-up
Daytime	Easy	Slow-to-warm-up	So-called difficult
Dusk	Slow-to-warm-up	So-called difficult	Easy

As mentioned earlier, you may have a problem squeezing your offspring into any one specific category. This is entirely normal – very few children, or adults for that matter, fit exactly. So you might want to produce a truly individual profile for your child. If you do, it will allow you to feel even more in control because you will be able to predict more closely your child's style of behaviour in various situations. This in turn means you will know roughly when to expect that you will need to be firmly in control, and when the loving fondness which you feel for your child can productively take the foreground. It can also indicate stormy weather periods and so alert you to the possibility of emotional flashpoints, enabling you to take appropriate action to defuse or circumvent the explosion.

How to build up an individual personality profile

● Take a large piece of paper and mark out three columns on it.

● Head the columns 'So-called Difficult', 'Easy' and 'Slow-to-warm-up'.

● Read through the lists on pp. 130–31 and copy down under the appropriate heading any of the characteristics which apply to your child.

● Take a second piece of paper and divide it into three columns as before.

● Read the table on p. 132 and copy into the appropriate column the description which most resembles your child at varying times of day.

The column which has the most features listed is, of course, the one that usually indicates your child's temperament. None the less take good note of the exceptions, because they point out individual traits. This activity is particularly enlightening if it is also carried out by someone else who knows your child well. Discuss the similarities and discrepancies in the profiles you each produce.

In my work with children and families, I have found that the notion of temperament, with its biological basis as mentioned in Chapter 3, can help mothers and fathers to understand why life with Tara is so difficult while that with the younger Alan is very much less stressful. Personality profiles are also an important factor for parents in their efforts to understand some of the cause-and-effect sequences in their interactions with their children. Issues of blame, guilt and responsibility frequently seem less intractable when you draft temperament into the equation; more on that in Chapter 5.

Parents' personalities are important too

What about your own personality, though?

● Does it mesh with one child, and cut straight across another?

● Do you and your partner have different temperaments?

● Does this allow each of you to contribute different, though equally valuable, elements to the process of raising your children?

In order to help you answer some of these important questions, I invite you to answer a questionnaire to establish whether you are predominantly an introvert, an extrovert or an interesting mix of both. It can be done in just the same way as the exercise for identifying your child's temperament profile.

Let's look at some of the typical characteristics of first an introvert and then an extrovert.

Introvert

- socially anxious in all but small groups of well-known people

- dislikes loud music and other noises

- is quite happy with solitude

- avoids novelty

- is very thoughtful and not given to rapid decision-making

- speaks only when he or she has something of importance to say

- is not given to public displays of feeling

- needs a generally peaceful environment if stress is to be avoided

- has some food fads, and some difficulty in sleeping

- is more vulnerable to stress than an extrovert

Extrovert

- likes large groups of people, many of whom are fresh acquaintances

- enjoys loud music and other noises

- needs lots of opportunities to be sociable

- embraces change and novelty in a positive manner

- is given to activity rather than reflection, and indulges in impulsive behaviour

- is frequently loquacious

- displays feelings without inhibition in public

- requires a great deal of stimulation in the environment if boredom is to be avoided

- has a good appetite and solid sleeping patterns

- has a robust reaction to stress

If most of your entries are under the 'Introvert' heading, it would be sensible to work out how you might modify your home, social and work environments to offer more calm and less stress. If you are mainly extroverted, ensure that you are receiving enough opportunities to revel in noisy, high-spirited social events. If you seem to be half and half, then in recognition of the complexities of human nature you need to fashion your life so that you can dip into and out of quiet and noisy settings at a rate which feels comfortable to you.

There are no value judgements in the business of personality type identification. Introverts and extroverts are not in competition for pole position in the personality stakes. Their differences should be celebrated for their contribution to the variety of daily life – heaven preserve us from a world peopled by all one or all the other!

When I say that everyone can change, should they so wish, I don't mean that extroverts can become introverts, or introverts extroverts. What is eminently achievable, however, is a toning down of the extrovert's expansiveness and a lightening up of the introvert's avoidance of social contacts, should that make for a better interaction pattern. Fortunately, many introverts are attracted to the company of extroverts, and vice versa.

Parent/child matches and mismatches

Now that you have had the opportunity if not to pigeonhole, at least to describe fairly accurately everyone in your family, what about that business of match and mismatch across the parent/child boundary?

I once worked with a family where the fairly easy-going extrovert parents were totally nonplussed by the arrival of their third son, a strong candidate for the so-called difficult temperament slot. Their two older sons were much more like themselves, though their ten-year-old first-born sometimes took a while to adapt to new situations. His mother and father had explained this to themselves as 'Dean taking his time to make up his mind'. Once that was done, they assured themselves, he would go for it just like their middle son, Perry. But nothing so comforting had been possible with their youngest, Marlon.

In their first session with me it was plain that Marlon's parents felt demoralized, deskilled and depressed by their failure to comprehend what made him tick. First we used a technique based on the simple logic of cause and effect. We worked out together what is called an ABC analysis of Marlon's guaranteed emotional flashpoints. Then the light began to dawn. As Marlon's mother and father gradually realized that he had been born with a temperament significantly different from their own or Dean's or Perry's, they began to relax. They also started to feel less riddled with guilt as they came to understand that it was not their fault.

ABC ANALYSIS OF DIFFICULT BEHAVIOUR

- A is for Antecedents (what sets it off?)

- B is for Behaviour (what happens?)

- C is for Consequences (what are the results?)

There will be more on ABC analysis in Chapter 5.

Antecedents
Let me tell you about some of the points covered with Marlon's parents. First of all, the most common antecedents of Marlon's 'turns' were worked out.

It seemed that on many occasions he 'went into one' just after either his father or mother had exclaimed, with exasperation, that they couldn't understand him. Fairly frequently, as a reflection of their genuine bafflement, they would remark, 'Why aren't you more like Dean and Perry?' At other times they would agonize aloud about how they had 'got it very wrong' with Marlon, adding: 'It all worked with your big brothers.'

As you might imagine, Marlon experienced a dramatic dip in his already prevailingly negative mood. This was coupled with a tearful tantrum which could last, said his wilting parents, for up to an hour. In order to reduce the number of triggers of this nature his mother and father were advised to try a spot of best guessing about the initial signs of an outburst. Providing Marlon with some activity options also proved to be helpful, as long as their son could exercise the final choice.

Behaviour

Deciding how to respond to Marlon's outbursts, were they to occur despite the measures being taken to defuse them, was the next part of the ABC to be tackled. For two weeks his parents kept a record of what he actually did during his explosions. Left to himself, Marlon would stomp, shouting, up to his room, often bursting into tears just before he slammed the door. The adult listening from below would immediately feel it was their fault that Marlon was upset. As a result, after enduring five minutes of sobs and crashes from upstairs they would creep up and tentatively start knocking on the door, calling out, 'I'm sorry, Marlon. Please stop crying. I'm really sorry.'

At this the noise inside the room would increase, and Marlon's mother and/or father would retreat. Five minutes later a replica of this little scenario would be enacted; and so on as the half-hour and then the hour dragged by. It usually ended up with a silence in the room which they did not disturb, tiptoe-ing away and muttering with relief, 'He's quiet now. I expect he's tired himself out with all that rumpus.'

What we agreed was that, in future, no one would follow Marlon to his room, and his parents would limit their remarks to something neutral when he reappeared downstairs. Mum and Dad charted the time it took before Marlon was quiet and how long it was before he came down.

Consequences

By not following Marlon with well-intentioned apologies and entreaties, his parents were already altering the consequences of his difficult behaviour. Remember the Attention Rule: 'Ignore behaviour you want to decrease. Give praise and rewards for behaviour of which you approve.' It applies to any type of temperament. Marlon's tantrum-less periods of behaviour therefore needed to be properly rewarded, and his parents and I discussed how best to do this.

His father suggested making sure that the rewards were to Marlon's liking by asking him. This was good thinking, and much appreciated by Marlon whose list was surprisingly long. The items included several which were less of a surprise, given his temperament. For example:

- earning 'points' towards a pet terrapin – possibly the quietest pet known

- time on his own with his father building model aeroplanes

- guarantees from Mum and Dad that neither Dean nor Perry would be allowed to destroy his complex Lego constructions

- Dean and Perry to stop calling him 'Sourpuss'

It was also agreed with Marlon's parents that, to reduce the possibility of sibling sabotage – always a positive move – Perry and Dean could earn 'points' for actively cooperating with the last two items.

The outcome was that Marlon remained more difficult to manage than his brothers, *and* his parents learned to show their love for him at the same time as being in control of the situation. Marlon himself, observably treasured for his specialness, became a happier boy, though there were, of course, still a few explosions. The boys' mother and father regained their confidence in setting limits and showing love to their sons by becoming much more Child Centred.

Before you consider trying out a similar exercise to the one which I undertook with Marlon's family, read through to the end of this chapter. You will then have at your fingertips all the necessary strategies and tactics.

ECHOES

Parent power accounts for a very great deal of the 'why' of 'how' you and I have turned out. Other vital influences include the economic, social, educational and occupational climate of your family. Health, both physical and psychological, plays an important part. The point at which you live your life, both geographical and historical, also has a powerful effect on your potential for development. In short, the interdependence of all these factors comes into play during every interaction which takes place within your family. To illustrate some of these dimensions at work in my own family (which displays most of the various temperament and personality profiles already mentioned), I am going to take a particular year and time, summer 1968, and describe in detail the weave of factors at work.

In 1968 my immediate family consisted of Rhiannon aged seven, Katy aged five, Nicholas aged nearly two, my archaeologist first husband and me. In late July every year we went off on a dig.

Rhiannon had a bosom pal, Alison, and a 'boyfriend', Martin, whose mother made fabulous cakes – no doubt part of the attraction. Rhiannon was quite happy both at home and at school, though she always had just a few special friends rather than being part of a larger gang. This left her open to some painful knocks in the social sense, especially as she was, and is, such a loyal person.

A relatively quiet child, Rhiannon was much more likely to be pushed by a peer than the other way around. She enjoyed routine, and liked to know what would be happening later that day or week. If tackled gently *and* firmly, she could also be persuaded to make faster adaptations to a change of plan if necessary. She was a very loving child, keen on cuddles, holding hands and snuggling up in the 'Big Bed' before breakfast. She was also prone to making caustic remarks about her younger siblings, though in general she loved them and was protective of them. Rhiannon was also capable of turning in an instant from being the sweetest of little girls into a shrieking, flailing vortex of fury should she be affected by anything remotely 'unfair'. At the time I failed to perceive this as the embryonic beginnings of what some people call 'moral development'. Instead, I simply worked hard at avoiding Rhiannon's emotional flashpoints and sorted out effective tactics to deal with the inevitable few that did occur.

Rhiannon always took a great interest in the preparations

for our summertime move to some remote spot in the country-side where her father was excavating a prehistoric monument. Identifying very closely with my own maternal role in attempting to ensure that nothing was left behind by mistake, she offered many helpful tips, such as 'Don't forget the cat' and 'Remember to tell Daddy we will be coming on Wednesday'!

Five-year-old Katy also had a special friend, Nicole, and a 'boyfriend' called Ian who lived next door but one. Ian's mother Shirley and I were close friends and our children were always in and out of each other's houses. Katy was also part of a larger group at school, and seemed to revel in the ups and downs of these fairly intense relationships. She was inclined to be the one who called the shots in terms of who was her current best friend. This led to some stormy scenes at teatime until I learned to ask just one of her friends at a time.

Katy was quite a changeable child who could veer from saint to sinner in nought seconds flat. She sometimes appeared to enjoy routine, though she was often happy to change plans without missing a beat. She needed very clear and firm limits laid down for her behaviour, as well as lots of demonstrated affection. A physical child, she liked some rough and tumble as well as short interludes for cuddles and kisses. Katy was, if anything, even more keen on her 'rights' than her older sister. She loved Rhiannon a lot, though she was also always looking for parity in terms of bedtimes, treats and clothes. This could cause fireworks, unless I had been able to defuse the situation. Katy's relationship with Nicholas was of the no-holds-barred type and she stoutly resisted any attempt to make allowances because he was the youngest. Looking back, I can see that her four years of being 'the baby' had been precious to her. She relinquished her position by demonstrating a mix of combustible outrage and adoration towards her little brother.

Katy's attitude to setting off for 'The Dig' was quite changeable. She could easily spend an hour meticulously sorting out which toys and books she would take, then sweep them all into a muddled heap as she sped out to play. None the less she was very excited about the trip, and eager to leave school behind and get going on what we often called the 'Big Adventure'!

Nicholas was quite simply a delectable bundle. He loved everyone and everyone loved him. Of course, at that age he had no special friends, though he was a very sociable toddler. He did have a slightly older 'mate', Edward from next door, with whom he spent a great deal of time in the sandpit – eating sand in a most companionable fashion and waving his red plastic spade about.

In terms of personality Nicholas was an easy child *par excellence*, and I have often wondered whether this was because experience made me more relaxed with him or because he was biochemically of this constitution. He slept at the right times, ate what was put before him, and spent the rest of the time beaming and stuffing everything he could reach into his mouth. He was fascinated by Katy and Rhiannon and loved to come with me when I went to collect them from school. They were very loving to him in return for his unstinting adoration, and bristled with desire to bath him, feed him, sing to him and play with him. He responded with delight. Nicholas was a truly physical little being, and at this point in his young life loved to kiss, chew, lick and mouth any part of your anatomy within his grasp.

As far as preparations for a summer in the country went, Nicholas was unimpressed. At that age he could not have any conception of what 'the future' meant. However, he remained affable and unworried by the frantic activity as the departure date approached. Whatever chaos surrounded him, he would smile through it all. In lots of ways he is still the same amiable, sociable creature now, in his thirties.

In describing just a small slice of my family life in 1968, I hope I have been able to show you some of the complexities of individual temperament at work as they interact with environmental factors. Those days were full of pleasure – which is not to deny that at the time they involved a great deal of hard work. But that hard work was much enlivened by the quirky nature of the differences in personality of my three children.

You might like to try 'spotlighting' a brief section of your own family's past life, comparing and contrasting your children's temperaments as illustrated by their style of behaviour. You could find it both informative and fun, as I have just discovered.

SETTING THE SCENE FOR CHANGE

I promised to explain here the strategy for dealing with sabotage elements in your family and yourself. I also want to tell you about the principles behind using what are called Alpha Commands.

Handling sabotage

Sabotage is a nasty word, particularly if you have to own up to having indulged in its illicit pleasures. There can be a terrible fascination in, for example, deliberately misunderstanding someone in the knowledge that it will lead to the row you officially protest you wish to avoid at all costs. I know – I have done it myself!

Social Learning Theory is a little quiet on such complexities, though Child Development Theory and Cognitive Behaviour Therapy principles have more to say. The Parent/Child Game does not specifically discuss sabotage, though it does infer that by providing your children with Child Centred attention you would be removing the discontent which seems to feed the actions of the child saboteur. Getting the Attention Rule right, and using Alpha Commands, can go a long way to reducing the frequency of both the desire, however subconscious, and the act of children's sabotage of family relationships. For the grown-ups it is rather more difficult: generally speaking, there are few others sufficiently lovingly in control of our behaviour to help us break our sabotage pattern once it is established.

Child Development Theory includes some discussion, grounded in Social Learning Theory, about how, if sabotage is the most rewarding activity around, then that's what children will go for. We are back with the point made in Chapter 1: children will do literally anything to gain your attention, no matter how circuitous the route.

Recognizing sabotage

Strategies for reducing sabotage must therefore start with clearly identifying who sabotages what, when and how, and the consequences for all involved. Think of yourself as a private eye; take a step back from face-to-face interactions and view the circumstances more objectively than is your normal habit.

Keeping the Attention Rule firmly at the front of your mind, set about first recognizing an act of sabotage. These are the behaviours which often have a double bind element. For example, your words are contradicted by your facial expression and body movements – damning with faint praise, for instance. So when you catch your son or daughter cooing over the latest infant interloper in the family, be vigilant. They may just be planning to pinch the baby. What they *really* want to pinch is, of course, the attention you give to the baby! Sibling rivalries are quite a hotbed of ferment where sabotage is concerned, no matter what your age. I suppose it is because, whatever their rationalizations and overt behaviour, most people secretly wish to be the favourite. Again, age seems to be no bar.

Responding positively
Supposing you are courageous enough to identify yourself in an act of sabotage? Perhaps you have, painfully no doubt, realized that you only feel really loved in the kiss-and-make-up aftermath of a flaming row with your partner or other beloved adult. Do you bury your head in your hands and repeatedly moan 'Mea culpa'? Or were you able to find the 'fault' with the other person involved?

Or perhaps you felt so overwhelmed with guilt and self-degradation that your mood plummeted and you believed you could do nothing to improve matters?

On the other hand, you may have reacted in a positive manner. This is the response required if your strategy for combating your own urges to undermine a relationship by sabotage is to succeed. In other words, Cognitive Behaviour Therapy principles need to be firmly activated at the first hint of disabling self-recrimination. Challenge such Negative Automatic Thoughts as 'I'm a rotten person' with the facts of the matter:

- your generosity

- your work

- your talent for putting others at their ease

- your strength in confronting an unpalatable aspect of your personality

Then vow to move forward by changing your behaviour. Tell yourself there are other ways to find the loving tenderness you crave. One of them might just be dishing out some dollops of this irresistible confection in the direction of your previously sandbagged partner. After all, what have you to lose except the exhausting rows?

Sounds quite easy put like that, doesn't it? Of course it's tougher to tackle in reality, though the rewards of a successful anti-saboteur action can be relaxing beyond belief. The emotional intensity of psychological terrorism is always draining, and ultimately depressing as the seeming inevitability of having to go on playing this dangerous and destructive game sinks home. You have everything to gain by devising a strategy to stop this pattern of behaviour.

Alpha Commands

A central tenet of the Parent/Child Game, Alpha Commands are the essence of effective instructions. The link between sabotage and giving Alpha Commands is that the latter can achieve real progress in a relationship, while the former merely creates an illusion of healthy interactions. I shall explain their exact nature in *What to do next*.

As part of your strategy to use these commands, it first has to be acknowledged that they run quite contrary to the way many of us think we should talk to others. For instance, the word 'please' is appallingly over-used in daily interactions. If you doubt me, spend a day counting the number of times it is used, during the course of an hour, by another grown-up. Try counting the number of times you yourself say it throughout half a day. I can hear myself quite clearly:

- 'Please put your dirty socks in the laundry basket.'

- 'Please get me a newspaper when you're out.'

- *'Please* don't cause a scene *now*!'

I met with some success, though I would have been much more likely to achieve my aims were I to have said instead:

● 'I want you to put your socks in the laundry basket, so they are sure to be washed.'

● 'I want you to buy me an *Independent* while you're out, then we could do the crossword together later.'

● 'I want you to be calm right now. We can talk about it when the visitors have gone.'

These are adult-to-adult Alpha Commands and virtually guaranteed to work, especially given the irresistible lure of the constructive tailpiece.

HOW TO ISSUE EFFECTIVE INSTRUCTIONS

Alpha Commands are simple unadorned instructions given with the firm conviction that they will be carried out. They achieve results.

Beta Commands are unclear instructions which often involve a question as opposed to a statement. They don't usually achieve results.

How to give an Alpha Command:

● Use a firm voice, just a little louder than usual

● Speak the person's name

● Get eye contact

● Give a one- or two-step command on what they should do next, starting with 'I want you to . . .'

● Congratulate yourself, if appropriate, on being a loving person who has taken control

---

A case from my own experience should help to convert any doubters. When I am doing a day's training course on, say, *Emotional Development in the First Five Years*, there are naturally coffee, lunch and tea breaks. These are usually accompanied by a fierce outbreak of animated conversation which reaches such a crescendo by the time the session needs to resume that you would need to be eight feet tall with a voice like a foghorn to make yourself heard. I soon learned that, at just five foot and with an ordinary set of vocal cords, politely asking the throng to return to their seats had no impact whatsoever. I decided to put an Alpha Command to the test.

Raising my voice, I now say: 'I want you all to come back to your seats *now.*' When order is restored and everyone is quiet, I smile and say a genuine 'Thank you.' It works like a charm every time. In a one-to-one situation an Alpha Command is even more effective.

So, whether your strategy is aimed at rooting out sabotage or ensuring compliance with your wishes, an Alpha Command followed by praise for the desired response can be enormously powerful. Try it and see for yourself. Throw away those lessons in being polite and always saying please, and instead practise being absolutely clear about what you want the other person to do. Always remember to give praise where praise is due, and you are on to a winner. The icing on the Alpha Command cake is always to mix fondness with the firmness in your voice.

Having, I hope, cleared away some of the debris that can lead to sabotage, and shown the helpful role which Alpha Commands can play in keeping subversion at bay, I want to move on now to the nitty-gritty of the tactics involved in preserving parent power as you put things into practice.

WHAT TO DO NEXT

The tactics I shall be setting out here are:

- Ground rules
- Alpha Commands
- Anger release
- Attention to victims
- Apologies
- Reparation
- Best guesses

They are all related to the business of being a loving parent who can take control.

Ground rules

These are best decided during discussion between the adults in the family. If you are a single parent, you could either steam ahead with your committee of one, or consult a trusted relative or friend. Agreement on the ground rules, and consistency in putting them into operation, are the keynotes of success.

Ten steps for getting the ground rule tactic off the ground

1. Discuss your ideas of suitable ground rules for family behaviour.

2. Be aware of each child's stage of development – don't make the mistake of expecting too much too soon.

3. Write out each ground rule clearly.

4. Stick up the ground rules sheets in each room of the house, including 'odd' areas such as passages, utility room and cellar.

5. Put the rules for garden behaviour in a plastic cover and pin it to the shed door.

6. Gather the family together for an introduction to the rules.

7. Spell out what rewards will be available for keeping the rules.

8. Make very clear the penalties for disobeying them, even if they have been conveniently 'forgotten'.

9. Make it clear that the rules apply to everyone in the family *including* the grown-ups.

10. Remember point 9 when you start sorting out ground rules!

Some additional hints are:

● Don't have a ground rule unless you feel strongly about the behaviours to be committed or omitted.

● Don't put down anything that you know *yourself* to be unable to stick to.

● It is *never* too late to start having ground rules.

● Have daily family meetings, or weekly if your children are older, to review each person's progress.

Each family will have different ground rules, the content usually dictated by the parents' threshold for explosion on any one behaviour. Commonly, ground rules often cover:

● Mealtime behaviour

● Hygiene

● Social events

● Destructiveness

● Aggression, including swearing, shouting and spitting

● Clothes

● Bathtimes

● School

● Pets

● What must not be touched

● Shopping

● The car

● The garden

● Dangerous activities or household items

● Noise levels

● Television and video games

The trick is to have as *few* rules as possible – at any rate, no more than you can predict you will be able to enforce. Try to draft the rules in terms of what you want people to *do*, rather than endless specifications about what they should *stop* doing. For example, have a shopping ground rule that it is only after acceptable supermarket behaviour that a treat will be provided. Or you yourself could decide to institute a rule that as long as the television is on at a moderate level, two programmes can be watched back to back.

RULES ON GROUND RULES – A QUICK RÉSUMÉ

● Have no more rules than you can enforce

● Make them positive– 'Do this', rather than 'Don't do that'

● Reward those who get them right

Put aside an evening to think this all through and get the ground rules written down. Some families put only one rule on a piece of card and tape it in the relevant place. For very young children try drawings, or cut out appropriate pictures from magazines and paste them up about the home, car, garden and so on. Ground rules will *not* work unless you carry them through to the letter. I don't mean to say that you, as the adult in control, should not on occasion say, 'OK, because it's your birthday you can watch as many videos as you like', one per day being the usual maximum. My own mother was exceptionally courageous in instituting the 'mad half-hour' early each evening, when we were allowed to climb all over furniture usually reserved for more sedate activities. She remained present, however, and woe betide anyone who was spiteful, one of her most strongly felt ground rules. You must, however tough at the time, be prepared to:

● take away a messed around meal.

● enforce an unwanted bath should 'private parts' not be washed properly.

● cut short a picnic for anti-social behaviour.

● banish certain toys that cannot be shared amicably.

● take away the day's fun opportunities after wanton destructiveness.

- remove privileges, and your attention, from an aggressor.

- stop allowing your children to choose what they wear if they put on silly things.

- withhold the bedtime story which would have followed OK bathtime behaviour.

- deliver them to school in pyjamas if they won't get dressed in time.

- take the pet to a friendly sanctuary for a while if it gets teased too much.

- withdraw your attention, and any object, if it has been touched when forbidden.

- not give treats, while shopping, in an attempt to quiet bad behaviour.

- refuse to drive off until all seatbelts are fastened.

- bring inside children who break rules about being in the garden.

- brook *no* deviations from the ground rules where danger is involved.

- make everyone speak in whispers for fifteen minutes, with you as a model.

- confiscate machines involved in breaking ground rules on TV and video games.

None of this will get a proper grip unless you are meticulous about rewarding those who stick by the rules. This could, and should, include yourself! Make a big number of it; remembering the Attention Rule at all times and so giving more attention to the rule keepers than to the rule breakers.

Using Alpha Commands

As already mentioned, there are some kinds of commands to go for and some to avoid.

Why Beta Commands don't work

The Parent/Child Game originators labelled ineffective and confusing instructions Beta Commands. These are often fuzzy and muddled, and tend to involve a question as opposed to a statement. For example, 'Cherry! Mark! What have I *told* you?' or 'Leo, I won't tell you again, will I?' The more confusingly phrased Beta Commands often take the form of 'That's it! You've been told a million and one times not to drop your coats on the floor, so I'm *not* going to say it again this time! What about a bit of cooperation before I *totally* lose my cool? I'm *warning* you!' Children (and adults), who don't know what to do next because of your unclear message, are unlikely to pop themselves straight back into your good books. Instead, they stand around looking blank or furtive, and feeling anxious and disapproved of.

Why Alpha Commands do work

How much more satisfying all round it would have been were you to have limited yourself to an Alpha Command, like this: 'Cherry and Mark [pause to get eye contact], I want you to come out of the bathroom right now. Go along to the playroom. I'll be there in a moment.' This one works quite well should you have a ground rule which dictates that modelling clay should not be played with in a sink of warm soapy water. Especially not with an electric toothbrush as a 'spoon' for mixing a cake!

Or, 'Leo [pause for eye contact to be made], you know it's a ground rule to carry your plate to the sink after you've finished eating. I want you to come back now and take your plate to the sink.' And finally, 'Emma and Joe [pause for you know what], come here now. Pick your coats up and hang them on the hook.'

The big temptation, when Cherry, Mark, Leo, Emma and Joe have done as they were told, via your Alpha Command, is to snort with derision, hiss 'I should *think* so' through your teeth, or even end up with yet another unanswerable question, a favourite being, 'Why didn't you do that in the *first* place?' Resist these lures with might and main, limiting your response to, 'Good. Well done. I want you to: make sticky clay cakes in the playroom/carry your plate to the sink/hang your coat up when you come home from school, *all* the time from now on.' Naturally you must then commend them every time they *do* stick to the rules. And you must *mean* it! They can tell the difference between genuine and insincere praise in a split second, as could you if you were on the receiving end.

What about explanations, though? Surely they are important. Indeed, though not absolutely essential to gaining compliance from your child, should you want to include them, they should come *before* your command on what to do next and *after* getting eye contact. Another successful format is to put the explanation *after* your command and then repeat the instruction again at the end.

As already mentioned, learning to use Alpha Commands may need some practice and dedication. It is all too easy, though wrong, to equate clarity with callousness. Try telling yourself that, in order to be a balanced parent, you owe your child three fundamentals:

● Show your love for them by providing Attends, Praise, Smiles, Imitations, Ask to Plays, Ignoring Minor Naughtiness, and Positive Touches.

● Reduce the number of Questions, Criticisms, Frowns, Teaches, Commands, Saying No, and Negative Touches.

● Provide them with ground rules and Alpha Commands which leave them with crystal-clear behavioural limits.

Also remember that in excluding Child Directives, confused rules and Beta Commands, you are offering yourself as a healthy role model that they can emulate in turn with *their* children – *your* grandchildren. The joys of watching your own children parent their offspring with firmness and fondness can be very sweet.

Constructive anger release

Just because you are being firm and fond towards your children doesn't mean that you aren't simultaneously grinding your inner emotional teeth with annoyance, irritation, hostility and anger. Children are exactly the same. Think of the number of times that Jeanette *has* done as she has been told, and yet is obviously steaming with fury inside. It is my view that there should be clearly stated, and permitted, tactics for harmlessly blowing off steam for all family members. Some of the most distressed adults I have worked with have told me how anger was never straightforwardly expressed in their family of origin.

Positively endorsing a child's dispersal of their rage in this way is still not as often used as I would advise. Many people believe that letting anger out can actually protect against stomach ulcers, heart attacks and cancer. Putting your energy into guiding your child down acceptable routes of exorcising their anger will, I am told, prevent hours of acid heartburn in later life.

I have talked a lot about emotional flashpoints and how best to avoid and defuse them. Now I want to tell you how to tackle the angry cat that just *has* to be let out of the bag.

For adults
The release of the physical tension which accompanies anger is the key. No doubt you will be able to come up with your own favourites, given a little time. Meanwhile here are some which work for me:

● Throwing a wet flannel very hard at a tiled wall: use the bathroom!

● Taking a deep breath and then shouting with all your might: use the cellar if you have one!

● Climbing on to an exercise machine and 'pumping iron' like fury: use a room with drawn curtains!

● Digging in a pile of compost around your special plants really vigorously: mind your feet with the spade!

● Kicking a giant beanbag cushion with serious intent to damage it: use your own beanbag!

● Poking your tongue out at yourself very fiercely as you look into the mirror: use a secluded bedroom!

It is *not* advisable to eat, drink, fight or destroy when trying to deal with anger. Stuffing yourself with chocolate, getting drunk, starting a punch-up or smashing crockery aren't nearly so effective as the ideas listed above.

For children

Children need the same escape hatches for their anger and frustration. The big difference is that they generally need you to approve of a specific tactic for letting off steam. Some ideas which have proved effective with children in the age range two to twelve are set out below. It is important for the child to understand that you will not be cross when they take up these tactics for real, and that everyone has some angry feelings that need to come out.

- Riding a bike furiously round the garden: keep the stabilizers on!

- Running very fast round the garden: mark out a special route that avoids the pond!

- Stomping up and down stairs: wear wax earplugs!

- Punching the 'Angry Pillow': held by you if necessary!

- Digging frantically in the sandpit: stand well back!

- Yelling loud and long: warn your neighbours!

- Chopping up modelling clay with passion: provide a plastic knife!

- Chucking the wet flannel at a tiled wall: you could join in!

- Pulling terrifying faces in front of the mirror: ditto!

- Kicking a large beanbag cushion ferociously: watch out for spillage!

- Slapping painted palms on to a large piece of paper: not the wallpaper!

- Painting fiercely with a large brush: the paper should be *enormous*!

- Writing out feelings intently: provide an unbreakable, thick-nibbed pen!

From my own experience I can tell you that, when you join in, laughter and a complete release of tension is often the result.

Do give these tactics a chance whether you are

- dealing with yet another outburst from your so-called difficult child

- helping to channel the sudden intense furies of the slow-to-warm-up child

- dealing with the easy child whose calm has finally been thoroughly ruffled

In my view, ten minutes of stomping, yelling or splashing paint around is much more constructive for everyone than hours of mutinous, barely repressed wrath – never mind the associated acts of sabotage!

Paradoxical Injunction: the art of manipulation
Anger redirection techniques also have elements in common with another tactic known as Paradoxical Injunction. Be reassured – the label is more difficult to pronounce than the tactic is to implement! The idea is that humans, when told to do one thing, regularly do the exact opposite.

I recently met an intelligent woman, successfully married for twenty-five years, who confided that her greatest tactical victory in her relationship with her husband was that she often asked him to do the opposite of what she really wished. If she wanted him to stay in, she urged him to go out. If she wanted him to mow the lawn, she would suggest he didn't need to, and so on. This lady was, without knowing its clumsy title, regularly employing Paradoxical Injunctions.

A variation on this theme that works well with five- to eight-year-olds would be delaying a child's expression of anger (though acknowledging it immediately) until a specifically designated time slot. For example, Heather could be boiling with rage that you have forbidden her to wear her pink fairy's dress/tiger leotard/Doc Martens to school. Instead of trying to avert the threatening storm or best guess its cause and intensity, you could try saying: 'Heather, I know you're angry but there isn't time for a scene because you have to leave for school now. You have my full permission to have a giant tantrum between 4 and 4.15 this afternoon. Right, off we go!' Operating a

Paradoxical Injunction in this fashion kills several tactical birds with one shot. For instance, you are simultaneously

- ignoring the tantrum in the making

- giving them permission to show their feelings later

- distracting them with the factual necessity of leaving the house within the next sixty seconds

From the child's perspective

- their distress has been noted

- they have not been scolded or slapped

- they can promise themselves a mega-explosion after school

Of course, by 4 p.m. life has moved on and they haven't got the time or energy to act out. You must remember to carol sweetly, at 3.59 p.m.: 'Time for your tantrum, Heather', or 'Jacob, you can explode now.' Add, 'You've only got fifteen minutes, so you'd better hurry up or tantrum time will run out!' The sorts of replies you receive can be both enlightening and funny:

- 'I haven't got time now, Dad. Roger and me are building a space station under the bed!'

- 'Mummy, can't you see I'm *busy*? This is a castle and I'm the princess!'

- 'Can't stop now, I'm off to my skating lesson.'

- And even: 'Mum/Dad! Don't be childish!'

I fail to understand why manipulation gets such a bad press, considering its ubiquitous presence in all human interactions. I suppose it depends on what is meant by manipulation. If it were to involve a gun to the head, I would certainly disapprove! But if it were the ordinary 'I'll scratch your back if you give me those chocolates' kind of manipulation I would be stating that there is nothing quite like it for making the world go round. Individuals, whether in family, social, educational, leisure or occupational settings, use each other. Every person's covert aim is to achieve their own ends.

So you will find no apologies from me about the 'manipulativeness' of strategies and tactics. Of *course* becoming more Child Centred is manipulative. Of *course* using the Attention Rule is manipulative. And yet what would you rather have: miserable family relationships and day-to-day life, or much more fun all round?

Attention to victims, apologies and reparation

This is a closely linked group of tactics that will add to your armoury.

Paying attention to the victim

This one sounds easy but is harder to do. Adults are often drawn almost irresistibly into focusing on the biter, rather than the bitten, for two reasons. One is the wish to punish the naughty child immediately; and while this is quite understandable, reprimanding, shouting or slapping them simply rewards them with that highly prized commodity, your attention. The other reason, to my mind, is that as the victim is rarely fatally injured, a quick 'Oh, poor little Becky!' often suffices. I think this is particularly likely to be the case when the demon of destruction is in your own child, while the innocent lamb belongs to someone else.

You know the scene. Your friends Terri and William and their kids have been invited round for Sunday lunch. This is to be followed by a walk in the park, which makes all the adults feel self-righteous after pigging out on a huge roast plus calorie-crammed pudding. Their Dionne and Cassandra have not really met your David and Deborah, though they are all in the age range of five to eight. The meal goes well, which means the children finished in five minutes and went off into the other room to watch a video. Peacefully. Together. Well, that was the idea. What actually happened will probably never be discovered. What the grown-ups saw was a weeping Cassandra run to her mother, followed by Deborah stoutly protesting her innocence. The exchanges go like this:

Her parents: 'Oh, Cassie darling! What's the matter?'

You: 'Debs, what *have* you done?'

Her parents: 'What, sweetheart? Deborah a nasty girl because she wouldn't let you sit on the sofa with the others?'

You: 'Debs, I've told you a hundred times you must be kind to guests!' This said in the knowledge that your beloved daughter has a decided tendency to boss, even bully, other children on occasion.

Her parents: 'Never mind, Cassie my pet, you can sit on my lap and help me finish this lovely pudding.'

You: 'Debs! Come back here this instant! *What* did you say? No, Cassie is *not* a spoilt baby and you should know better because you're three years older than her!'

Her parents: 'Take no notice, darling. Debs is *usually* a nice girl, aren't you, Debs?'

You: 'Deborah! That's *enough*! Come with me this *instant!*'

In this vignette Cassie and Debs both got masses of attention from their parents. The trick would be for you virtually to ignore Deborah, apart from saying quite firmly, 'Debs, that sort of behaviour is out of line. You'll have to miss your 5.30 TV programme today', and then join in with the commiserations for Cassie.

It is partly embarrassment, I believe, that leads you to focus on your own miscreant child. 'What *will* they think of us?' is often the internal agonized wail as you are once more 'shown up in public' by the behaviour of your children. Instead, I recommend that you are really strict with yourself next time you are in the company of any child who is mean to another, and ignore the former while you lavish attention on the latter. It really does work, in that the 'beast' is likely to be less beastly in future when you use this tactic.

Meanwhile, the guests having departed, Debs's mother would be well advised to sit down with her daughter and sort out where the bullying came from. For example, Debs might be a victim herself at school, or admire a rather bossy child in her class but be unable to distinguish the fine line between assertiveness and aggression. It is very Child Centred to talk things through with your children, especially if you actually spend a lot of the time listening to them rather than moralizing at them.

Apologizing and making reparations

An additional tactic, which can frequently be tagged on to the one above, is that of making an apology and some form of reparation. For example, I would have insisted that Debs apologize to Cassie. Next I would take Cassie by the hand and ensconce her in the middle of the sofa: this would be part of the reparation sequence. Debs would be allowed back to the video, though she would have to sit in another spot, and she *would* miss out on the 5.30 TV programme.

You may well wonder about the value of a 'forced' apology; about the usefulness of reparation carried out only because you have insisted. Many parents are extremely sceptical at first, believing that saying sorry if you don't mean it is a waste of time. A lot of people lay claim to the moral high ground in this matter. These adults are convinced they know, without a shadow of a doubt, when a child is 'really sorry' and when they are only pretending.

Sadly, no one individual can truly know what is going on inside another. You can assume. You can estimate. You can observe. You could also turn cartwheels. You would still, in essence, be guessing.

My own position on saying sorry is that, unless you help your children to practise, they may never learn this essential aspect of putting things right after they have gone wrong. And when would you be most effective in aiding them? Right! In the heat of a real-life incident, when their emotions will be stirred up and swishing around at high speed. At moments like that children are desperately in need of parent power in action. Your capacity to be simultaneously fond *and* firm is a much-required resource for a child reeling with the inner impact of strong, confused and rather frightening feelings.

You can't, on the other hand, necessarily expect to be thanked at the moment when you step in to insist on an apology. Mothers and fathers engaged in the hard slog of attempting to socialize their young should not expect instant acknowledgement or thanks from the objects of their activities.

So what's new, you ask? What's new is that, as no one can *really* tell what another human being is experiencing emotionally, you now know that trying to insist on a 'genuine' apology is a waste of time.

At the point where Debs's heinous crime was revealed, and Cassie was due an appearance in the spotlight of adult attention, surely it is more than enough that the transgressor actually articulates 'Sorry'? At that moment even Debs does not know if she means it. She may feel angry, unfairly accused, displaced as the special girl in your life, bored, miserable, triumphant, humiliated, sulky and misunderstood – simultaneously! Quite a heavy number for an eight-year-old to handle!

I think the business of a 'real' as opposed to a 'pretend' apology is a matter for later discussion at home. You could track down a suitable story book which focuses squarely on the issue yet in an entertaining manner. Read it together. Tell Debs how mixed up and cross you used to feel when her Nana or Grandad made *you* say sorry, when you weren't at all sure if that was how you felt inside. Act out some little 'morality plays' with dolls, toys and cuddles; or use cut-out figures for the older children. The important point is to show that you understand how muddled they felt; that you love them all the time; and that they must learn first to *say* sorry, even if it means they sound more saintly than is really the case!

The reparation tactic is based on a principle which probably pre-dates written history. It isn't a particular part of the Parent/Child Game. It isn't necessarily a part of every aspect of Child Development Theory. Neither is it a fundamental tenet of Cognitive Behaviour Therapy. And it doesn't take up page after page in any exposition of Social Learning Theory. Yet it is central to the science (or should that be art?) of all long-term relationships.

The same is true of making an apology, though it is often the behaviours labelled 'reparation' which convince the recipient of the genuine regret of the guilty party. 'Saying it with flowers'; using 'The gift of love' (I like that one – it seems to mean gold *and* diamonds, if the adverts are to be believed!); 'Kiss and make up'; 'Making a new start': all these clichés and more continue to exist because, having transgressed, most of us want to be allowed back into the fold.

When you are guiding a child in acts of reparation, it is helpful if you use a little imagination. Flowers are good, though a funny card, a little home-made cake, a box of coloured paper clips, a cheap book, a seashell – anything, in fact, can be used in 'making up'. Children themselves often have quite brilliant ideas, so remember to ask: 'What would you like to do to say sorry?' Questioned recently along these lines, three-year-old Eoin pondered for a moment and then announced: 'I think Geoffy would like a roastie potato. That will make him feel better.' Right on the button! Another example of imaginative reparation, as suggested by a child of ten, was that they would read their erstwhile victim a story every bedtime for a week.

Take care with over-correction

There is, of course, a balance to be struck between reparation and over-correction, another technique used to punish wrong-doing. In reparation some gesture of recompense is made, which may or may not be directly related to the 'crime'. In over-correction, the post-iniquity tactic is to ensure that the perpetrator of the misdeed puts back exactly what they have previously disrupted or destroyed, and then does a whole lot more of a very similar activity. For example, when at lunchtime Theo accidentally on purpose sweeps half his hated cabbage on to the floor, he first cleans up the spilled vegetables and *then* has to help clear the table and *then* clean the floor around everyone's places. '*Boring!*' as most children, and grown-ups, would agree. Which is the whole point, naturally.

Over-correction is not meant to be painful, humiliating or totally exhausting. It *is* meant to be boring. It is a punishment tactic, however, and should be reserved for behaviours by your child that are clearly beyond the pale. There are developmental aspects, too. For example, a two-year-old who throws cabbage on the floor cannot reasonably be expected to clean the whole floor as part of over-correction. Neither should a fourteen-year-old be required to clean the entire house simply because they have broken the ground rule requiring them to hang used towels on the towel rail as opposed to dropping them on the floor. It remains a very potent tactic *providing* you keep it in reserve for some of the nastier of your beloved child's efforts.

Using the best guess approach

I want to finish by explaining how to use the best guess tactic in the context of delivering Alpha Commands, using five-second warnings, and anger release approaches. The principle is the same as before: you offer out loud your best guess of how your child might be feeling about particular incidents, issues and circumstances. As well as being used retrospectively and in the present, best guesses can be employed as a kind of predictor of feelings, behaviours and thoughts.

Best guessing with Alpha Commands

In the case of an Alpha Command, for instance, you may want to key your child into your new way of giving instructions. You might set the scene by saying: 'In future when you're to do something, I'll say, "Chuck, I *want* you to clean your teeth now." It's a special way of letting you know what I want you to do, and it will help you to get on with whatever it is without any trouble.' All this is to be uttered in tones of sparkling optimism, even though you secretly fear that your children will turn out to be just as 'deaf' to this mode of command as they have proved to be with all the others you have tried. Remember to follow up with praise for compliance, plus an Attend and Smile; 'Chuck, that's brilliant! You've cleaned your teeth until they really sparkle.' Add: 'It's all much easier when I tell you exactly what I want you to do. Well done!'

Best guessing with a five-second warning

The five-second warning system comes in very useful when you have uttered your impeccably styled Alpha Command and *still* Hannah makes no move to comply. Instead of waiting 'patiently' – that's when you grind your teeth and feel like stamping your tiny foot! – simply count to five. You can do this silently or out loud; experiment and see which version works best for you and your child.

The point is that you often wait too long at this 'patient' stage, with your emotional tension rising so that when enough is enough you have already lost your cool, calm and consistent handle on the situation. Counting to five nips in the bud any question of escalating anger on your part; there is just not enough time to get wound up. Five seconds is also ample time for your child to *start* doing as they have been told. They don't have to have finished complying within the one-to-five count, merely to be making those moves which tell you that they have heard you and are about to spring – well, dawdle – into action.

You might like to make a predictive best guess that your children *will* have started to obey your crystal-clear Alpha Command by the time you have counted to five out loud. This is similar to, but more effective than, the old, 'If you haven't put your sock on/eaten your last bit of pasta/taken that tee-shirt off the dog by the time I count to three, there'll be trouble!' This approach works less well than the five-second warning plus predictive best guess because with the latter you are focusing upon positive cooperation, whereas the 'count to three' technique is a threat which you may or may not follow through.

Best guessing with anger release

As far as best guesses and anger reduction techniques go, they can prove to be a truly effective combination. Imagine the situation for an adult. When I am angry I often want to escape the sight of the person who has so enraged me, so that I can vent my spleen in luxurious and unobserved privacy. The trouble is, as an adult I have to organize that for myself, aiming to chuck wet flannels at the bathroom wall a moment *before* I let rip in front of others.

You can give your child a much better start by best guessing to get rid of their anger, in an approved style, before they too explode in the middle of breakfast/practising for the school concert/playing with their best friend. I believe that you will be pretty expert at recognizing the signs which precede your child 'throwing a wobbly'. The sooner you nip their rage in the bud, the greater the chance that the moment of conflagration can be effectively by-passed. The same goes for adults.

Combine the best guess with an Alpha Command to go and practise an anger reduction technique, and your child should comply quite willingly. For example:

- 'Toby, I can see you're getting wound up, so I want you to go and run round the garden until you're puffed out.'

- 'Annie, you seem to be feeling really annoyed, so I want you to go and chop up modelling clay with this plastic knife until you feel calmer.'

- 'Joel, you're on the way to an outburst, so I want you to go and throw the wet flannel in the bathroom so that you can simmer down.'

If you get in early enough during the children's sprint towards an explosion you can even offer them a choice of anger reduction techniques, for example:

- 'Karina, instead of losing your temper completely, I want you to choose between punching the beanbag and riding your bike round in the garden until you've relaxed.'

- 'William, I know you're getting tensed up and angry, so I want you instead to choose to do a big messy painting or write it all out on a big piece of paper.'

- 'Liam, you've gone all red and sulky, so I want you to choose between running up and down the stairs and shouting your head off until you calm down.'

When you stir in your expert knowledge of your child's temperament type, it will be even easier for you to choose the right moment to use your best guess, Alpha Command and anger reduction tactic combination. Give it a trial run, so that you can see for yourself how constructive this approach can be in averting the blood, sweat and tears of a major blow-up.

A QUICK FIX ON CHAPTER 4

1. Knowing your child's temperament type, and your own personality, helps you to make the best moves towards calmer family relationships.

Example: Chloe, aged ten, and her mother Caroline are not on the same personality wavelength. Chloe is a slow-to-warm-up child, while Caroline has an extroverted style. Caroline therefore has to remember to give Chloe plenty of forewarning when a new event or experience is in the offing, even though she herself can happily switch plans at a moment's notice. Chloe can respond quite positively once her mother has provided a gradual introduction to the novel situation. Chloe's approach to 'surprises' is much improved by the fact that neither of her parents expects her to be as rapidly adaptable as her younger brother Harry, who has always had an easy temperament.

Evidence: Long-standing research into children's temperaments shows that, although the reason for an individual child having a specific temperament type is as yet unclear, the three subdivisions of so-called-difficult, easy and slow-to-warm-up are clearly reflected in children's styles of behaviour. Introversion and extroversion, in adult personality types, have also been shown, via comprehensive research, to account for most grown-ups' styles of interacting with the people and world around them.

2. A clearly phrased Alpha Command, using eye contact and the child's name, is much more effective than a muddled Beta Command.

Example: Charlie, aged three, is discovered by his father in the act of screwing up the Sunday papers. He calls his son by name to alert him and get him to look at his dad, who then says, 'I want you to get up off the floor and come over here to me.' As Charlie obeys, after giving the Arts section a last scrunch, his father says 'Good boy.' Charlie is then taken off to play in the garden while his father retrieves and smooths out the papers, possibly on the ironing board.

Evidence: The Parent/Child Game technique of giving Alpha rather than Beta Commands has been demonstrated, in research on both sides of the Atlantic, to ensure a much higher rate of compliance from children. However this is generally found to be true only when the child is rewarded for doing as they are told.

3. Anger release, or reduction, tactics can decrease the number of exploding emotional flashpoints in a family. Combined with a best guess and an Alpha Command to go and let off steam, anger release tactics are very effective ways of lowering the emotional temperature.

Example: Sammy, aged eight, is a child with a so-called-difficult temperament. It is important for the whole family that his descents into rage and tears are kept at a minimum. June and Jon, his parents, know the signs of an approaching emotional flashpoint: Sammy hunches his shoulders, mutters fiercely and cannot keep still. Whenever they notice this behaviour starting up they use a combination of a best guess: 'Sammy, you look very cross'; an Alpha Command: 'I want you to . . .'; and an anger release technique: 'Go up to your room and shout it all out.' This gives Sammy an acceptable route of escape from the threatening storm, and also allows his mother and father to stay lovingly in control.

Evidence: Investigations of anger management techniques show that when two or more tactics are used in combination, emotional flashpoints are defused more effectively than when one tactic alone is employed.

5. Hard Graft

The Rough Guide to Tough Love

WHAT THIS CHAPTER IS ABOUT

This chapter looks at how parents want and need to achieve **consistency**, and at how difficult it can be for them to do so under pressure. Pressure and parenting often seem to be synonymous, and a great deal of sheer **stamina** is needed if parents are to stick to the principles and practices which they espouse. The central issue of **contingency**, which is all about timing, and cause-and-effect relationships will be looked at in order to find out why, just when parents know they should be consistent, many give in simply to achieve a little peace and quiet. I shall also be discussing tactics for dealing with very difficult behaviour, and describing an assessment strategy that parents can use when faced with children who have big behavioural problems.

MORE GOOD DAYS, FEWER BAD DAYS

All parents know that there are good days and bad days in family life. Everyone has their own individual threshold for staying perky – no more than one bad day a week, say, or it might be as high as three bad days a week. Most people seem to cope as long as the good times occupy at least 50 per cent of family life.

One of the major features in the varying quality of most parents' day is the behaviour of their children. For example, you take your nine-year-old shopping for school clothes; they are cooperative; you, and they, have a good day. You take your nine-year-old shopping for school clothes; they are totally uncooperative; you, and they, have a bad day. So your day can be made or ruined by your child's propensity to behave either well or badly. If 'badly' becomes 'horrendously' you will need special tactics to remedy the situation.

Parents' responses can and do at times inadvertently prolong the agony of one bad day followed by another, and another, and another. This sort of pattern is undoubtedly destructive for children, parents and the fun factor in family life. You want the bad days to decrease dramatically in number, and the good ones to replace them.

You could start off by putting into practice all that you have learnt about being Child Centred, about the Attention Rule, about your own baggage, about emotional flashpoints, and about being a loving parent who takes control. But you might, despite your very best efforts, find that there are still too many promising days being devastated by your children behaving in an absolutely unacceptable manner. What else can you do to reduce the ghastly grip of truly bad behaviour?

Being consistent can be the solution. Accurate timing ensures that your impact on your child's behaviour is as potent as possible. An ABC assessment of the trouble spots (remember the ABC analysis on p. 137?), will enable your use of particular tactics to be based on a good understanding of who goes wrong when and where, and how it all ends up. Further helpful tactics covered here include Time Out, which is a very powerful tool for decreasing a child's utterly objectionable behaviour. In essence, this technique involves responding to such behaviour by making the child go to a place where there are no interesting stimuli such as toys, games or people to talk to. It is meant to be unbelievably boring!

Some of the most challenging children I have ever worked with were those who, though responding positively in many areas in which their parents became more Child Centred, still exhibited totally off-the-wall behaviour on too many days per week. The sheer intensity and scale of the damage and hurt stirred up on these bad days can infect family relationships on a grand scale. My most helpful advice to the parents was to urge them to be consistent, contingent and Child Centred, and to use Time Out.

Some readers may already have tried Time Out, with varying degrees of success. I want to lay out here, in considerable detail, exactly how to make Time Out work best for you and your child. Other parents may have read disturbing reports about how time out can be misused and abused. But don't dismiss it out of hand as – properly operated – it is one of the best alternatives when you are trying to manage your child's behaviour without becoming physical.

In fact some people consider Time Out to be the backbone of tough love, where loving parents are managing to take control, praise OK behaviour, ignore minor naughtiness and punish anti-social rampages. Tough love is another way of describing the mix of fondness and firmness talked about in Chapter 4, with perhaps more of an emphasis on punishment for truly unacceptable behaviour. Tough love, when properly balanced so as to highlight praise for sociable offerings from children, covers all the options known to increase parent power, without recourse to smacking or shouting. It certainly doesn't exclude being Child Centred – indeed, tough love would not work were it to consist only of punishment.

The meaning of 'punishment'

Time Out is a punishment, but not in the sense in which the term is normally understood. 'Punishment' usually refers to an extremely unpalatable experience, such as imprisonment, as retribution for outlawed behaviour. But when the word is used in Social Learning Theory, it has a different meaning: it is defined in terms of its effect upon the likelihood of an unwanted behaviour recurring in the future. In other words, the punishment itself is not intended to be painful. Rather, as with over-correction, it is just meant to be very dull.

It is vital to keep this discrepancy in mind when using the Time Out tactic to reduce the frequency of really bad behaviour.

The aim is not to subject children to a damaging experience, but to teach them that the consequences of good behaviour are much more fun than are the results of playing up big-style

So, if you are dedicated to giving your children tough love, read on for ideas on using hard graft in your efforts to realize your ambition of having more good days than bad.

Consistency

In terms of managing your child's behaviour effectively, consistency is one of the main watch-words. Conversely, the very thought of being so perpetually on the ball is not only daunting but positively boring. Perhaps this is partly so because you and I know that 100 per cent success in being consistent towards children is, quite bluntly, unachievable. Or you may find the notion of consistency a decided turn-off because so much stamina is needed to put it into practice on a daily basis.

None the less, the fact is that the more consistent you are in dealing with your children, the more rewarding your relationship with them will be. This is in large part due to the positive impact on your children of their being able to predict, with certainty, the likely consequences of any one of their many behaviours. This in turn increases children's feelings of security in their relationship with you, their parent. As a result children become quite eager to comply with your Alpha Commands and ground rules. In *Giving and receiving* I shall be providing more details of the whys and wherefores of consistency at work in your family.

Contingency

You may remember from Chapter 2 the discussion on different patterns of consequences which can influence the likelihood of a behaviour being shown again. Just to recap:

● When you receive something you like *after* a particular behaviour, you are more likely to come up with that same behaviour in the future.

● When something you like is withdrawn *as a result of* a specific behaviour, you are less likely to do it again.

● When you experience something noxious *in consequence of* a behaviour, you are less likely to repeat the performance.

● When something you dislike is removed *following* an individual behaviour, you will be more likely to behave in a similar fashion in future.

The phrases in *italics* express the contingency aspects of these statements. Think of it as: if A, then B. The cause and effect dimensions of actions, and interactions, is in essence contingent in that behaviour A is followed by consequence B.

The other important strand of contingency is timing, the general rule being that the shorter the gap between behaviour A and consequence B, the more powerful the impact on future behaviour patterns. This is particularly true of children, whose grasp of time is much more immediate than your own. Hence the confusion felt by children when a parent trots out as punishment that old chestnut: 'Just wait till your mother/father gets home and hears about this. *Then* you'll be in trouble!'

There is also a huge overlap between contingency and consistency, as you have probably already gathered. This is because, when used in combination, each increases the power of the other. In other words, when you are being fairly consistent, using the contingency laws will improve the effectiveness of your parent power, and vice versa. In *Setting the scene for change* I shall be talking about the influence of contingency on your ability lovingly to take control of your family life.

Stamina

Probably most noticeable by its absence at those moments when you need it most, the elusive commodity called stamina is part physical, part psychological. Your stamina can be significantly reduced by any number of factors:

● fatigue

● physical illness

● low mood

- job worries
- economic pressures
- partnership problems
- and, it goes without saying, pushy kids

Parents of very young children are probably in the midst of the most stamina-demanding phase of family life. Balancing work, home, children and possibly an embryonic social life can prove utterly exhausting. Add to that the inevitable broken nights, and you have a recipe guaranteed to deplete your stamina levels.

One of the problems is that no one really tells you how much sheer hard graft is involved in bringing up children. Those rosy advertising images of family life do absolutely nothing to prepare you for the numbing tiredness that follows clearing up four lots of sick in one night. Yet there they are the next day, your loved ones, still needing your attention and energy – still needing the stamina which seems to have leaked from your fingertips during the dark hours before dawn, leaving you quite unprepared to meet the challenges of the day. In *Echoes* I shall explain how, despite apparently overwhelming odds, you can bump up your stamina quotient sufficiently to cope with even your child's most taxing behaviour.

GIVING AND RECEIVING

In this section of the chapter I want to focus on consistency and stamina as they relate to the balance of give-and-take in dealing with children's very difficult behaviours. By 'very difficult behaviours' I mean this sort of thing:

- Hitting other children, and adults
- Kicking other children, and adults
- Biting other children, and adults
- Dangerous behaviour in the street
- Dangerous behaviour in the home

- Dangerous behaviour in the park
- Setting fires
- Torturing animals
- Running off
- Spitting at people
- Destroying the home
- Wrecking the garden

You have probably already had to deal with some of these unwelcome exploits on a one-off basis. The real trouble starts when your child persists in them time after time, day after day, at a high level of intensity. That is when your consistency and stamina will be at a premium. It could even be that your past inadvertent inconsistency and lack of stamina are the factors now maintaining your child's very difficult behaviour. Certainly, it has been proved beyond all reasonable doubt that when you ignore a behaviour one day, reward it with a telling-off the next, and insist on Time Out the day after that, your child is *more* likely to go on dishing it up in future.

In other words, if you want your Child Centred approach, your behaviour management techniques and your various tactics to have a powerful impact on your child's behaviour, you must do your very best to be consistent. That means getting the Attention Rule right at least 50 per cent of the time; getting it right 60, 70 or 80 per cent would be a huge bonus for you and your children.

Use powerful combinations of resources

In the context of making inroads into a very difficult behaviour, consistency is even more important – paramount, you could say. Without it you are unlikely to make much of a dent in your child's dangerous behaviour, relative both to themselves and to others. That does not mean to say that you can only use one tactic, simply that you should use the most powerful combination of responses at your disposal.

Your reactions to very difficult behaviour need to be protective, as well as effective, since you are responsible for your child's safety and that of their companions, young or old. For example, ignoring dangerous behaviour – and you will notice that all the very difficult behaviours listed above are dangerous ones – is not a safe option. Running out into the road presents a very different level of risk from spitting out your broccoli and saying 'Yuk!' in a loud voice. Employing a Paradoxical Injunction would also be unwise, as would be scolding and physical punishment. Your best bet is to combine lots of Child Centred attention for acceptable behaviour with a clear and consistent policy of Time Out for dangerous actions.

When unacceptable gets worse

Recognizing the point at which an unacceptable behaviour pattern becomes a very difficult one is quite hard. You often only realize in retrospect that things have gone from bad to very much worse. That is no reason to blame yourself, yet it is a clear indication that your previous tactics have not had the desired effect.

As such, not only would you need to switch to a mixture of Child Centred attention and Time Out, but your consistency in applying this approach would be vital to its success. Naturally, it can all become something of a juggling act when you are attending to your child's victim and trying simultaneously to put Time Out into practice for your erring offspring. Putting out a small conflagration in the playroom whilst operating Time Out is also a pretty complex business. These high-octane situations can push you to the edge.

Parenting in extremis might be an apt phrase to describe the intense pressure felt by the mothers and fathers of children who are showing very difficult behaviour on a regular basis. So, as usual in family life, the very minute when you most long to crawl into bed and pull the cover right over your head is the one when you are called upon to exercise all your parenting skills. Life is so unfair!

However, though your optimism might be at an all-time low, you can comfort yourself with the knowledge that dealing effectively with a very difficult behaviour *now* will significantly reduce the likelihood that you will have to cope with it again in the near future. That is where one version of the give-and-take involved in managing very difficult behaviour can be seen: they give you hell and you take action. Parents are squarely responsible for the emotional flavour and behavioural profile of the interactions that take place within the family. That includes shouldering the burden of responding to your child's behaviour consistently, most especially when it has graduated to being very difficult.

How to improve your consistency rating

It must be acknowledged, though, that promising yourself you will be more consistent in future does not in itself bridge the gap between your intentions and their realization. So now I am going to describe some of the ways in which you can help yourself gain your goal.

Ten steps to becoming more consistent

1. Decide on a particular behaviour of your child's that you really want to change.
2. Write down on a sheet of paper the tactics you will be using in future.
3. Photocopy your tactics sheet and stick the copies up around the house.
4. Put the same message on postcards cut in half, and stow them in various pockets or your bag or briefcase.
5. Make up a little rhyme or jingle that contains reminders to be consistent.
6. Repeat it to yourself once every half-hour.
7. Tell a close friend what you are doing.
8. Ring them every day and give them a progress report.
9. Tell yourself you don't have to be perfect, you just have to do your best and be consistent.
10. Give yourself a little treat at the end of each week.

Don't expect miracles overnight. Give yourself a four-week initial trial and then review the situation. At that point ask yourself these questions:

● Has your child's very difficult behaviour changed in any way?

- How has it changed?

- Do you think you have really been more consistent?

- How could you sharpen up your act?

- What other tactics could you usefully employ?

- Are you still being as Child Centred as possible?

- Are you and your child less at loggerheads than before?

- Do you feel more loving towards your child?

- Is your child being more loving towards you?

- Are things getting easier on a day-to-day basis?

- Do you deserve an extra treat for your best efforts? (The answer is always 'Yes'!)

So they have given you hell and you have taken action. What do you receive in the way of rewards from your children? Because they now feel more secure as they experience you being consistent, firm and fond, it is to be hoped that they will begin to *want* to please you. Their general behaviour and mood will improve. You can start to have more fun together. Family life will lighten up considerably as the very difficult behaviour gradually reduces.

There is a very simple principle at work in the giving and receiving here which characterizes a family trying to deal with a child who is showing very difficult behaviour: the more of 'the right stuff' you give your child, the more you will receive from them in the way of cooperation and affection. Quite a bargain! Especially when you now know so much more about the exact constituents of 'the right stuff'. When I have explained the proper use of Time Out, you will have even more effective tactics at your fingertips. I shall be doing just that in *What to do next*.

Recharge your parental batteries with sleep

Where is the energy for all this change going to come from? That is the question you may be asking yourself as you set out to be more consistent with your child. Your daily schedule is a miracle of complex organization to fit in work, family and the very occasional spot of fun; and the last day you spent pleasing yourself was so long ago you can't remember.

Fortunately, as a physical entity you are almost inexhaustibly rechargeable. Like all good batteries, when you are fully charged you will function with as much gusto as you did yesterday and the day before that. Instead of electricity you need sleep, but it's such an elusive commodity when you are a parent. If it's not the baby waking you up three times a night, it's the school child with a bad cold or the teenager coming home late.

There is no doubt that sleep is a most precious thing. Everyone needs to have a modicum of dreaming time if their brains are to do their 'filing' job efficiently. Your body needs to rest if your batteries are to start up first thing next day. However, the amount of sleep required by the average adult is still in dispute. Some authorities say that much of the world's population, particularly in the industrialized countries, is permanently sleep-deprived. Conversely, many world leaders claim to survive quite nicely on four or five hours' sleep per night. What is without question is that individual sleep require-ments vary enormously. Most parents, though, have one thing in common – they don't get *enough* sleep.

How can you increase the amount of sleep which you cur-rently get? A lot of parents tell me that they consider they have been sleep-deprived for several years, so a good deal of catch-ing up may be needed. Apart from simply enduring the torture of permanent fatigue until your children reach the stage where they want to sleep in, what can you do? I have a few ideas for you, some derived from my own early 'Sleepless in South London' experiences, others garnered from other parents who have wrestled with the same demons and won. Try some of them and see if they put the zing back into your energy reserves.

Ten ways to catch up on sleep

1. Go to bed early, even if this means taking lessons in video recording so that you don't miss your favourite TV programmes.

2. Review your diet, especially if you know you are consuming too much junk food at irregular hours.
3. Develop a soothing bedtime routine. Go on: pamper yourself for half an hour.
4. Get your child's sleeping pattern sorted. Try this when you have clawed back some of your lost sleep.
5. Cat nap during the day, even if the opportunity arises when you feel you *should* be awake.
6. Aim to catch up on sleep over a four-week period, even if this means that you don't party for a month.
7. Avoid taking a wakeful child into your bed. No one sleeps properly when there are three in a bed meant for two.
8. Decide how many hours' sleep you need, then count back from when you know you will have to get up in order to identify your optimum bedtime.
9. Remember that you need sleep more than 'relaxation', even if this means missing out on some of your favourite evening activities.
10. Make sleep a priority. In years to come there will be plenty of time to give reading a novel top priority.

Keep a positive outlook

Another important ingredient of stamina is mood. When you dread tomorrow, even when you are getting enough sleep, it is time to bombard yourself with Positive Automatic Thoughts. Sometimes it is a question of challenging an instinctive Negative Automatic Thought ('I *can't* . . .') and turning it into a Positive Automatic Thought ('I *can* . . .'). Here are some helpful examples:

- 'I *can* cope quite well with tomorrow.'

- 'I *can* make parts of tomorrow really fun.'

- 'I *can* manage it all today, because I know I will be in bed asleep by 8.30 p.m.'

- 'I *can* be more consistent tomorrow.'

- 'I *can* find time to get most things done.'

- 'I *can* leave some jobs for another day.'

It can also be helpful to pinpoint times during the next day when you will be doing something you enjoy, and recite them out loud to yourself.

- 'I *can* look forward to . . .' List the things you enjoy.

When I say 'doing something you enjoy' I am not talking Mediterranean cruises. I mean little everyday things such as

- watching a favourite TV programme
- drinking a cup of freshly brewed coffee
- planting some bulbs in a pot
- having a snack in the garden
- playing a special CD all afternoon

There are millions of ideas available, and only you know the ones which give you that pleasant buzz. You could try spacing them out across your waking hours, so that not the morning nor the afternoon or evening looms before you like a joyless, empty desert.

Neither do you need to sit passively waiting for such small pleasures to happen. You can make them a part of your own life by setting up a daily treats schedule for yourself. Looking after yourself in this way will improve your mood of the moment as well as your perspective on tomorrow. An elevated mood is associated with greater energy and stamina, while a depressed one leads to tiredness and lethargy. Even when times are tough – *especially* when they are tough – set out to treat yourself to several mini-rewards each day.

I believe that whether you are trying to manage the ordinary ups and downs of your child's behaviour, or attempting to tackle a very difficult behaviour, your prospects of being successfully consistent will be much enhanced when you put into practice the tactics shown above. It *can* be done. You must give to yourself in order to come up with the goods for your children. You will then receive from them the rewarding company that you so wish for.

ECHOES

My mother often told me about how, when I was little, she would take me out for a walk 'round the square'. This was just a small English town, not London or New York. None the less she apparently found, and pointed out to me, lots of small miracles: a flower, an insect, a tree, a postman, a cat, a big car, a brightly painted front door. I cannot actively recall these mini-idylls, yet I have vivid memories of doing exactly the same when my own children were young. Perhaps today, when many parents regularly transport their children from one venue to the next by car, these rewarding little perambulations are less frequent.

I believe that via our excursions and her later behaviour my mother taught me an enormously important lesson. I learned that when you focus daily on the small joys of life, instead of waiting for your big dreams to be magically fulfilled, it lifts your heart. Put more prosaically, drawing enjoyment from everyday occurrences can be the key to an improved mood and increased energy and stamina.

Daily treats

Engineering my own small rewards is a very reliable source of pleasure. Here are some of my favourite daily perks:

- Standing still for two minutes and looking up at the sky.

- Cuddling a baby or toddler and sniffing their lovely new skin.

- Drinking hot milky coffee mid-morning.

- Deciding what TV programme or video to watch later on.

- Choosing what to wear.

- Listening to music which suits my mood.

- Curling up with a book.

- Massaging moisturizing lotion into my body.

- Eating a cream cake.

- Walking round the garden.

- Looking out of the window at the trees.

- Buying myself a bunch of flowers.

- Deciding what jewellery to wear.

- Clearing out my briefcase and knowing that everything is organized.

- Eating a cheese and salad sandwich.

- Running a bubble bath.

- Eating a chocolate.

- Buying a magazine.

- Driving the pretty way to the supermarket.

- Chatting with family and friends.

- Popping into the garden centre for two plants and coming out with twelve.

- Telephoning or writing to someone far away.

During a particularly stressful phase in my life, I put aside half an hour each day to practise yoga. Those thirty minutes, plus one or two items from the list above, saved the day. I found my energy levels, and the stamina to mother three children increased when I was treating myself. As my children grew older and I went out to work, just the contrast between being a psychologist by day and a mother the rest of the time was a source of joy.

Too little sleep cheats everyone

One of the major treats I make sure to give myself regularly is enough sleep. I know that I can only cope with the following day when I have had nine hours' worth. I used to be much more casual about staying up late and getting up early, but in the early 1990s I developed the debilitating condition known as ME or Chronic Fatigue Syndrome. So instead of trying to wring a last hour from my day, as I had been doing since my children grew up, I realized that I now had to conserve my energy by protecting my sleep just as I had tried to do when they were young.

In those years, when they were waking up at the ungodly hour of 5.30 a.m., I'm afraid I was not going to bed early enough. The result was that I was more irritable during the day than they deserved. No wonder that I stared, bleary-eyed and unenthusiastic, when they bounced on to the bed at what seemed like dawn.

I know now that I should have gone to bed much earlier if I was to face the next day with sufficient energy. Yet I made the decision to stay up. Why? Misguided ideas on 'having my own space' probably; it was the sixties, after all. Maybe it was linked to my age. As a very young mother of three, perhaps I felt I had been cheated of my share of what would now be called 'rave' nights out. Whatever the cause, I see now that I was cheating myself and my children of my top-notch daytime energies. Shame you can't live your life backwards – such mistakes would be drastically reduced in number!

Muddling through

As for using Time Out properly, forget it! I had no real idea of punishments apart from an outraged yell, the very occasional slap, sending the offending child to bed early, and withdrawing sweets or TV. I realize now that only the last of these reactions was helpful or effective. It is no small wonder that my children have grown up to be such lovely people, given my state of ignorance about parenting.

The only information available came from my own experiences as a child, and from Dr Spock's fat little paperback. I was very fortunate in having had good parents myself. Without their positive example I would have been well and truly lost. It was not until I was in my mid-thirties and doing a master's degree in clinical psychology that I understood the concepts of consistency and contingency of consequences and how important they were.

I think that, despite getting the punishment tactics wrong, the day was saved by my giving my children enough Child Centred attention to swing the emotional balance for them. In other words, by some miracle I managed to get the Attention Rule right at least half the time.

So you see, ignorance about parenting is not bliss, it is actually dangerous for our children and ourselves. The credit for my own children's narrow escape lies not so much with me as with my parents for all the fond firmness they used in bringing me up in such a balanced fashion.

Trying hard to be consistent

My attempts at consistency were, well, rather inconsistent. I knew that, as a parent, you should mean what you say, and say what you mean. This, thankfully, gave me a strong nudge in the direction of following through on whatever edict I had just issued, whether a promise or a threat of retribution. I also worked out that scolding a child for loud noises one day, and joining in with them the next, was at best confusing.

The big problem which I experienced in my aim to be consistent was the sheer volume of idiosyncratic and distracting factors around whenever I was supposed to be sticking to the party line. Factors like

- one of the children being ill

- three solid days of rain and everyone suffering from cabin fever

- low energy levels on my part

- the family kitten being lost

- the gas cooker going on the blink

- the weather being stiflingly hot

- the pudding being burnt

Each time these sorts of influences were at work – which seemed to be all day every day – my resolve to be more consistent was very sorely tried. To be honest, I often wilted and ended up being only fairly consistent instead of consistent enough. Thank heaven children don't need us to be perfect!

Acknowledging the good things in life

One last blast from the past is about how I used to try to keep up my mood, and therefore my energy and stamina, in the face of the daily grind. When I was feeling discouraged or out of sorts I would go through a list of the different compartments in my life, working out the ratio between those that were going well and those that were currently a no-no. The compartments were labelled:

- children
- family
- friends
- partner
- work
- money
- sex
- health
- fun
- practicalities

This list is not in strict order of priority, as you have guessed.

As long as six of the ten were all right, I could tell myself that I was more blessed than downtrodden. Seven or eight out of ten would forcefully remind me to acknowledge the many good things in my life. Nine or ten, and I would be unable to ignore the fact that I had every reason to be happy and full of get-up and go.

My rule, if the balance should be on the minus side, was to decide what to do next to improve the situation. That at least gave me a feeling of control which bumped up my mood, even if the decision reached was to do nothing at all for a while except concentrate on all those little treats waiting in the wings.

It would have been even more helpful if I had carried out an

ABC analysis when there were problems in the 'children' area of my life. Sadly, I knew nothing of such approaches, though you can now learn all about them from reading this chapter's *Setting the scene for change* section.

SETTING THE SCENE FOR CHANGE

The notion of contingency (which was explained on p. 171) is central to understanding how the ABC exercise works. As you may remember from p. 137:

A (antecedents) $\longrightarrow$ B (behaviour) $\longrightarrow$ C (consequences)

So you can see that the behaviour is contingent on the antecedent, and the consequences are contingent on the behaviour.

The ABC pattern therefore has real meaning in terms of a sequence of behaviours over a particular timespan. Often the timespan is very short indeed. You approach the check-out in your local supermarket. While you are waiting, your children start to demand chocolate in loud, penetrating voices. You wear this for a minute or so and then capitulate, often rather ungraciously. 'Oh, go *on*, then! *Have* some sweets if it will keep you quiet.' That's an ABC sequence all over in about four minutes tops.

And it can be more rapid still. You are all watching TV. One of your children flips channels without so much as a by-your-leave. You shout, 'Don't *do* that! You've been told a hundred times!', and snatch the remote control from their hot little hand, muttering about who pays the TV licence. Another ABC, over this time in less than a minute.

These two examples show how difficult it can be to come up with a planned contingent response at times of parenting stress. When you are also trying to be consistent, the challenge to your stamina and good intentions is considerable. However, it *can* be done, especially when you get into the habit of looking at your interactions with your children through the ABC framework.

Learnt behaviour can be unlearnt too

It was realized several decades ago that human beings repeat patterns of behaviour when interacting with others. The more often a sequence is repeated, the more likely it is to become an entrenched part of a person's behaviour in the company of others – particularly when it is those others who trigger the learnt response.

Interacting with your child is a regular feature of your day, so you will appreciate how easily ABC patterns can develop. They can be helpful or damaging, and either kind can become an intrinsic aspect of family relationships before you can say ABC. Luckily, because these sequences have been learnt, unsuccessful ones can also be unlearnt.

Supposing you and George, aged seven, had lurched from one confrontation to another over the past two weeks. An ABC analysis would be a helpful way of understanding and dealing with the problem. First discuss the situation with your partner or anyone else who has regular contact with your child. Getting them to do the ABC exercise with you is best, though as long as they understand that they must behave differently come lift-off day it will probably be OK for you to do the exercise on your own.

The consistency of adult reactions is a very powerful and effective tool for first provoking and then maintaining positive change in a child. What I mean here is consistency between adults – not each parent being consistent in a different way from the other. When grown-ups are consistent in this way a child has a much greater chance of learning that anti-social behaviour doesn't pay, and learning it rapidly.

The table below shows how to set about an ABC analysis, followed by an explanation of it using George as an example. In the table:

A	=	antecedents
B	=	behaviour
C	=	consequences
M	=	maintenance factors which keep patterns going
I	=	intervention
ABC	=	sequence of contingent events

How to do an ABC analysis

The behaviour
Write down the specific behaviour of your child on   B
    which you want to focus

Description of the behaviour
Write down an accurate description of the   B
    behaviour itself

Immediate antecedents
Write down each thing that seems immediately to   A
    precede the behaviour

Other triggers
Jot down any other triggers, in terms of time of day,   A
    people present etc.

Grown-ups' behaviour
Write down a description of exactly what you do   C
    during and straight after the behaviour

General consequences
Add an outline of what general consequences, for   C
    the child, follow the behaviour

Factors which reduce the behaviour
Pinpoint and list anything that seems to be associated   M
    with less of the behaviour

Factors which increase the behaviour
Put down things related to the behaviour being   M
    more frequent

ABC patterns
Read through your notes, making a list and looking   ABC
    for ABC patterns and contingency relationships

Manipulating the antecedents
Determine how you might manipulate the   A
    antecedents to reduce the rate of the behaviour

Manipulating the consequences
Decide which consequences you can modify to make   C
    the behaviour less likely

Child Centred inputs
Work out which Child Centred inputs you can   I
   make to help your child feel valued

Attention Rule lapses
Pick out the points where you can see that you   I
   have let the Attention Rule lapse

Useful tactics
Make a list of the tactics you might usefully   I
   employ to reduce the behaviour

Intervention plan
Write out your intervention plan   I

Starting date
Pinpoint a specific day to get started on your plan   I

Consistency
Be determined to try out the plan consistently for   I
   two weeks and then review the situation

Let's look at the whole process in terms of George and his parents. Step by step it should go roughly like this.

The behaviour
George's temper tantrums.

Description of the behaviour
George stamps his feet and makes karate moves dangerously close to others. He first looks really angry and shouts, 'It's not fair!' or, 'No. Won't, so there!' Then he spins round wildly with his arms flailing, while he shoots out one leg in half-aimed kicks. The next phase is when he begins to dodge around doing straight-arm jabs and kick-boxer movements. When he is doing that he *almost* hits and hurts people, but always manages just to miss them. He doesn't seem to care who is involved. It could as easily be a little child or a grandparent as his father and mother.

Immediate antecedents

  ● When someone has told him to do something he doesn't fancy

  ● If he can't be first

Other triggers

- When George has been awake very early

- It happens more often in the late afternoon, usually shortly after school

- It is especially likely if friends come round to play

Grown-ups' behaviour

Father: 'I often shout and try to grab him but he dodges away from me and I end up chasing him around. I've usually lost my temper by the time I catch him. Sometimes I smack him, especially if he's frightened the little ones. At other times I just let him get on with it and we all go into another room.'

Mother: 'He doesn't do it when I'm around – at least, he might start but I just say, "Pack it up", and he does. I had four younger brothers and they were always up to daft stuff like that. My parents just used to ignore them unless they were literally tearing the place to pieces, when they all had to go out in the garden, rain or shine, until they'd cooled down.'

General consequences

- Everyone is stirred up and distressed after George has had a tantrum when Dad is in charge

- His father feels a failure and doesn't like George much

- His mother remains unruffled because the tantrum doesn't really get going, so there's no upheaval when she is in charge

- George's younger siblings avoid him and sometimes seem to be afraid of him

Factors which reduce the behaviour

- Mum being around

- George having had a good night's sleep

- George not being hungry

- Saturdays, Sundays and school holidays

- No friends being present

Factors which increase the behaviour

- Dad being in charge

- George having been at school

- George having friends round on Monday through to Friday afternoons during termtime

- Going shopping after school

- George being told it's time to wash his hands for tea

- George being told to switch off the TV because it's teatime

- George being told to take off his outdoor shoes and put on his slippers

ABC patterns
There seem to be several patterns where ABC contingencies are going on (see following table).

A	→ B	→ C
George hasn't had enough → sleep for a school day	He has a tantrum	→ His father shouts and chases and perhaps smacks him
He comes out of school hungry at 3.30 p.m.		
He has friends round to play at teatime when his father is in charge		
His father tells him to wash his hands/turn the TV off so he can eat his tea hygienically and without distractions		
Any of the above	→ He has a tantrum	→ His father lets him get on with it and the rest of the family go into another room

Exactly as above	→	George starts to have a tantrum	→	His mother responds in a low-key but firm way which nips the tantrum in the bud
It's a weekend or no friends are invited in after school	→	George is cooperative at teatime	→	The family remain on friendly terms

Manipulating the antecedents

As going to school is an inescapable fact of life for seven-year-olds, that particular A has to stay in place. The As that can be manipulated are

- George's sleep quota
- George's hunger at 3.30 p.m.
- George's friends coming round straight after tea
- Shopping after school

Manipulating the consequences

The consequences which most need modifying are George's father's shouting, chasing and smacking him. George's mother's response to the beginning of one of his tantrums should be left as it stands, as should the consequence of the rest of the family leaving George alone and going into another room.

Child Centred inputs

- Praise
- Attends and Smiles
- Imitation
- Ignoring Minor Naughtiness

Praising George every time he does as he is told would be a very good start. Giving him lots of Attends and Smiles when he is being friendly and cooperative, especially at teatime, could be very helpful. Imitating some of his pro-social behaviours and asking him what he would like you to do would no doubt increase George's feeling of being valued, as would more hugs and strokes. Ignoring the vast majority of his other minor naughtinesses would be a clincher.

Attention Rule lapses

The most obvious one is when George's father gives his older son lots of dramatic attention which is directly contingent on the child's tantrum behaviour.

Useful tactics

- Getting the Attention Rule right

- Manipulating the antecedents

- Being Child Centred

- A reward scheme for calm teatimes Monday through to Friday

- Time Out (see p. 194) to be held in reserve for when George actually hurts someone during a tantrum

- Being more consistent and contingent in your reactions

Intervention plan

Manipulating the As

- Ensure George goes to bed early enough on Sunday through to Thursday

- Take a banana or something similar for George to munch directly he comes out of school

- Do the shopping while he is in school

- Only invite friends in to play *after* tea on weekdays

Manipulating the Cs

- Isolation

- Reward

Instead of George's father shouting, chasing and smacking, he will either isolate George in another room until he has calmed down or he will take the rest of the family into another room until that moment is reached. The second option might be best as it means George's father won't have to wrestle his flailing son into another room. Add in the reward scheme for calm teatime behaviour.

Manipulating the B

● You have already managed it!

Starting date
It could be useful, in George's case, to start on a Monday.

Consistency
Use the tactics discussed earlier.

WHAT TO DO NEXT

In this section I shall be explaining Time Out in detail; talking about five-second warnings as part of Time Out; and looking at a tactic where, in exchange for allowing your child limited opportunities to do something fairly harmless that you none the less abhor, they come up with lots of behaviours of which you approve. I shall also be discussing the whys and wherefores of giving children an explanation about how you intend to tackle their very difficult behaviour.

How to operate Time Out

The full, if rather heavy-handed, title for this powerful technique is Time Out from Positive Reinforcement. What it means is removing your child from all sources of rewarding stimulation. That is one of the reasons why making a child go to their room (often known as 'grounding') as a Time Out procedure doesn't work particularly well – children's bedrooms are a cave of toyland delights. What you must do is put your child in a boring place away from everyone and everything that could provide 'positive reinforcement'.

In practical terms, this leads many mothers and fathers to put a chair in a dull corner of a room, or in the hallway. Choose a hard wooden dining chair (or a little plastic one for very small children) rather than a comfortable armchair. The chair should be used only for this purpose and should remain in place all the time. I used to call it 'The Naughty Chair', until a six-year-old boy told me he called it 'The Magic Chair' because it helped him to be good. Talk about positive thinking!

Timing is crucial, and you need to follow a set sequence. By timing I mean not only how swiftly you act but also how long your child should stay on the chair. The set sequence ensures that you and your child, while having a built-in chance to move back from the full procedure, also both know what will happen next should you not retreat to cordial cooperation, full apologies and so on.

Twelve steps to using Time Out effectively

1. Carry out an ABC analysis of the behaviour that is worrying you.
2. Decide exactly when you will put Time Out into operation.
3. Identify the chair and the place to be used for Time Out.
4. Put the chair into position.
5. Explain to your child that they will have to sit on the chair every time they do 'x' behaviour.
6. Explain that they will not be able to leave the chair and join in with everyone until they have sat quietly for one minute and can be friendly again.
7. Tell your child that they will get a warning, but if they continue to do 'x' they will have to go into Time Out.
8. Show them the Time Out chair and add that it is very boring to have to sit there.
9. Make sure they understand that even if they are quiet for one minute, should they start to do 'x' again once they are off the chair they will have to go back on it until they can be friendly.
10. For your own guidance, write out a Time Out programme and put it where it can easily be seen.
11. Ensure that you have a parallel reward programme worked out and written up, so that your child knows there are benefits to be derived from refraining from 'x' behaviour.
12. Go to it!

So that you have a clear picture of what the Time Out programme and its associated reward programme look like, here are two examples. After that, I shall be talking about some of the 'Yes, buts' that always seem to pop up whenever Time Out is discussed.

Time Out programme to stop Andrew spitting

● Every time Andrew spits say, 'Andrew, I want you to keep your spit in your mouth. Close your mouth now.'

● Wait five seconds for Andrew to start to obey.

● If Andrew keeps on spitting or refuses to close his mouth, say in a firm, clear voice, 'Andrew, this is your warning. Keep your spit in your mouth and close your mouth *now*. If you carry on spitting you will have to go on the Time Out chair.' Wait five seconds for Andrew to start to obey.

● If Andrew does as he is told at this point, you say, 'Good boy for keeping your spit in your mouth and closing your mouth.' Then carry on with your routine.

● If Andrew ignores your warning, say, 'Andrew, you have to go on the Time Out chair now.'

● As you guide Andrew on to the Time Out chair, don't say anything apart from, 'You can come off the chair when you are quiet and sit still for one minute, and keep your spit in your mouth and close your mouth.'

● Don't start bargaining.

● Don't say anything else.

● Stand behind the chair, ready to press down on Andrew's shoulders should he try to escape.

● Don't touch Andrew unless to keep him on the chair.

● Don't make eye contact with Andrew once he has ignored your warning.

● Start counting up to sixty once Andrew is quiet and has stopped spitting.

• If Andrew is quiet and doesn't spit for one minute say, in a neutral voice, 'You can come off the Time Out chair now, Andrew.'

• Don't praise Andrew for being quiet and not spitting.

• Simply pick up where you left off, and carry on with your usual activities or routine.

• Should Andrew start spitting again once he is off the Time Out chair, repeat the whole process from the beginning.

• Repeat as many consecutive times as necessary.

The importance of a reward programme

As I hope you can see from this programme, Time Out is not a physically cruel tactic, though you may need to be quite firm in keeping your child on the chair. It should be reserved for very difficult behaviour – if you use it for every minor annoyance that your children exhibit it will lose a lot of its power. Neither should it ever be carried out unless accompanied by a reward programme for pro-social behaviour.

Reward programme to help Andrew to be friendly

• Every time Andrew is friendly towards someone, praise him generously. Say, 'It's so lovely when you are friendly, Andrew!'

• Every time Andrew doesn't spit for fifteen minutes, praise him enthusiastically. Say, 'Well done, Andrew! You have kept all your spit in your mouth! What a good, friendly boy you are!'

• Make sure Andrew understands that, when he is friendly and doesn't spit for a whole morning (or afternoon or evening), he will get a nice little reward when that time period has finished.

• Concoct a 'reward board', with a selection of treats, or pictures of treats, that Andrew can win up to three times a day for being friendly.

- When Andrew has won three treats a day for three consecutive weeks, change the programme so that:

  ○ Andrew is praised every half-hour for being friendly and not spitting.

  ○ Andrew has to be friendly and not spit for half a day at a time before you give him a reward treat.

- When three or more successful weeks have passed, change the programme so that:

  ○ Andrew is praised every hour for being friendly and not spitting.

  ○ Andrew has to be friendly and not spit for a whole day before you give him a reward treat.

- Gradually change the programme until Andrew receives a praise twice a day and a treat once per week.

- By this time, Andrew should have stopped spitting altogether so you can space out the treats to once per month, with praise being given once a day.

- The whole programme can be allowed to lapse – you will probably be focusing on another behaviour by now.

- Be ready to revive the programme should Andrew start spitting again.

The main thrust of the reward programme is that Andrew finds it much more fun *not* to spit. You may well find that you have to use Time Out only a few times at the beginning of your onslaught on a very difficult behaviour. Your main energies and stamina will be needed for the reward programme, which is absolutely central to success.

Yes, but . . .
Now about those 'Yes, buts' on the topic of Time Out. Here are some of the ones I hear most frequently, along with my perspective on each of them.

- 'Yes, but what if Maggie won't stay on the chair?'

Maggie *will* stay on the chair, because you will put your

hands on her shoulders and press down firmly enough to keep her there. Should she do the 'Floppy Doll' bit and slide off the chair, you have two options. If she is small enough, you can silently lift her back on to the seat. If she is too large for you to lift, let her stay on the floor but continue with every other aspect of Time Out. Next time you could try pushing the chair right up close to the dull corner chosen, so that there is no room to slide off. Do *not* speak to Maggie during this time, except to say, 'You will have to stay in Time Out until you are quiet and friendly.'

● 'Yes, but what if we're out shopping and I haven't got the chair with me?'

Being out of the house is no bar to using Time Out. For toddlers you can use the buggy, pushed into the nearest boring corner. For older and bigger children, my friend and colleague Martin Gent has come up with a brilliant idea for a mobile form of Time Out. Martin tells parents to carry with them, in a pocket or bag, a small square of vinyl floor covering. When your child exhibits in public the behaviour which would have been Timed Out at home, simply lead them to a dull and uninteresting spot, pop the vinyl on the ground and go into your Time Out sequence. You will need to steel yourself, of course, in order to deal with the likely social embarrassment involved in other people looking at you as if you are insane and/or wicked. However, it does work, partly because older children will not want to be 'shown up' in this way. Unfortunately, toddlers don't appreciate this added dimension to Time Out in public!

● 'Yes, but what if Jack just laughs at me when I say, "Time Out"?'

The fact that Jack snorts with derisive laughter when told he has to go into Time Out should be completely ignored as long as you have the physical edge – by which I mean as long as you are taller than he is. (As this proviso indicates, Time Out ceases to be much of an option for larger-than-you teenagers!) Laughter, sneering, giggles, blowing raspberries, pretending to fart or pulling grotesque faces should all be ignored. They are just childish attempts to put you off the planned Time Out track.

You must show Jack that clowning around has no effect on you, and even if he laughs like a hyena Time Out will still proceed inexorably. It is very important for Jack that you stick to your guns, otherwise he will feel out of control and scared even if he is grinning fit to bust.

Jack's attempts to distract you with merriment or contempt have no bearing whatsoever on the efficacy of Time Out. The only gauge you should use to measure whether it is having the desired impact is the frequency of the obnoxious behaviour you are attempting to decrease. When its rate drops, then, despite Jack's heroic efforts, Time Out is working effectively.

- 'Yes, but what if Julia keeps on spitting or making a noise when she's on the chair?'

Your response here should be the same as for Jack and his guffaws. In other words, you totally ignore it and continue with the Time Out procedure. You would then, however, not be able to start counting to sixty until she was quiet. If Julia is still spitting after two or three minutes, which can seem like a lifetime, simply say in a firm but neutral tone, 'Julia, you can only come out of Time Out when you have kept your mouth closed, stopped spitting and been quiet for one minute.' Don't respond when she says, 'Well then, I'll stay here all day and you'll have to stand there and watch me!' Should your child be under three and therefore rather less vocal, the same Time Out rules apply as for older children.

- 'Yes, but what if Rory won't go on the chair?'

Getting him on the Time Out chair depends to a considerable extent on your own air of unbudgeable authority and his physical size compared to yours. There is little point in having to wrestle Rory to the ground in order to drag him towards the chair, only to find he has become such a dead weight that you cannot lift him into it. For larger and older children whom you cannot pick up and deposit on the chair, you need an extra incentive. Try out a ground rule which states that for every fifteen seconds delay, Rory loses fifteen minutes of a favourite TV programme. A small cut in weekly spending money for every second of prevarication can also work wonders with a recalcitrant child. Don't be drawn into a physical tussle unless you are absolutely sure that you can win, without either you or your child getting hurt in any way.

- 'Yes, but I've tried Time Out before and it didn't work.'

My response is always the same: try again. Often Time Out has not been used either consistently or contingently enough. Parents may simply not have realized that a reward programme is an essential part of the procedure. When used properly, Time Out is an enormously potent tactic. In the course of my work I have seen it modify some of the most disturbed child behaviours ever encountered. Don't be put off by other mothers or fathers who say it is no good. If you are consistent, contingent and include a motivating reward programme, you will be well on the way to success.

- 'Yes, but why should I have to bribe Tamsin not to spit? She should know it's not nice.'

It is only when you reward Tamsin for doing something antisocial that you are bribing her. Rewarding anyone for acceptable behaviour is simply that – a reward. There is no way that even giving a child money for being friendly, rather than vicious, is bribery. Nor are you corrupting their moral development. You are in fact teaching them a lesson that must be learnt if they are to function as an acceptable member of society throughout their lives.

Neither are children born with an in-built system which allows them to distinguish right from wrong. Socialization is a long and tortuous, though essential, journey on which none of us would embark voluntarily.

Parents are the most powerful agents of socialization in a child's life. Knowing that 'spitting is not nice' does not come naturally. You have to *teach* your children that spitting is not acceptable, particularly as it is an intrinsically rewarding action, especially if you are under five! Your belief that a child *shouldn't* know that spitting is an unsavoury habit is really rather irrelevant, as it will not make one jot of difference to the fact that Tamsin is spitting and needs you to teach her how to stop. Using a reward programme is an essential part of helping to socialize your child, and socializing your child is one of the major responsibilities of every parent.

● 'Yes, but is it normal to go to these lengths to get Peter to stop spitting?'

It all depends what you mean by 'normal'. There are three definitions of the word. 'Normal' can mean most frequently occurring, desirable, and exemplary.

According to the middle definition, operating Time Out and a reward programme to stop Peter spitting does not qualify, as every sane parent would simply prefer their child not to spit in the first place. From the point of view of the first definition, using Time Out and a reward programme with Peter would again fail to qualify. This is because, in my view, such sensible measures are not taken often enough to quell a child's anti-social behaviours. What *is* normal, in terms of high frequency, is children's spitting behaviour itself!

So that leaves 'exemplary'. I would agree that putting Time Out and a reward programme into operation in order to make a significant reduction in a child's difficult anti-social behaviours is exemplary parenting. In other words, parents who put the scheme into action should be regarded as admirable models of successful parenting.

A little of what you *don't* fancy can do you good

No, the heading is not a misprint – I am referring to a technique squarely founded in Social Learning Theory. Researchers and clinicians (parents too) have found that some behaviours which are rewarding in themselves can be extremely difficult to stop. I mean things like:

● sucking your thumb

● twiddling your hair

● carrying round a comfort blanket

● insisting you go nowhere without your favourite, if rather grubby, toy

● 'fiddling about'

This last item is just one of the many euphemisms used to describe children's masturbatory activities. Thank heavens all those earlier rumours about masturbating making you mad, blind, very hairy or all three have been thoroughly debunked! Playing with their genitals can be a great source of comfort and pleasure for children. None the less, it can be quite difficult to get your young ones to keep this interesting behaviour for their moments of solitude.

The tactic goes like this: in exchange for you positively allowing your child to suck, twiddle, carry a comfort object or masturbate for a limited amount of time in a specified situation, they must come up with lots of non-sucking, non-twiddling etc. the rest of the time.

Supposing your four-and-a-half-year-old is still sucking their thumb for more than 40 per cent of their waking hours, not to mention furious dedication to this activity when dropping off to sleep. You know that, once your child is at school, regular thumb sucking may well be ridiculed by the other children, and is likely to be disapproved of by teachers. So you want to help your child to stop.

Unfortunately, getting a child to refrain from a truly pleasurable behaviour is exceptionally difficult. So be realistic about what you can achieve. In other words, aim for control and not eradication of the comforting activity. With the four-and-a-half-year-old thumb sucker, your best bet would be to use a reward programme to get them to limit their indulgence to bedtime. You would also, of course, tell them that *big* children who go to *big* school do *not* suck their thumbs. If you are consistent about when and where sucking is allowed, and silently remove the offending thumb at other times while simultaneously operating a reward programme, you are undoubtedly on to a winner.

This approach can also work very well with the other types of self-pleasing yet unwanted behaviours previously mentioned. I have, for example, seen parents of comfort object-attached schoolchildren turn up at 3.30 p.m. in the playground with the said comfort object held discreetly available for their child. I am talking here about five- to eight-year-olds, many of whom will have been thoroughly taxed by their day in school and therefore be in need of immediate comfort as soon as it is over.

Explaining things to children

Should you offer your children an explanation of how, and why, things are about to change? Having worked with learning-disabled children and adolescents who were unable to understand even the simplest of explanations, I know that behaviours can be changed without them. I take the view, therefore, that you don't have to wait until your child's language comprehension has fully developed before explaining to them that you are trying to change their anti-social behaviours.

After all, when your child starts to crawl you don't teach them to stay away from the stove by explaining the principles of heat conduction. You either pick them up and move them away, saying, 'No! Hot! Ouch!', or put a gate up in the kitchen doorway. 'No! Hot! Ouch!' is of course an explanation, though at a very primitive level. Nevertheless it is perfectly appropriate for a baby who has just started to crawl.

The older your child becomes, the more able they will be to understand your explanation of how, and why, things are going to change. You should always explain at a level which you know your child will understand. For younger children, accompanying your new actions with a simple statement of 'When you bite/scream/kick, I will put you on your Magic Chair until you are quiet and kind,' does very nicely. You can use more complex explanations when the growing sophistication of your child's speech tells you that they will understand.

In general, I would strongly advise you to involve your child in planning and then implementing the changes you want to accomplish. This should be quite possible from the age of three. Let me give a few examples of the sorts of explanations you might need to use:

● 'Gerry, I've noticed you seem to be finding it difficult to stay calm lately. So I'm going to help you to be more relaxed. What's going to happen is . . .'

● 'Mandy, Dad and I both think you need some help in getting ready for school in time. So this is how things will be in future . . .'

● 'Ryan, it seems difficult for you to settle down at night, so we're going to start a new routine. It will go like this . . .'

- 'Beth, I know you want to have fun when your friends come round, so I'm going to help you, and so is Dad. What will happen is that . . .'

- 'Mikey, you must be more friendly and kind to baby Jonathan, so I'm going to help you by . . .'

- 'Jasmine, you know I want you to leave the matches alone, so I've worked out a way to help you. It's . . .'

You will notice that there are four stages to these explanations:

1. Saying your child's name and getting eye contact.
2. A statement about the fact that you have noticed, not the problem behaviour itself, but that your child is having difficulty in achieving the behaviour you *want* to see. That is the one to focus on – not on the behaviour you wish to reduce.
3. Next is the important part where you clearly say that you are going to help. This is very much more effective than saying that you 'cannot stand for another second' their tantrums/messing about at breakfast/refusing to go to bed/ pushing and shoving their pals/pinching the baby/setting little fires. It helps your child to feel that you are on their side, and also decreases the likelihood of their experiencing your explanation as an exercise in blaming them.
4. Your intervention plan, giving your child a clear picture of who will be doing what, when, how, to whom and for how long, once the new deal starts.

It is particularly central, at this point, to emphasize for your child the reward programme aspects of your plan for positive change. If you were about to try being much more Child Centred, I think an explanation would be rather less necessary. However, you could always mention that, because you love them so much and they are so great, you are going to make sure that you show them all that love by giving them lots of praise and cuddles. Choose a time for explanations when neither you nor they are tired or fraught. It is a good idea to begin the reward board, or its equivalent, as soon as possible after the explanation. That way you can bump up your child's, and your own, motivation to get going on the new scheme.

A QUICK FIX ON CHAPTER 5

1. A parent's consistency towards their child/children is often the key to much happier family relations.

Example: Ted and Nicola had been trying for several months to help their son Matthew, a large three-year-old, to be more friendly towards other children and to stop pushing them over. They had tried numerous reward and punishment tactics to no avail and were beginning to feel desperate, because it was clear that Matthew would become socially isolated if his aggression could not be reduced.

After deep discussion they decided to be more systematic and consistent. Their consistent application of the first approach they had used (though only for three days), that of having just one little pal round daily for half an hour, plus giving Matthew a slice of apple, one of his current favourites, every five minutes while he played in a friendly fashion, was surprisingly success-ful. They combined this with Time Out for one minute every time he did push a child over, plus lots of attention for the victim. After ten days of consistent use of this package of tactics, Matthew had virtually stopped his anti-social behaviour.

Evidence: There is a massive body of research evidence showing that, when parents behave in a consistent and balanced way towards their children, not only does the child's behaviour become more socially acceptable but the parent/child and child/parent relationship improves.

2. When you want to change your child's behaviour pattern, make sure that you provide contingent consequences.

Example: Joshua's father Daniel had been hoping to help his son, aged six, to stop his dangerous climbing activities. As Joshua often carried out his acts of derring-do in public places, and Daniel felt embarrassed by his lack of parental control, Joshua was often not told off until the pair were safely home. He carried on climbing.

Daniel then decided on a new tactic. Explaining to Joshua that he could earn a penny a minute for staying close to him, he set off with laden pockets. All went well until Joshua found a wall he couldn't resist. At this point Daniel, instead of frantically trying to get Joshua down, stopped walking and stood with his back turned towards his son, though he could still see him out of the corner of his eye. After only two or three minutes of 'Yah, yah, you can't catch me!' Joshua came down off the wall of his own accord, for the first time in living memory. Daniel had cracked the problem by making sure that the consequences for sociable and unsociable behaviour alike were immediately contingent on their appearance.

Evidence: Social Learning Theory work has for decades shown that, when consequences are not contingent on the appearance of a specific behaviour, the likelihood of any significant behaviour change is vastly diminished.

3. Time Out can be really effective in reducing very difficult behaviour *only* when used with a reward programme to encourage pro-social behaviour.

Example: When Cherie heard about Time Out from another mother, she couldn't wait to try it out on Stella, aged eight, who had recently become rather impatient and spiteful towards her three younger sisters. However, after a week of sitting Stella on a chair in the hall every time she was mean to Sandi, Terri and Daniella, things were not improving at all.

Meeting the other mother by chance, she poured out her story. When it became clear that Stella needed a reward programme to go along with Time Out, Cherie hurried to put one into action. The results were more encouraging than she would have believed possible, and Cherie had learnt a very important lesson about balanced parenting.

Evidence: Painstaking investigation of Time Out repeatedly concludes that the use of a punishment tactic alone is not only an unethical way to treat a child, it is also ultimately ineffective. Combined with a reward programme, the picture is significantly reversed.

6. Whose Fault Is It Anyway?

Casting Aspersions

WHAT THIS CHAPTER IS ABOUT

Chapter 6 will focus on the effects of **blame, labelling** and **guilt** within family relationships. The reason for casting aspersions at others, putting them in the role of culprit in our misfortunes, will be discussed, as will the sharing of family **responsibilities**. Differing roles for mothers and fathers, sons and daughters – always a rather sensitive area – will be considered in terms of their impact on a family's emotional equilibrium. Another tough topic will be sibling relationships and how to help sisters and brothers to spend less of their time arguing.

FAMILY RELATIONSHIPS AND RESPONSIBILITIES

In this chapter I shall be taking a family perspective on the whole knotty problem of the interactions between blame, labelling, guilt and responsibilities, as I believe that each member of your tribe makes a contribution. Not everything is down to Mum and Dad. Family attachments are also influenced by sons, daughters and grandparents, and each role has its own attendant responsibilities. Blame and guilt can cripple the demonstration of love between members of a family, adult and child.

In my work as a therapist, I often find that one of the major tasks is the fair apportionment of responsibility for particular actions or behaviours. It might be that an adult has always assumed responsibility for what, in factual terms, should be squarely laid at the door of their own parents. The guilt which often accompanies these skewed attributions can ruin lives. As indeed can a mother's or father's blaming themselves for problems which are in essence due to the interactions of the differing temperaments and personalities within their family. I have found during my decades of work with children and their families that single parents are often more prone to disabling emotions of self-blame and guilt. Though understandable, casting yourself as the baddie riddled with guilt, deserving the label 'Failed mother' or 'Failed father', is rarely constructive. Nevertheless these ultimately destructive emotions, if not addressed, can hold powerful sway over family life, making it unnecessarily painful. I hope to be able to illuminate for you how best they might be dealt with.

Mothering and fathering

In the Introduction to this book I spoke about how there was no such thing as a parent – that you were either a mother or a father. None the less, in order to avoid too frequent use of the rather clumsy 'mother or father' I have often found myself using the term 'parent'. Not very consistent of me!

In *Giving and receiving* I shall concentrate on the differences and similarities between mothering and fathering, and the changing roles of men and women in their children's upbringing. In *Echoes*, I want to compare and contrast mothering and fathering patterns as witnessed in my own family over the last three generations. There is little doubt that in the second half of the twentieth century the generally accepted face of being a mother as opposed to being a father, and vice versa, has significantly changed. These changes have brought with them high levels of uncertainty and confusion, which can complicate even further the delicate balance between fathers and mothers.

Sibling rivalries

This in turn can influence the relationships between the children of a mother/father partnership. Whatever the combination of brothers and sisters, there can be complex and frequently problematic attachments. Families where siblings are unfailingly kind and considerate to one another appear to be almost unknown.

There are, of course, many reasons why sisters and brothers clash. One reason is the struggle of each child in the family to identify with, and then model themselves upon, the parent of the same sex. 'Girly girls' and 'real boys' are understandably often at loggerheads on a day-to-day basis. Their specific gender orientation, divergent interests and growing sense of themselves as destined to become either a woman or a man are bound to cause ructions between brothers and sisters. For same-sex siblings, the contentious issues often centre around quite fearsome competition for the attention of their mother and father. Should they have a single parent, the intensity of the fight to reign supreme can reach destructive heights if not carefully handled.

Sons and daughters are different animals

Neither, in my view, are daughters and sons the same. This goes against the grain of modern politically correct thinking, yet I cannot deny the evidence of my own eyes. It seems to me that those who wrestle daily with the differences between girl and boy children have always known that there are significant discrepancies. However, in recent years mothers and fathers have been encouraged to blur the edges between rearing sons and rearing daughters. It may be that, in striving for equal opportunities for girls and boys, sons and daughters, the defining differences between the two sexes have become lost and muddled. My own view is that having identical chances in educational, social, occupational and leisure spheres is a separate issue from whether girls and boys are themselves identical – which they clearly are not.

Blame

- 'It's *your* fault!'

- 'You're the one to blame!'

- 'It wasn't me!'

- 'You started it first!'

- 'Who's to blame for this?'

These are all phrases bandied around in pursuit of pinning down a culprit, preferably not yourself! In *Setting the scene for change* I shall be telling you about some tactics to reduce the flood of acrimonious accusations that plague some families. Here I simply want to mention a few of the psychological reasons why people seem to be so enthusiastic about identifying the perpetrator of the latest domestic outrage.

When you are a child, fear is one of the most powerful motivators for blaming someone or something other than yourself or your actions. Fear of punishment. Fear of ridicule. Fear of failure. Or, perhaps most painful of all, fear of your mother's and father's disapproval or withdrawal of their attention. High levels of anxiety are known to impair performance, whether you are on your toes in a tutu, disposing of used cat litter, or sticking a plaster on a grazed knee. This is not some wacky idea of my own, it is a tried and tested research finding.

Given, then, that a very fearful child will find it difficult to account for themselves in a calm and reasoned fashion, don't mistake symptoms of stress for evidence of culpability. That makes the whole business of establishing 'whose fault it is,' very much more dicey, however fair and just your intentions in trying to get to the bottom of why Mark has a bruise on his arm while Bettina has a smug look on her face.

I have already laboured the point that children will do anything to gain their mother and father's attention, whether congratulatory or castigating. This means that, having had an 'accident', or committed a 'crime' of some sort, children are really left between a rock and a hard place. Still longing for your attention at any price, they none the less fear retribution. What better way to solve their dilemma than by pointing the finger of suspicion at someone else?

Hence some of the rather tall stories offered in explanation of why for example,

- Tonia's hair is suddenly very uneven in length
- Bobby's building bricks are covered with chocolate pudding
- Your briefcase no longer locks as it used to

You can see the temptation for a frightened child who has broken your latest CD of *Eine Kleine Nachtmusik*, of fiercely intimating that it was their pal Malcolm, or even the dog, who had mashed up the Mozart. For what would be the consequences of admitting their error?

Children fear that, should they own up to their misdemeanour, you will hurt them physically and/or emotionally. So, instead of vilifying them for their attempts to pin the blame on others, you could usefully view their transparent little strategies for maintaining their own innocence as a manifestation of your unrivalled power as their parent. Dealing with their pathetic cover-up stories for what they really are, attempts to retain your love and favour, can have a much more positive impact than simply labelling your child a liar.

Adults, too, have a decided tendency to shift blame for any mishap or misunderstanding on to a handy scapegoat. Though you may, as a grown-up, make some sterling efforts to admit responsibility for your actions, there is no getting away from the psychological fact that you would probably much rather avoid unpleasant consequences than stand up to admit your offence. Adults, after all, experience the same compulsion to survive intact as do children.

You know what it is like:

- You fluffed the important presentation
- You missed the vital train or plane connection
- You failed to complete the project by the deadline

Even if you do have sufficient 'moral fibre' to admit your error, I suspect that, like myself, you would also urgently wish for a cast-iron reason for some other unfortunate to take the drop. We grown-ups too often fear punishment, ridicule, failure and the withdrawal of approval by the authority figures in our lives. It is simply part of being human. I believe that, just as you and I forgive and understand in ourselves, so should children be treated.

If that sounds a touch pious I am unrepentant, because this business is just one more example of the double standards that adults sometimes operate when evaluating a child's behaviour. I strive to stay away from double standards, though not always successfully.

Labelling

Labels are powerful. Ask any child to choose a pair of trainers and you will immediately be given a string of them – only certain 'labels' or 'logos' will do. Adults are no different: most of us at some time or other succumb to the pulling power of 'brand names' or 'designer labels', whether in the supermarket, the car showroom or the fashion boutique.

Nor are personal and household goods the only items to be treated in this way. People are labelled, for good or ill, all the time. I have been using labels throughout this book, for example when defining personality types. When you are discussing another person, it is extremely difficult to paint a vivid picture without using labels. That's fine – just another human characteristic at work. Or is it?

One of the major concerns in my work is to ensure that any labels I employ are as accurate and constructive as possible, used at the right time, in the right place and for the right reasons. Yet I admit that in personal conversations I am rather less careful. In my work I feel a powerful sense of responsibility for, and accountability to, the families who trust me to do my best for them. In contrast, when I am 'at play' I feel I can be a little irresponsible in doling out labels.

So into which category does parenting itself fall? Is it as serious as work? Or should it be regarded as an equivalent to play? Realizing that your responsibilities as a parent rank equally with your commitment level outside the home is a watershed in many adults' lives. When this happens, the whole business of labelling within the family setting cries out for a thorough spring clean.

Have you ever called your child

- lazy

- clumsy

- slow

- dim

- crazy

- hopeless

- pathetic

- a failure

- a waste of space

- a worry

- a nuisance

- too short

- too tall

- too fat

- too thin

- or, worst of all, stupid?

It is easy to be driven by parental exasperation to use derogatory labels. The list of damaging labels is almost endless.

- There are the ones framed as questions: 'Do you know what an absolute *pain* you are, Joe?'

- The ones phrased as a plea: 'What am I going to *do* with you? You're so aggressive!'

- The rapid-fire version with the humiliating sting in the tail: 'You're useless, pathetic, slow and stupid! *What* are you?'

● The reflecting type: 'Get out of my sight, you worthless, lazy lump!'

And so on, ad infinitum.

If you stop to think about it logically, little is accomplished by such epithets. Are children supposed to respond by:

● translating the negative adjectives into their positive counterparts

● vowing to show their parents that they are really in the latter category, and

● enacting their promise?

Surely not. Yet this is presumably the castigating adult's intention.

Or is it? Perhaps when a parent uses such devaluing labels towards their child it is actually the verbal equivalent of a smack. If this is so, it would follow that the adult received the same immediate but short-term discharge of tension achieved by slapping a child. Grown-ups usually only let fly with a string of damning labels when their ability to stay on top of a child management problem has reached a point of ultimate exasperation. Character assassination might seem preferable to physical punishment, but that does not deny the hurt and psychological damage that can stem from a tongue-lashing.

In my experience most children react not with a toughened resolve to prove their critical parent wrong but with the very opposite. Their rationale for their response is frequently along the lines of 'Well, if she/he thinks I'm lazy/dim/a miserable nuisance, then I might as well *be* lazy/dim etc. That'll show them!' A psychological bullet through the foot for the adult, who probably regretted their outburst as rapidly as would have happened had they hit their child.

Try asking yourself what would be your likely reaction to a dressing-down from a loved partner or friend. My own experience is that I feel first alienated, then outraged and often uncooperative. I know I *should* view their criticisms as constructive, though I also believe 'should' is a dangerous word as it allows little room for valid emotions and far too much for social conventions.

If I, a supposedly mature woman, can react in such an emotionally primitive fashion to what is ostensibly 'constructive' criticism, how on earth are children supposed to cope with a stream of destructive labels? Just because your child may be slow or hopeless on occasion does not mean that either they, you or your relationship will benefit from your telling them so in no uncertain terms. In *Setting the scene for change* I shall be talking about how best you might avoid defeating your own ends by using derogatory labels to describe your child.

Guilt

Psychologically speaking, guilt is a fascinating process. In relationship terms it is a killer, unless it leads pretty swiftly to constructive acts of reparation. What I am talking about here is regret for having been emotionally insensitive, including smacking a child.

Everyone has done things which they regret, especially having been hurtful to someone else for no good reason. Whether your transgression is inadvertent or intentional, remorse for your actions can be just as real and painful. Not that these internal emotions do either yourself or your victim much good unless they are openly acknowledged, apologized for and channelled into repairing the damage done. The guilty party can otherwise be tempted to luxuriate in the *'mea culpa'* aftereffects of doing the dirty on someone, a piece of egotistical indulgence which is most undesirable and achieves nothing.

Why then do so many succumb to the temptation? I know that when I have found myself doing a great deal of breast-beating, it often precludes my making any effective reparation towards the person to whom I have been insensitive, unkind or unjust. Why do I, or you, take this path?

The reason is probably associated with unresolved feelings and attitudes about self-worth. When you are mean to someone, you can be forced to get in touch with those aspects of your personality and behaviour of which you disapprove. While this can be uncomfortable, it may be less daunting than taking the risk and trying to right the situation, only to be rebuffed and ridiculed by those towards whom you have behaved badly.

Naturally, guilt as a brief precursor to taking that risk can serve as a useful stimulus to action. Your definition of 'brief' is likely to be subjective. People who are extremely reluctant to admit bad behaviour may consider a year to be brief. Others may need only seconds before they embark upon repairing the damage done. There is bound to be an enormous range of reactions because each individual's psychological reasons for the guilt experienced are so complex, as well as deeply rooted in the distant past.

Whichever way you cut it, the fact remains that guilt is an unproductive emotion unless it is firmly and rapidly linked to reparations. In *What to do next* I shall be offering some tactics which can help you to be constructive with your guilty feelings. These ploys will not only help the victim but will also allow you to feel more positive about yourself.

Responsibility

I have already alluded to parental responsibility when talking about blame and about labelling. By inference, the issue of what you do when you feel guilty is linked with personal and parental responsibility. Everyone has 'responsibilities'. They may range from remembering to feed the family pets to refusing strong liquor just before piloting four hundred passengers halfway round the world. One of the major characteristics of responsibilities is that, if you shirk them, problems may ensue.

When you become a parent there is an immediate cosmic shift in your responsibilities. Infants, toddlers, schoolchildren and adolescents all depend on their parents to provide a safe, nurturing and sufficiently stimulating environment. No doubt you yourself are currently embroiled in the exhausting task of seeing that your child's emotional, physical, social, intellectual, educational and behavioural needs are properly met. Matching up to the challenging and extensive responsibility of being a parent is not easy. However much effort you put into it, you are bound to achieve only partial success. Not much of a motivating package, is it? Yet, impelled by complex and intensely powerful urges, becoming a parent is still an option that many of us choose above life without a child.

PARENTAL RESPONSIBILITY DEMANDS PARENTAL SUPPORT

'Parental responsibility' has become a political buzz phrase in recent years, with emphasis being placed on adults' role in ensuring their children behave well in school and out in the community. Juvenile crime statistics and reports of increasingly violent classroom and playground behaviour seem to be the main triggers for attempts to make parents legally as well as morally responsible for their children's behaviour. This trend seems to be occurring in many countries. Information from the USA, Australia, New Zealand, France, China, the Caribbean and parts of India indicates that similar attempts are being made to break the vicious circle of very troublesome children turned juvenile delinquents who finally emerge as anti-social adults who then produce very troublesome children . . . and so on ad infinitum.

Not long ago I was invited to be an 'expert' on a TV programme which debated hot topics in current affairs. The motion was whether parents should be fined if their children behaved badly in school. In essence, the issue was about who was responsible for schoolchildren's behaviour during their daily education. Cases were made for the responsibility lying with teachers, parents, children themselves, the media and the state.

My point was that, until parents were given educational, practical and financial support to enhance their ability to meet their responsibilities to their children, everyone was wasting their breath in trying to find someone to blame. In my experience, to highlight the crushing nature of parental responsibilities without providing such help simply doesn't work. I am a passionate protagonist of education in parenting, advice and treatment centres for parents, and sufficient state money to provide truly effective versions of both. Until such services are universally available by right, I don't believe that either crime or other anti-social behaviour can be noticeably reduced.

Were I to elaborate on each and every aspect of parental responsibilities, I could write a whole book. Perish the thought – unless I were also to draft a companion volume on the fun, joys and rewards of parenthood. In this book, particularly in the *What to do next* sections, my aim is to alert you to some of the ways in which you can help yourself to rise to the occasion again and again and again!

Having dealt with the four key words of this chapter, I shall now tackle the business of sex and gender roles as they influence family life. I shall be looking at some of the ways in which, on a daily basis and for both children and adults alike, being a daughter or son, mother or father flavours the giving and receiving in your own family relationships.

GIVING AND RECEIVING

It is virtually impossible to discuss women and men, girls and boys, without reference to the stereotypical roles each has been ascribed. In all the areas of human functioning the debate continues to rage. Are males superior to females or vice versa? The reasoned answer to all the rhetoric would be that men and women, girls and boys, are equal *and* different.

The focus of this section is the realities of family life as currently experienced by most people. That means concentrating on the interplay between the male and female members of families, and their likely patterns of giving and receiving. Such patterns are often determined by expectations, which are themselves usually an admixture of stereotypical attitudes and brave attempts to move away from such well-worn ideas.

Mothers and fathers: equal and different

What exactly is currently expected of mothers, and what of fathers? Certainly there have been many developments in this area, particularly over the last half-century. Fifty years ago women were positively encouraged to retreat from their vital contribution to 'the war effort' and return to home and hearth, supposedly to free up jobs for the men no longer needed in the forces. Today women have moved back into the workplace en masse, while still attempting to fulfil their responsibilities as mothers. The path of men has been almost the reverse in that many now have equal, or *almost* equal, responsibility with their female partners for child care and domestic tasks. Well, that's the theory, though a dispiriting number of surveys claim to show that men's lives go on very much as they always did. Meanwhile, women are left if not having it all, then doing it all!

But however 'equal' men and women may be nowadays, they are still quite distinctly different. Whether you go out to work, work from home, or work *in* the home, you remain either male or female. However, the apparently inevitable tensions of female/male intimate relationships infiltrate most family exchanges. It seems that expectations of gender roles still play a central part in family life.

In today's society mothers are still expected to provide most of the child care. That is so even for the many working mothers. For instance, mums are expected to

- organize family life

- ensure their children have a healthy diet, wear shoes that fit and go to the dentist regularly

- be especially sensitive to their offspring's emotional highs and lows, and to be able to skilfully calm the first and lift the second

They are expected to be a fund of knowledge about

- what clothes their children should be wearing

- what TV and videos they should be watching

- what books they should be reading

- at what point the doctor should be called when they are running a temperature or vomiting their little hearts up

For fathers, the modern expectations are that they should play a much more participatory role in their children's lives:

- take their turn at getting up during the night to tend to fractious babies and toddlers

- do half the housework, laundry and shopping
- be sensitive to their children's emotional needs
- share the cooking
- change the baby
- and *still* take the household rubbish out for collection!

Quite a tall order, especially when many of today's fathers had fathers who went out to work and were treated like minor royalty when they came home. *Real* men, so the story used to go, were 'strong and silent'. Today's man is supposed not only to be 'in touch with' his feelings, but to be sensitive enough to appreciate the various mood states of his partner. Tough, especially when you are pumped full of testosterone and have reduced *social* sensitivity (more on this below).

Mothering and fathering: what's the difference?

Given the official closing of the gap between what mothers and fathers contribute to the welfare of their children, what distinguishes mothering from fathering? In my view, the answer lies partly in the use of the word 'official'. While the list of expectations of mothers and fathers seems set on a convergence course, the emotional and psychological realities for children are another matter.

Many children, at bottom, believe their father is there to fight for their safety, while mothers are for cuddling and making you feel better. Thankfully, there is a growing band of children who have experienced the reverse, or indeed interchangeable mother/father behaviour. This is much closer to meeting a child's requirement for flexible role models, though it cannot be denied that young children are keen on slightly more categorical thinking – in their eyes, you tend to be either 'a goodie' or 'a baddie'.

Part of a child's emotional and psychological reality is heavily influenced by the physical differences between mothers and fathers. Mothers are generally smaller, rounder and have softer voices; fathers are larger, leaner and louder. In the first year or two of a child's life, most of their emotional and psychological experiences and development are processed via their sensory functions – seeing, hearing, tasting and so on. In other words, they are very physical beings at this early age, and your physical interactions with them are the mortar in the building blocks of their personality.

That does not mean that babies need only the mothering input. Nor should it lead to an assumption that a father's contribution is paramount. The point is that babies benefit from a balance of small and large, round and lean, soft and loud. On the other hand, babies are quite robust and adaptable, so that having two small and soft, or large and loud, parents is not going to upset them unduly either.

Both males and females have a 'social sensitivity gene' – an inherent awareness of and responsiveness to the 'messages', such as body language and facial expression, that other people are giving us about how they are feeling. The recent discovery that this gene is only 'switched on' in women seems to account in part for the observable differences in mothers' and fathers' social/emotional attitudes and behaviour towards their children. When children are asked which parent they turn to most readily when upset or ill, most respond without hesitation, 'My mum/mother/mummy.' This applies equally to boys and girls. When adults are asked about their own childhood experiences, the same choice is noted. This would seem to show that, however, *simpatico* fathers may consider themselves to be, the chance of being comforted or nursed by their mothers is often what children would prefer.

Does this mean children can tell that their mother's social sensitivity gene is switched on while their father's is not? My idea – and it is only that, because there are as yet no research findings on this topic – is that from infancy children are aware of the subtle, and not so subtle, differences between how their mother and father behave towards them.

This is not such a far-fetched notion as it might initially appear. There are solid research findings about how men and women hold boy or girl newborns. The women fold both sorts of babies towards their bodies, cradling them in their arms, while the men react like this only with girl babies, yet hold the boy babies out towards the world while jiggling them up and down.

However, this little story has a sting in the tail as far as my theory goes. By the end of the first week of a baby's life both mothers and fathers enfold the girls and jiggle the boys. Nothing is ever simple, it seems. In other words, adults are not just acting on their children – the characteristics of the baby influence the manner of the adults' behaviour. A reciprocal interaction, in fact – exactly as would be predicted by the Parent/Child Game and Child Development Theory.

So where does that leave my idea that the effect of a mother's active social sensitivity gene prompts behaviour that children can distinguish from that of their father? I think it still has something to offer, though who knows how much? Here are a few typical examples of discrepancies that I have observed over the years. You have probably come across very similar ones yourself.

● Richard, father of Charlotte aged four, responded with, 'Never mind. Be a brave girl and don't cry', when his daughter fell and scraped her knees.

● Amy, mother of Sean aged five and a half, said, 'Oh, my poor little love. Come here and let me kiss it better', when her son fell and bruised his hands.

● David, father of eight-year-old Aaron, told his son when he had bumped into a concrete post, 'Come on now. You'll be all right. Big boys don't cry.'

● Marianne, mother of Kelvin aged ten, responded with, 'Kelvin! Sweetheart, are you hurt? There, there. Let Mummy take a look. I'll be very gentle', after her son had fallen off his bike.

Boys and girls: the subtle distinctions

It has long been accepted in folklore that girls and boys are not only different shapes, but are made up of very discrepant elements. You may remember that boys are supposed to be made of 'Frogs and snails and puppy-dogs' tails', while girls are made of 'Sugar and spice, and all things nice'. This idea has been thoroughly researched over recent decades, and some interesting findings identified among boys in general and girls in general.

Type of Development	Girls	Boys
Intellectual and language	Verbal skills are ahead of boys' in the early years	Visuo-spatial skills are in advance of girls'
Social	Good at negotiating when problems occur	Prefer a more confrontational and physical solution
Educational	Generally behave well in school	Schooltime behaviour is often limit-pushing
Play	Favour quiet domestic, creative, family or romantic themes	Delight in noisy fights and fearsome adventures
Physical	Often more poised in their physical actions	Fling themselves about quite readily
Emotional	Generally very empathetic	Take a more spartan attitude
Psychosexual	Seem to masturbate less frequently than boys	More enthusiastic about masturbation
Personality	Known to be caring and sensitive	Less interested in subtleties of feeling

Are the differences determined partly by the social sensitivity gene discrepancy between boys and girls? Almost certainly. To what extent? No one knows at present.

A further source of information that points to distinctive girl and boy characteristics is the reports of parents themselves, who have persistently made these general comments:

Boys	Girls
Noisy	Quieter
Enjoy rumbustious games	Enjoy sitting-down activities
Push behaviour limits	Are more acquiescent
Play competitively	Play cooperatively
Like getting muddy and messy	Value cleanliness and neatness

Adjust your expectations

So how does mothering being different from fathering, and daughters and sons being unlike work out in practice? 'Complicatedly' is the most accurate answer, I think. Still, that isn't going to help you much when Jimmy has split his lower lip falling out of a tree while simultaneously Liza is spring cleaning her dolls' house, and your partner walks in and starts to handle things in a noticeably different style from your own. I suggest that the most positive response to realizing that mothers and fathers, sons and daughters have distinctive gender-bound characteristics is to adjust your expectations. When you have accepted the interesting divergences between one sex and the other, their differing roles within the context of the family life could well become much less troublesome.

● Expecting your son to get dirty at the local park can make it much easier to handle any irritation you might feel when you spot him rolling around in a grubby corner of the playground.

● Expecting a mother to be more emotionally in touch with her children could quite easily lift some of a father's pain at not being chosen to dole out the comfort and kisses.

● Expecting your daughter to enjoy craft activities means you will not make the mistake of buying her an evil space alien villain for her birthday.

● Expecting a father to be hotter on children sticking to ground rules than their mother is might be a useful way forward when tempers get frayed and arguments flare between the children.

All this is, of course, relevant only within the parameters of your detailed and intimate knowledge of your own partner, daughters and sons. I am simply trying to make the point that in my opinion it is time to stop lumping together under the label of 'parenting' the varied contributions of mothers and fathers to bringing up their sons and daughters; just as it is my view that children are done a disservice when they are not further differentiated into boys and girls. Perhaps, instead of just two categories of family members, parents and children, it would be more constructive to acknowledge that there are in fact four, mothers, fathers, sons and daughters.

ECHOES

The three generations in my own family which I am going to describe in terms of the gradual twentieth-century evolution in mothering and fathering, are:

- my own parents

- myself and my first husband

- my two daughters and one stepdaughter, and their partners

First generation

The pattern of mothering practised by my own mother ensured a distinct difference from what my father provided. Kathy did not go out to work after she married Harry, even though it was eight years before I, their eldest child, was born. Neither did she work when we children were older, apart from a Saturday job in a clothes shop when the youngest was about ten.

As a result we children grew up expecting our mother to be constantly available at home. She did not seem to resent this arrangement at all. Indeed she rather gloried in being a mother and took her responsibilities in that direction very seriously. I believe Kathy would have been actively unhappy if she had had to go out to work rather than be at home with her children.

In her view, it was the job of mothers to take on all child care, as well as the housework, laundry, shopping, cooking, nursing, educational liaison and healthcare arrangements. She also made sure that all birthdays, anniversaries, high days and holidays were celebrated in style, even when money was scarce. An active part of Kathy's mothering efforts involved making all our clothes on her trusty sewing machine. Another role was to provide interesting, stimulating and rewarding play opportunities. I know that Kathy strove at all times to be fair, to avoid having favourites and to mould her children into acceptably socialized human beings. I can understand why she found being a mother a full-time occupation!

My father's contribution to bringing us up was slight when compared with my mother's heroic efforts. They both agreed, however, that Harry's daily priority was to earn the money which kept the family ticking over financially.

For years Kathy made his lunchtime sandwiches after he had brought her an early morning cup of tea in bed, cooked breakfast for him, then kissed him goodbye as he cycled to work. When he returned in the evening it was a priority to have his dinner ready in time, and she always changed into an attractive outfit to greet him.

My father would kiss everyone hello, then listen relatively patiently as we children told him the high spots of the day. My mother then made it abundantly clear that Dad's meal was not to be interrupted, so she organized quiet activities for us while he ate and read the evening paper. Next came the opportunity for a bit of a romp around with our father, after which he read us a story once we were tucked up in bed. And that was it, apart from weekends and very rare holidays.

After finishing work for the week at midday on Saturday Harry would either work in the garden, watch a football match or set off with his farmer pals to watch birds on the nearby marshes. Both football and birdwatching were fully approved by my mother, as 'a man needs a hobby'. We didn't see much of him on Saturdays.

That left Sunday as the 'family day'. My mother went to church, having put the roast into a slow oven. We children quite often went with her, so it was not until 11.30 or so that we were all together at home. For the rest of Sunday, apart from an hour's nap after lunch, my father gave us his attention – when he wasn't painting, wallpapering, plumbing, fixing the lights, tidying out the shed, sorting out the family finances or mending and polishing our shoes.

Yet, although he wasn't around much, I don't remember feeling that he was 'absent' in any way, apart from during the Second World War when millions of men were separated from their families. In my recollections, the times that were spent with my father were 'special': a supply-and-demand mechanism at work, perhaps. It's as if my mother provided the fabric of daily life, while my father added little patches of colourful embroidery.

In the 1940s and 1950s there was nothing strange about the way in which they brought us up. Mothers looked after the children and home, fathers earned the money – simple as that!

Second generation

You might think that when I had children in the early sixties I would have moved on and chosen a more modern pattern. I didn't. Why? I suppose my mother and father's division of labour seemed quite acceptable to me. After all, I had enjoyed life at home with them – at least until I was about fourteen and started to want to spread my wings! Also, I am sure that my mother's way of explaining how important it was for women to be where their children needed them – at home – was extremely persuasive.

I trained as a nurse, got married to my first husband at nineteen and left my job to travel with Geoffrey, as his work demanded, and produce and care for our children. Until my eldest child was fourteen, although I studied part-time, I did no paid work. So what did I do all day?

Surprise, surprise, I did almost exactly the same as my mother! I cooked, shopped, laundered, sewed clothes, knitted, did the housework, took my children to school and then collected them, organized family life, nursed sick children and my husband, made Christmas a delight and family holidays fun, and arranged interesting activities. I too strove at all times to be fair, and to ensure that my children became socialized individuals. I also had a meal ready for Geoffrey when he came home, and had changed my clothes, tidied up and got the children into their nightclothes for story time with Daddy.

Naturally, this pattern altered as my children grew older and my educational activities as a 'mature' student took off. I put a meal in the oven and hired child care as my studies took me into London on three and then four evenings a week. It was this which led me away from the pattern of mothering learnt at Kathy's knee, and it was all done with Geoffrey's total support. He was quite marvellous throughout the long years of study, upon which I embarked with his full approval. I cannot see that my father or mother would have considered this a 'proper' pattern for a mother, though they encouraged me throughout.

I eventually went out to work full-time, having gained a degree in psychology, when my children were aged fourteen, twelve and eight and quite able to get themselves to and from school. After that point I juggled job, home, family, friends and fun just like all working mothers. As the years passed my input to my children became less hands on and more conversational – in fact I looked forward to our daily chat times as a rewarding activity after a long working day.

Geoffrey's pattern of fathering was not unlike my father's. On weekdays, after first bringing me a cup of tea in bed, he left for work, returning promptly at 6.30 each evening. There would be hugs and kisses, a brief fun time and then bedtime stories which he read with gusto. He would make deliberate mistakes in well-loved tales, only to be delightedly howled down by his rapt audience. We quite often ate together. At weekends, apart from regular attendance at football matches, Geoffrey spent time with his children at home, in the garden, out shopping or on interesting trips. I believe the great bonus for my children in their relationship with their father was the very considerable time they spent together on his archaeological excavations. To be part of their father's work, to trot around with him in their wellies, enjoying their niche as the boss's child, was visibly a great delight for Rhiannon, Katy and Nicholas. In this way, my own children enjoyed much more of their father's company than had been possible for me with my father. A definite plus.

Third generation

Now that my two daughters and step-daughter are all mothers, it seems as though some old patterns are being repeated while new ground is being broken too. Katy found she did not want to make the compromises and sacrifices involved in juggling motherhood and a career. As a result she spent four-plus years at home with Ben, following a pattern of mothering rather similar to that of myself and my mother. Katy has since worked part-time, and is currently available to take Ben to school and collect him, whizzing off to her job during his school hours.

Ben's father James also has a rather traditional pattern, in that he works full-time and is available for Ben mainly in the evenings and at weekends. The change I notice in James's fathering, compared to that of the previous two generations, is the very open demonstrations of love and affection which he shows to his son. My own father, Harry, was quite a cuddler for his generation, as was Geoffrey, yet I do believe that James and Ben are physically and emotionally closer than were Harry and my brother, or Geoffrey and our son.

Sarah, after a horrendous pregnancy, spent the first eighteen months of Elliott's life as a full-time mother. As such – you've guessed it – she did most of the cooking, laundry, housework, shopping and so on. The main difference for Elliott is that his daddy, Alan, is around much more than might be usual, as he is an actor.

Alan too is delightfully affectionate to his son, and shares in his care and amusement when not working. I find the trend of modern fathers to be openly loving towards their children very heartening. It would seem that the young dads of today may well be significantly more Child Centred towards their offspring than their predecessors, and that society may at last be endorsing demonstrations of love between fathers and sons.

Rhiannon's mothering has followed a rather different pattern: apart from taking maternity leave following the births of Maeve and Eoin, she returned to part-time work. This has involved complex child care arrangements and regular daily contributions from Mickey, the children's father, to the tortuous transport plans. None the less, Rhiannon's mothering has included many of the elements common to myself and her grandmother. She too shops, cooks, launders, organizes family life and provides Maeve and Eoin with interesting outings and activities – as does Mickey.

I have noticed that, in comparison to previous generations in my family, the young men who are presently new fathers *expect* to play a more active role in sharing tasks that used to be regarded as 'woman's work'. Bully for them! They are providing their children with a model of fathering which may lead, in future generations, to a more equitable pattern of mothering and fathering.

SETTING THE SCENE FOR CHANGE

The principles of Social Learning Theory, Child Development Theory, the Parent/Child Game and Cognitive Behaviour Therapy all contribute towards understanding the blame and labelling which goes on in families.

The part played by Social Learning Theory

Social Learning Theory reminds you that if you give attention, albeit critical, to behaviour, it is more likely to occur again in future. In terms of blame and labelling, it can often happen that the very processes involved guarantee that attention is provided contingent on unacceptable behaviour.

For example: suppose you heard a wail from the next room and rushed in to find that seven-year-old Ian and his pal Rufus, aged eight, were lying on the floor surrounded by a mass of cushions and the remains of your Aunt Edna's precious antique vase. Your rapid assessment of the situation tells you that the boys have been bouncing off the sofa on to the cushions; an expressly forbidden activity. Before you know it, you have shouted, 'Well! Who's to blame for this mess? *And* Aunty's vase has been broken in the process. You're so clumsy, Ian – and you're no better, Rufus! I blame you both for this, and I don't care if it's supposed to be an accident. You'll both clear everything up straightaway and then come into the other room to talk to me!'

You would certainly have achieved some success:

- you have not smacked them

- you have made them clear up

- you have told them what you want them to do when order has been restored

Unfortunately, you have also both blamed the boys and labelled them clumsy, in such a way as to increase the likelihood that they will again 'perform' in this way, probably at their earliest opportunity.

How could you have played the scene to reduce the future incidence of such mini-disasters? Mainly through being

- calm

- consistent

- contingent

Like this: 'Ian, Rufus, get up off the floor and clear up all the mess right now. I'm not interested in who did what. All I know is that when everything is straight I want you to come into the other room to talk to me.' Then, while they are scurrying around doing your bidding, you have time to sort out exactly how you want them to make reparation for breaking Aunt Edna's vase and the 'no bouncing' ground rule. You might make them forfeit some spending money, or not let them watch their current favourite video for two days.

According to Social Learning Theory the second method, where you avoid blaming and labelling entirely, is the one which will make it least likely that Ian and Rufus will repeat their misbehaviour. As an important adjunct to this welcome outcome, neither Ian nor Rufus will be wrestling with the idea that you don't care for them any more and that they are clumsy boys. And you will have stayed in charge of the situation. All this points to better behaviour and relationships in future. What more could you want?

The part played by Child Development Theory

Child Development Theory too would very much substantiate the benefits of option number two for dealing with the bouncing boys and the non-bouncing vase. The emphasis would perhaps be more on the emotional reaction of the boys, and the potential damage to relationships were you to exercise the first type of response. Blaming and labelling children really knocks their self-esteem and undermines the attachment between you, unless of course the blame is left out and the label is a positive one.

The part played by the Parent/Child Game

The Parent/Child Game principles stoutly confirm that avoiding emotional statements of blame and negative labelling is much more advantageous than a tongue-lashing about how it is all your mean/aggressive/stupid/thoughtless child's fault. The combination of

- Alpha Commands
- reparation
- punishment by withdrawal of privileges

as shown in version two of dealing with Ian and Rufus is right in line with being properly Child Centred. You would, to all intents and purposes, at first be ignoring the boys' unacceptable behaviour by focusing on how they should deal with the mountain of cushions, if not the damage to Aunty's vase! Your Alpha Commands on what they *do* to make things right, alongside a reasonable punishment, would exert a powerful influence on whether they do or don't bounce in future.

You would, in fact, have taken them one step nearer to being sociable and responsible children, which would *not* be the case were you to blame and label them. Neither would you have driven them to believe themselves, and in future act as, clumsy, naughty boys.

The niceties of punishing someone else's child I leave to your good sense. Negotiation with Rufus's parents would be, however, advised!

The part played by Cognitive Behaviour Therapy

The founding principle of Cognitive Behaviour Therapy – that thoughts impact directly on mood and behaviour – is clearly applicable to Ian and Rufus's plight. Children are not only subject to Negative Automatic Thoughts, just as you and I may be, they are in the process of building up fundamental assumptions about themselves, their world and their future. This makes them particularly vulnerable to the destructive influence on their personalities of blame and critical labelling. Were you to best guess their reason for fibbing about who was at fault, rather than blaming and labelling, you would be doing much to improve their mood, their behaviour and their view of themselves.

Going back to Ian and Rufus: supposing, when you arrived on the scene, either one or both of the boys had looked up at you with stricken face and loudly affirmed, 'I didn't do it!'? Putting Cognitive Behaviour Therapy ideas to work, one of your tacks, when you had got them in the other room for a talk, would be to best guess the reason for their denial of culpability. Your helpful best guess remarks, after you had told them what their punishment was, could be along these lines.

'Now, I think that one of the reasons children say, "It wasn't me", or "I didn't do it", is because they are afraid. I know that when children have had an accident, maybe through bouncing on the sofa when they know they shouldn't, they can be afraid that their mum or dad will be so cross that they will give their children a smack. Often, when parents smack their children, or shout at them, the children think that their mum and dad don't love them any more. That's not true, though. The mums and dads *do* still love them, like Daddy and I love you, Ian, and your mum and dad love you, Rufus. It's just that parents don't allow bouncing on the sofa because it can be dangerous. So we love *you*, and we *don't* like bouncing.'

Summing it up

It seems clear, then, that, instead of blaming and labelling, you should treat your children to this sequence of events:

- an Alpha Command telling them to do the sociable/ constructive behaviour you would rather see

- instructions for reparation

- a suitable punishment for bad behaviour

- your best guess

For instance, when your child has been lolling around in front of the TV for the three hours since school ended, *don't* say, 'You lazy lump! You never do anything!' Do say, 'I want you to put lots of energy into your homework this evening, Danny/ Daniella. I know how good you are once you get cracking!' Then stand back and cross your fingers!

Getting it right on blame and labelling means that you bite your lip when you would usually be dishing the dirt, and go instead for positive commands and comments. This will actively encourage the behaviour which you want to see, instead of entrenching the kind that drives you mad. Sounds good, doesn't it?

WHAT TO DO NEXT

In this section I shall be talking first about ways in which to deal effectively with parental guilt and sensibly with issues of parental responsibility. Then I shall move on to helping you cope with the sibling arguments that are the bane of even happy families' lives.

Guilt, as I have said before, is a destructive and sometimes self-indulgent emotion. Cognitive Behaviour Therapy can be particularly productive in dealing with it. My adult patients often tell me they feel a great deal of guilt over what they see as their past failures and misdeeds, and this is frequently expressed in the form of a Negative Automatic Thought. For example:

- 'I'm a completely horrible person, because I'm never kind enough to my mother.'

- 'I'm a failure, because I always let people down.'

- 'I'm no good, because I can never get the children organized.'

- 'I'm a really wicked mother, because I smacked Rosie this morning and she's only four.'

● 'I'm a rotten father, because I don't spend enough time with my children.'

Even if you only ever say these things to yourself, and whether your lips simultaneously move or not, these are dangerous statements. They are dangerous because they perpetrate a self-image which is likely to disable you further, due to its negative slant. You could see it as a kind of destructive self-labelling and blaming, and yet you probably actually *want* to be different:

● kinder

● more reliable

● better organized

● using less physical punishment

● spending more time with your family

Identify, then challenge

The best way to defuse the destructive nature of such guilty ruminations is first to identify your Negative Automatic Thoughts, and then challenge them by coming up with an opposing Positive Automatic Thought on the same topic. For instance, taking the negative examples quoted above:

● 'I *can* feel much better about my mother by sending her a card, giving her a phone call and inviting her round for a meal. I can also apologize for having been unkind in the past. That's *much* more sensible than wallowing around in pointless self-recriminations.'

● 'I *can* be much better at keeping my promises by putting up a big notice in the kitchen/bedroom/bathroom/hall on which I list all of my appointments. I can also say sorry to people I have let down in the past. That's *much* more constructive than creeping around muttering, "Mea culpa, mea maxima culpa."'

● 'I *can* organize things better for my children by planning a week ahead at a time. I can also tell them I'm sorry I've been a bit chaotic lately. That's *much* more positive than berating myself for my failures.'

● 'I *can* find other ways of disciplining Rosie by getting some information on methods that avoid physical punishment. I can also apologize to her for losing my temper in the past. That's *much* more productive than going around moaning about how awful I am.'

● 'I *can* make sure my children know how much I love them by being really Child Centred when I'm with them. I can also say how sorry I am that I have to be out such a lot, and how much I would rather be with them. That's *much* more loving than stabbing myself in the back with guilt.'

Putting your energy into coming up with a Positive Automatic Thought and then acting on it will simultaneously allow you to spring out of the destructive psychological trap that is guilt and to put right the hurt you may have caused others. You will also be restoring your self-image, which is good news not only for you but for the rest of your family as well. A further very productive step is to forgive yourself for being merely human and therefore not perfect. It can also be helpful to remind yourself that you had very probably not *intended* to:

● be unkind

● let people down

● be chaotic

● smack Rosie

● hardly see your children

It makes forgiving yourself much easier!

Parental responsibilities

Though quite likely to be linked to feelings of guilt for not having fulfilled them, parental responsibilities are a rather different kettle of fish. Only you can decide what you consider to be the exact nature of your own parental responsibilities. And given that your likely intention is to do your very best to ensure that your child's development will be suitably encouraged and protected, you will probably run through your list of priorities from time to time.

Parental responsibilities which I believe should be at the top of the list are:

- To be as Child Centred as possible.

- To protect your child's physical and emotional safety.

- To provide a stimulating environment for your child.

- To be your child's champion as they struggle with the world outside their family.

- To be sensitive to your child's changing needs.

Hints on how to keep yourself on your toes, in terms of your parental responsibilities, would include:

- Make sure to tell your child, at least once a day, that you love them.

- Nourish yourself with little treats for doing your best at an incredibly difficult task.

- Regularly remind yourself that being Child Centred, and getting the Attention Rule right at least half the time, is central to your child's happiness and social adjustment.

- Tell yourself daily that all the energy, time and effort you put into fulfilling your parental responsibilities will be fully rewarded, if not today, then tomorrow or the next day.

- Talk seriously about parenting issues with other mothers and fathers whom you know.

Difficulties with siblings

Now I want to discuss some of the ways in which you might best handle the inevitable arguments and fights between your children. Even if your child has no brothers or sisters I would advise you to read on, as you will probably still have to try to resolve conflict between your child and their friends.

If you have read this far, you will already have made lots of progress towards being able to tackle the thorny problem of sibling dust-ups. For instance, you already know how to do an ABC analysis of the problem behaviours which you wish to modify (see p. 188). You also have information about

- being Child Centred (see p. 14)
- Ignoring Minor Naughtiness (see p. 18)
- Best guessing (see p. 120)
- Reward programmes (see p. 197)
- Time Out (see p. 194)
- Reparations (see p. 160)
- Ground rules (see p. 148)

That gives you quite a lot of techniques to help deal with sibling teasing, bullying, aggression and downright meanness.

In addition, I am going to tell you about some tactics that have been found particularly useful in keeping the peace between brothers and brothers, sisters and sisters, and sisters and brothers. Sibling arguments are, in fact, so common that even when physical fighting is involved parents often don't view this as unacceptable aggression. Certainly it is to be expected that brothers and sisters under school age will find it difficult to be considerate, kind and sharing to one another. It is as well to remember this when your three-year-old thwacks their little eighteen-month-old sibling round the legs with a yo-yo for the third time in as many minutes!

Thankfully, as children mature, so too does their ability to appreciate fairness and sharing as the way forward. None the less there is often not a great deal of difference in the techniques used for subduing troublesome younger siblings whether they are three-year-olds or fifteen-year-olds. This does not mean to say that you should be condoning regular fist fights, though it does indicate that occasional pushing and shoving is quite definitely to be expected as a normal part of family life. Always keeping in mind that your child must only be expected to behave in line with their age and stage of development, there are several approaches you could choose from. These include:

- Ignoring both protagonists equally, and instead rewarding sibling friendliness and cooperation.

- Discussing ground rules and feelings with your children when they quarrel.

- Pointing out clearly and forcefully to young children the adverse consequences of being unkind and aggressive.

- Helping your children to learn how to resolve conflicts by comforting and apologizing to each other.

- Showing your children positive ways of dealing with conflict by avoiding bullying, teasing and aggression yourself.

A QUICK FIX ON CHAPTER 6

1. Parental blaming and using negative labels are destructive behaviours. Giving an Alpha Command, followed by the child 'putting things right', a suitable punishment and your 'best guess' as to why your child may have lied, is much more constructive. Never call a child 'stupid'.

Example: Max, a single father, often became exasperated by his son Gavin, aged five and a half. At these moments of irritation, sometimes up to twelve times a day, Max would say to Gavin in frustration, 'Gav, you're nothing but a pest. It's your fault that we never get through a day without a row!' Gavin's teacher, worried by this bright little boy's attention-seeking behaviour in class, suggested that Max get an appointment at the local Child Guidance Clinic.

In the very first session the staff noted Max's blaming and negative labelling of his son. Max was persuaded to ignore his son's irritating behaviours for one week and, instead of blaming and labelling, to praise him for his good behaviour. He also tried giving Alpha Commands, making Gavin restore order if he had destroyed anything or hurt anyone, imposing a brief punishment and best guessing why his son lied about having been destructive/aggressive.

In the second session, Max reported that there had been 'a miracle' at home, and that for four of the last seven days he and Gavin had managed to stay friends all day. Gavin was also whining less and becoming more fun to be around.

Evidence: A good deal of research has demonstrated the damage which can be caused by a parent blaming and negatively labelling their child. Avoiding these parental behaviours and substituting the kind of Child Centred approach outlined above allows both parents and children to feel more positive about themselves and each other.

2. When you are working out your expectations of your family members, remember that girls and boys, men and women, are equal *and* different.

Example: The Boy with the Pink Trainers is just one small example of the still prevailing differences between boys and girls. Four-year-old Josh was in his first year at infant school and going through the exciting, stressful business of becoming a proper schoolboy. His brave non-sexist parents decided that, as the trainers which Josh fancied most were pink, he should be encouraged to wear them. The pink trainers were duly worn to school on Monday morning.

Collecting his son that afternoon, Josh's father found the little boy crying and distressed. The other boys in his class, and some bigger boys in the playground, had spent the day teasing and bullying him.

The reason? The said pink trainers. Josh had been called 'Girly', 'Poof' and 'Mummy's little baby girl', much to their glee and his consternation.

The fate of the trainers? To be worn only at home or in the garden, when no other children were present.

Josh's fate? With his gender clearly established by a new pair of black trainers, he was fully accepted by his male peers as a 'real boy'!

Evidence: Investigations into children's views on gender differences have repeatedly shown that they have quite categorical
ideas about what is 'girls' stuff' and what 'for boys'. They see
the differences extending across play activities, toys, clothes,
leisure pursuits, books and, to an extent, TV and video viewing.

**3. Arguments between siblings are normal and to be expected.
However, vicious teasing, bullying and physical violence are
damaging for both aggressor and victim. Parents can use ordinary
arguments as hot opportunities for lessons in sharing and caring.**

Example: Marcy and Jack, seven and three respectively, bickered
persistently over what videos to watch after tea and before
bedtime. Their parents studiously stayed out of these
arguments until the day when Marcy pushed Jack off the end of
the sofa and he broke his wrist. After this episode, their parents
laid down clear ground rules on each child having their own
choice on alternate days.

Evidence: Studies of sibling arguments show that there are
several approaches which parents can constructively take. It is
likely that unless there is physical violence or intense bullying,
in which case parents should intervene, ignoring verbal rows
between brothers and sisters is quite effective.

7. Reaping the Rewards

Giving Change a Chance

WHAT THIS CHAPTER IS ABOUT

As a parent, it can be scary to **risk** doing things differently. Likely gains and losses of giving change a chance will be discussed here, as will some of the safety nets – the **protection** factors needed when mothers and fathers go for the balancing act of a Child Centred parenting style. The delightful **family fun** which can result from courageous and positive change on a parent's part will be emphasized. The links between a change to being Child Centred and improvements in family relationships will feature, as will that sometimes elusive quality, **parent pride**.

GRASP THE NETTLE!

In my work with troubled children and their parents I have seen great unhappiness. The children's problems have ranged from non-compliance and aggression through to attempts at suicide and murder. The parents' difficulties have included unresolved baggage, lack of information on useful parenting tactics, marital problems, mental ill-health, learning disabilities and outright child abuse.

Since you are reading this book at all it is likely that you yourself are experiencing some non-compliant and maybe aggressive behaviour in your child. You might also have unresolved baggage left over from your own childhood and be wrestling with the intricacies of an intimate adult relationship. That is all quite normal.

If your problems, or your child's, however, persist even though you have religiously put into consistent and contingent practice all the strategies and tactics I have already suggested, I would strongly recommend you to seek some professional help. Most professionals working with children and families are really quite approachable and can be very helpful. On p. 271 you will find information on how to make the necessary arrangements. I know that a high proportion of the families with whom I have worked made significant progress. All these parents felt they should give change a chance – after all, they had a lot to gain despite their fears of the risks involved.

Risk

There is always a risk associated with making changes. The living room did not benefit from the vivid green wallpaper you tried last time, but it could look even worse in yellow sponge-effect paint. Your lawn is a mess now, but would substituting gravel really be the best solution? Your summer gear is a little unadventurous, but you could look even less appetizing in the safari suits that are the 'in' thing this year.

It is all about the uncertainty associated with departing from known and established aspects of your life in order to pursue a novel, and as yet untried, idea. When uncertainty increases, so does stress. When both are elevated, anticipated change can also bring anxiety.

So there you are; thinking about changing your parenting style to a more Child Centred one, and full of uncertainty, stress and anxiety. A likely reaction to such experiences is to avoid all thoughts of changing the status quo. However, there is an alternative way forward: instead of allowing yourself to become stuck in the old Child Directive rut, forever fearful of any changes, *approach* the feared situation.

The rationale for moving towards being more Child Centred

is linked to the principles of Cognitive Behaviour Therapy. It is this: since no one can predict the future accurately, you simply cannot be sure that your expectations of difficulties are correct. So why not say to yourself, 'Although I can't predict progress after making the change to being Child Centred, neither can I say with any accuracy that it will be a failure.' That is a statement of fact, and when you take it on board you will want to give change a chance. After all, what have you to lose? Your dented self-image and feelings of parental inadequacy, from which everyone who is bringing up children suffers at times.

When I started to be truly Child Centred – or as truly as I can manage – nearly twenty years ago my self-image visibly strengthened and my feelings of inadequacy as a parent took much more of a back seat. My message to you is this: grasp the nettle and see for yourself that being more Child Centred improves the quality of family life.

Protection

If you were asked to do a bungee jump for charity, you would doubtless enquire about the safety precautions. Were you to be shown a piece of knicker elastic and a baby's pram harness, you would presumably decline the opportunity since the risk of death or injury would be too great. Alternatively, if you were shown a professional-looking set-up with all the proper safety equipment, you might well be encouraged to go ahead. This 'Go for it' feeling would be even further enhanced were you to talk things through with other people who had already successfully made the jump.

There is a parallel with changing your parenting style. Before you take the leap of intentionally trying to be more Child Centred, it would be eminently sensible to weigh up the balance between the risks involved and the protective factors. In *Setting the scene for change* I shall be listing what I regard as the risk and protection elements. You may well have additional items which relate to your own individual life and situation – throw them into the scales too. But for now let me assure you that I would certainly not be trumpeting the virtues of the Parent/Child Game were I not convinced of its great potential.

Family fun

Families enjoy themselves in very different ways. For some, a Disney video and a take-away Chinese meal are a guarantee of a good time. Visiting zoos, museums, parks and the seaside are, of course, old favourites. Then there are theme parks, bowling, ice skating, circuses and fairs. You might be into kite flying or roller blading, boot fairs or garden centres.

Not long ago I saw an entire family, from teens to toddlers, all wearing crash helmets, out on sturdy bicycles for a ride in the country, and apparently having great fun. Or were they? For all I know, they might have been in the throes of a mega-disagreement about their destination that day. Or perhaps the families making their slow progress round the zoo, with the children insisting on 'talking to' every species, have just learnt that their adolescent offspring has been expelled from school. And something as straightforward as a video and a take-away can still be the scene of intense family rivalry and hostility.

Even when families are *officially* enjoying themselves, unless their relationships with one another are at least partially healthy the fun factor will not be available. In *Giving and receiving* I shall be highlighting the joy and laughter that can become a frequent aspect of family life when you take the plunge and start to be much more Child Centred. When children and parents are getting on well together, even a trip to the corner shop can become a happy excursion!

Parent pride

Your daily efforts to be a good parent are probably the hardest work you will ever do in your life. Yet most parents are deprived of even duly earned plaudits for their incredible dedication towards their children. As a result, many millions of mothers and fathers feel isolated, worn down and generally unappreciated. Apart from Mothers' Day and Fathers' Day, you are unlikely to hear those magical words, 'You're such a lovely Mum/Dad', unless one of your children is sufficiently moved, on one of the other 364 days of the year, to deliver the occasional accolade.

So where is this parent pride to come from? From yourself, or, if you are particularly fortunate, from your partner, a close relative or a friend. I would like to see a system of merit badges set up so that there could be some public acknowledgement of the enormous energy which mothers and fathers put into parenting their children. However, I don't advise you to hold your breath while awaiting this brave new world! In *What to do next* I shall tell you about some of the ways in which you can bump up your parent pride ratings.

GIVING AND RECEIVING

Before anyone makes a significant change in their lives, they tend to work out the costs and benefits. You and I are unlikely to make alterations voluntarily unless we are pretty convinced that the said benefits will clearly outweigh the costs. You would be unlikely to buy a more expensive car if you expected it to be a poorer performer and less reliable than your current one. You would certainly shy away from changing to a new style of parenting unless you were convinced that it offered a good pay-off in terms of improved harmony and happiness.

I naturally hope that, having read thus far, you are already encouraged about the prospect of becoming a Child Centred and thus more balanced parent. However, I am aware that in previous chapters I may, in my desire to be absolutely honest and up-front, have placed greater emphasis on the 'hard slog' elements. So now I want to focus on what you, and your child, will receive in the way of 'rewards' for your efforts to be more Child Centred.

Your just rewards

To bring the whole thing alive, I am going to tell the stories of two of the many hundreds of families who have found that the Parent/Child Game and Child Centred parenting brought them lashings of family fun. I believe these stories will give you a good deal of positive motivation for change.

Tara's story

Tara, mother of two sons aged four and six, came to me because she felt she had lost control of her boys' behaviour. Tara, Dillon and Cal had been very traumatized by the sudden death of the boys' father a year and a half earlier, and they all still missed

him terribly. Tara herself had been clinically depressed for some
months following her husband's death, and though now feeling
that she could cope with her grief, she was frightened by the
extent to which Dillon and Cal had got beyond her control.

The sort of scenario which I observed included both boys
totally ignoring their mother's requests to

- come in from the garden

- eat their meals sitting up at the table

- share their toys

- play quietly

- get dressed or undressed

- bath without flooding the place

- get into bed and stay there

Tara had such compassion for the boys at the loss of their
father that she felt she could not discipline them. However,
neither did she consider that their difficult behaviour was to
anyone's benefit. Cal's behaviour in class had also become
problematic, and Dillon was rather isolated at his nursery
school.

I introduced Tara to the principles and practice of the Parent/
Child Game. The emphasis was put on being Child Centred,
and so Tara started to

- praise sociable and compliant behaviour

- ignore minor naughtiness

- cut down on Child Directive behaviours

- issue Alpha Commands

- best guess

- use reward programmes

- and, only when necessary, use Time Out

It took several weeks for Tara to begin to feel at home with
the new approach. She said that at first she had found it very

hard to stop asking questions of her sons, saying 'No' to them and criticizing. However, she also reported that combining being Child Centred with giving Alpha Commands was working wonders in terms of the boys' compliance and observing ground rules.

After three months of using a Child Centred parenting style, Tara was able to tell me of the improvements she had noted in Cal and Dillon. These included:

- being much more obedient
- fighting less
- going to bed more calmly
- smiling more
- whining less
- being more able to separate from Tara without prolonged clinging
- less faddy eating
- rather more sharing

Tara also told me that she had gained confidence as a mother, and now felt able to cope quite adequately with most things which the boys might 'try on'.

When I last saw Dillon and Cal they were certainly still quite 'bouncy' physically, as would be expected. As well as the obvious improvements in their mood and behaviour, there were clear signs that they were now feeling much more secure in their relationship with their mother. Instead of dodging away, running off or squirming when Tara offered them a cuddle, as had previously been the case, both boys could now relax into a satisfying hug with their mother.

So Tara changing her parenting style to a much more Child Centred one had produced, within three months, not only behavioural progress in Dillon and Cal but a palpable improvement in the degree of harmony and happiness within the home. Instead of feeling despair at being overwhelmed by the task of bringing up two boys alone, Tara felt her self-confidence, competence and mood all increase to a level where she was coping with the challenges of single motherhood very well indeed. She had, in fact, become able to show her undoubted love for Cal and Dillon in a way that they found meaningful.

Martin and Ruth's story

Martin and Ruth had three small children, all under six. Josie, five, Stella, three, and Nathan, one and a half, were certainly something of a handful when I first met them. Both Martin and Ruth worked full-time, so while Josie was at infant school, Stella and Nathan went to the same pre-school nursery. All three were picked up around 3.30 p.m. by a childminder, Shirley, who gave the children their tea. The children were then collected by either their mother or father at around 6.30 p.m.

Martin and Ruth told me that they felt they needed help, as the couple of hours before bedtime on weekdays was 'pure hell'. When I asked them to tell me what I would see, Monday through to Friday, between 6.30 and 8.30 p.m., they poured out a vivid description of children who seemed dedicated to testing out their mother and father to the absolute limit. Martin and Ruth were also finding that the family weekends, to which they so much looked forward, had become a living nightmare.

When I visited to see the situation for myself, these were some of the 'snapshots' I witnessed:

- Josie smacking Stella

- Stella pushing Nathan

- Nathan responding by throwing himself on the floor, howling with outrage

- Nathan trying to hug Josie

- Josie taking no notice because she was too busy bossing Stella about

- all three children running, squealing, in opposite directions when told it was time for bed, with both parents in hot pursuit

- the chase ending in tears and tantrums from the children and acute irritation on the exhausted parents' part

Ruth and Martin told me that, when they went shopping or on outings at the weekends, it all ended in a similar fashion: escaping children, exasperated parents, tantrums, tears and sometimes smacks. The couple had begun to question whether they should ever have had children in the first place. Martin wondered out loud how they 'might not be able to carry on if something doesn't change, and fast!' Ruth worried that she was a failure as a mother, and was somehow ruining the lives of her three beloved children by being unable to cope with their behaviour. Both parents declared that they were at the end of their respective tethers. They seemed to me to have lost both control and heart in their parenting.

It became clear during our first discussion that Ruth and Martin had very different ideas on child rearing, based on their own childhood experiences. Martin had been brought up in the country and his own mother and father had very much allowed him to go his own way. He was therefore in favour of 'letting kids get on with it'. Ruth, on the other hand, came from a family where routine ruled and everything happened according to a rigid plan. She had hated this, and yet found that, as a mother herself, she swung from being authoritarian to laisser faire in an unpredictable fashion.

I spent time with Martin and Ruth emphasizing the importance of consistency, contingency and an approach to managing their children to which each could subscribe. I talked about the Parent/Child Game and said how helpful many parents had found it. In the absence of any other appealing options, they agreed to give being Child Centred a trial run. I left them some literature on the Parent/Child Game and said I wanted them to draw up a list, together, of

- what naughty behaviours they were willing to ignore

- what ground rules they considered vital

- what dangerous behaviours they wanted to stop

Gradually Ruth and Martin decided that their trial of Child Centred parenting was beginning to pay off as they extended it week by week. They found themselves working much more as a team in the evenings and at weekends, which was bringing

them a sense of shared experiences and goals. Of course, they
had lots of questions and a good deal of time was spent practis-
ing the Alpha Commands to be used instead of the plaintive
and hopeless questions they had previously been employing
with their children.

● Out went, 'Are you ever going to go to bed?' In came,
'Josie [pause for eye contact], I want you to come upstairs
with me now', spoken in a firm and clearly audible voice.

● Out went two adults chasing three children round the
house.

● In came sensible ground rules about staggering Josie,
Stella and Nathan's bedtimes.

Martin and Ruth also decided that on alternate weeks Ruth
would put Josie to bed while Martin saw to Stella and Nathan,
and vice versa. As a result they were finding it much easier to
manage their three children on weekday evenings, and invited
me to come round to see their new Child Centred style in action.

The first difference was that there were far fewer 'push and
shove' incidents with the three children. Not only that, but the
whole emotional temperature in the home had become less
frantic. In fact the children, and their mother and father, had all
been able to relax now that it was quite clear that Martin and
Ruth were the ones in charge. They themselves had decided
that it would be a good idea to have a 'family focus' for the
evenings, so I saw all five sitting up to a snack meal together,
followed by them all watching two short favourite video clips
together.

Stella and Nathan showed only token resistance to Martin's
Alpha Command on bathtime, and Josie and Ruth happily
settled down to a precious half-hour of 'staying up late because
I'm a big schoolgirl'. Martin battled through the bubbles
upstairs in the bathroom, managed to get the two little ones into
their nightclothes without much trouble, and then called Ruth
so that she could come and kiss them goodnight before he read
them their bedtime stories.

Downstairs, Josie and Ruth discussed the possibility of a
weekend outing, while snuggling together; all such activities

had been on hold for several weeks while Martin and Ruth got the evenings 'sorted out'. Martin came down wreathed in smiles, enormously pleased with the success of his new parenting style, and Ruth acknowledged him with: 'Well done, darling.' When I left, Ruth had just said to Josie, 'In five minutes from now, Josie, I want to take you upstairs for your bath and afterwards I will read you a story. You can choose which one.'

A month later I learned that, although the family's weekend trips had been renewed with some trepidation on the part of Ruth and Martin, they had been very pleased with the children's behaviour. Nathan had escaped momentarily in a clothes store, but had been calmly brought back into the family fold by Martin. We agreed that the children were all much happier now that their mother and father were being consistent, contingent and Child Centred. I said goodbye not to two overwrought adults who felt that their children were running the show, but to a mother and father flushed with their own success and sure that they were all a much happier family now that the Attention Rule truly ruled. The image of Ruth and Josie peacefully cuddled up together will remain with me for a very long time.

I hope you have found these two stories encouraging, perhaps even inspirational. Remember, too, that though in these families the children were all under six, exactly the same effects can be achieved with older offspring when you adopt a Child Centred parenting style. As long as you are sensitive to your child's developmental stage, there is every reason to try your new balanced parent approach on all ages from tinies to teenagers!

ECHOES

Thinking back to some of the family fun that I had as a child, there seem to have been two distinct categories. One was the high-days-and-holidays type, the other much more home-based. Grand outings were in the minority, as my father's salary only rarely ran to such extravagance. Family fun at home was much more available as it cost almost nothing apart from parental ingenuity and the generous spirit of my mother and father.

The high-days-and-holidays kind is probably best exemplified by the way in which our family Christmas was celebrated in the 1940s and 1950s. The preparations were as enjoyable and exciting as the holiday itself. They began in September, when the whole family would visit a church autumn fair. There would be numerous stalls devoted to toys, books, plants, cakes and sweets stall, together with others packed with crochet pigs, monkeys and dolls, knitted teddy bears and donkeys, and daintily stitched and embroidered hankies, teacosies, placemats and traycloths.

From amongst these delights we would carefully decide on Christmas gifts for particular relatives and friends. My mother would encourage us with any suitable purchases and gently steer us away from the non-starters. My father, sociable and jokey, could be relied upon to top up our spending money so that we were not only able to complete our Christmas 'shopping' but also indulged in hoop-la, shove-ha'penny and the coconut shy, as well as being treated to an ice cream, a ride on the bored-looking donkey and a dip in the bran tub. By teatime, everyone was sticky, exhausted and happy!

When we got home, while my mother saw to our baby brother and Dad went to do some work in the garden my sister Lizzie and I would race up to our bedroom with our prized purchases. No one was allowed in while we pored over our treasures, deciding and then redeciding on the best recipient for each. Our examination of these objects was so intense and enthusiastic that they were often in danger of being demolished before they got so much as a sniff of Christmas wrapping paper!

The preparations continued. Making Christmas puddings took our mother a whole day. The major concern of us children was trying to work out where the traditional silver sixpences were hidden – always a fruitless task. The puddings bubbled away, filling the whole house with a festive aroma which made us dribble with anticipation. Then there was the ritual of the Christmas cake, each of us being allowed to scrape the basin and eat small spoonfuls of the rich uncooked mixture. After that came the making of spicy, fruity mincemeat for the dozens of little pies to be made the day before Christmas Eve.

My favourite preparation was making the decorations. I can still vividly recall the delicious taste of the gum on the strips of brightly coloured paper which we made into long chains to festoon the house. Both my mother and father joined us in this activity, keeping a pot of glue and a brush handy for repairs on the strips licked clean of glue by the over-enthusiastic young participants.

Then there was the ritual preparation of the Christmas stockings to be hung at the end of our beds on Christmas Eve. Each year my father produced a new hand-made stocking for each of us. He cut out, pinned, stitched and decorated each stocking in full view of a rapt audience – truly a wonderfully exciting operation.

The day itself followed a routine which later became the blueprint for the Christmas Days orchestrated for my own children. Stockings were rifled any time from 4.30 a.m. onwards, accompanied by squeals of delight and much running in and out of our parents' bedroom so that they too could see what wonderful presents Father Christmas had left. We weren't allowed downstairs until we were washed and dressed in our special Christmas finery, all made by my mother.

Then, while she made our breakfast, we were taken into the lounge to be transported by the large and magically decorated Christmas tree: baubles, tinsel, stars, bells and little parcels all fought for space. Sometimes there were lighted candles – dangerous but beautiful. We duly fingered the nuts, the chocolates, the sugary orange and lemon slices, the Turkish Delight, the dates, the preserved figs and anything else within reach. After breakfast we each gave our special presents to the other family members and the room ended up knee-deep in ripped wrapping paper.

Of the actual food at lunchtime I remember very little, though I will always remember the fun with the crackers and the extra little gift that sat beside each person's plate. Next on the agenda, after the washing up, were games, followed by lusty renditions of 'Silent Night', 'We Three Kings' and 'Ding Dong Merrily on High'. Lizzie and I obliged by offering a solo of 'Away in a Manger' and a Christmas Fairy Dance respectively. Then it was time for tea, and prolonged discussion of the cake's texture, moisture, content, fruit quantities and novel decorations. After a final crazy half-hour it was bath, bed, prayers and sleep, full of the wonders of family fun on Christmas Day.

We had no realization, then, of the huge amount of energy and commitment put in by our mother and father so that we might experience such a fantastic day. As we grew up, it slowly began to dawn on us that it took hard work and a great deal of love, though only when we became parents ourselves did we properly appreciate their gift to us of a children's Christmas. When, much later, I asked my mother what exactly she herself received from all her sterling Christmas efforts, she smiled, we hugged, and she said, 'Oh, but your little faces all lit up, of course. That was the reward for your Dad and me.' I now know exactly what she meant, as I went on to re-create my parents' kind of Christmas for my own children and experienced the same sheer joy.

The more domestic family fun time were great too, especially when I include picnics in the countryside and down by the river Thames. The delights of making a camp under the kitchen table, the pleasure of cooking largely inedible biscuits, the excitement of planting peas, catching tadpoles, leaving bread and milk out for the hedgehogs, and toasting crumpets on a brass fork – all these are an enormous source of warm feelings for me even today. Sounds almost too *Rebecca of Sunnybrook Farm* to be true, doesn't it? I could continue to list family fun things because my parents, by giving us so much Child Centred attention, created an atmosphere in which even the most mundane activity became yet another opportunity for enjoyment. They wouldn't have called it being 'Child Centred', of course. They would just have said they were doing their best, which is all that can be expected of anyone.

SETTING THE SCENE FOR CHANGE

Giving change a chance is usually much easier when you have the protection of a solid body of evidence to show that others who have taken that risk have ended up successful rather than suicidal! However it is always sensible, when contemplating change of any sort, to look at the risks involved. In this section I want to outline what I see as the risk factors in moving to a more Child Centred style of parenting, as well as looking at the associated protective features.

Risk factors and counter-arguments

Risk
Your own anticipatory anxiety.

Or not?
When acknowledged as a natural part of giving change a chance this should be ignored as it is a destructive process.

Risk
Your own fear of failure.

Or not?
This is also an accepted aspect of giving change a chance, and should be ignored as it is another destructive process.

Risk
Extra demands on your concentration and energy.

Or not?
Similar amounts of concentration and energy are needed whether you are giving Child Centred parenting a trial or sticking to your usual style. Following the Parent/Child Game can actually be *less* taxing, as many parents tell me.

Risk
Negative reactions from relatives and friends.

Or not?
These are always a possibility when you give change a chance. However, you may already be subject to criticism, whether veiled or not, from these same people. In any case, their disapproval of your proposed changes may well be much more to do with their anticipatory anxieties than with the realities of what you could achieve by starting on a Child Centred parenting approach. As such, negative reactions from others are best ignored.

Risk
Feeling confused by the novel approach to be undertaken.

Or not?
A degree of confusion at the outset of giving change a chance is almost inevitable. When you regard it as your cue to take

another look at the relevant information, and/or start testing out the new ideas, it can be seen as a quite natural feature of becoming more Child Centred.

Risk
Failure of the novel techniques.

Or not?
There is, of course, always a possibility that anything new will fall flat on its face. However, as you will see when I list the protection factors, the Parent/Child Game, which has already been successfully tried and tested by tens of thousands of mothers and fathers in the UK and USA, will prove to include its own in-built provisions against failure.

Risk
Cost of reward programmes.

Or not?
Paying out for the goodies which provide the material positive reinforcement in a reward programme needs not cost an arm and a leg. With a little ingenuity on your part you will realize that, for example, a box of marbles, a packet of felt-tips or a sheet of stickers can be handed out one small item at a time. You will also remember that activities and praise are an important part of reward programmes, and these often make no call on your pocket.

On balance, I would say that changing to being a Child Centred parent has very few, if any, significant attached risks. There are certainly none that cannot be satisfactorily dealt with by a parent determined to give their child their best shot at showing them how very much they are loved. Remember too, that getting the Attention Rule right only half the time protects your child's development and their secure attachment to you.

Protection factors

The protection factors inherent in the Parent/Child Game are closely related to Social Learning Theory, Child Development Theory and, to an extent, Cognitive Behaviour Therapy principles. So that you can be properly reassured about giving change a chance and really zap up your balancing act as a Child Centred parent I shall spell these out again here rather than asking you to turn back to an earlier chapter.

CONSIDER YOURSELF WELL PROTECTED!

● Social Learning Theory, Child Development Theory, Cognitive Behaviour Therapy and the Parent/Child Game have all been subjected to rigorous research for several decades on both sides of the Atlantic and further afield.

● In a study carried out by Joanna Swindles-Carr in 1993 and 1994, she found that the mothers who attended a children's psychiatric clinic because their offspring were having problems managed to keep up the optimum 6:1 Child Centred to Child Directive behaviour for only a third of the time or less. Conversely, those mothers whose children never needed to be referred to professionals had the 6:1 ratio right for half the time or more.

● Finally, you have my own clinical and research experiences to rely on. For more than a quarter of a century I have been using the concepts which I have explained in this book, with great success for thousands of families. That's not because I am uniquely talented or have magic powers. It's because the ideas work. If I weren't 100 per cent convinced myself, I would never have written this book. So take heart, and take the plunge!

Social Learning Theory

Any behaviour rewarded with any type of attention is likely to recur in the future – often the near future. As a parent, you need a structured approach which will enable you to get the Attention Rule right at least 50 per cent of the time. The Parent/Child Game undoubtedly shows you how to do this.

Child Development Theory

When a child feels secure in their attachment to their mother and father, their behaviour is extremely likely to remain within acceptable social boundaries. A securely attached child is therefore not only much more self-confident and sure of their own positive worth, but will in all probability be cooperative, friendly and fun to be with most of the time.

Cognitive Behaviour Therapy

When an individual has taken to heart the negative, critical and too directive behaviour towards them of the people most important in their lives, they are likely to suffer from long-term psychological, emotional and behaviour problems. When parents follow advice on being Child Centred and getting the Attention Rule right, they are directly protecting their children from such difficulties by being positive and approving.

WHAT TO DO NEXT

Parent pride is an elusive quantity. Parents pat themselves on the back for doing their job well much less frequently than they congratulate a child on their achievements. Yet everyone who has attempted to raise children knows in their heart that it is probably the greatest challenge of their lives. Why are parents so good at blaming themselves for their faux pas, and yet so poor at self-reward when it's clear they are having a successful year, month, week, day or even five minutes? When you accept that rewarded behaviour is more likely to be repeated in future, you also acknowledge that this applies to all human beings, young and old alike.

The main trouble as a parent is that you are highly unlikely to get positive immediate feedback from your children themselves. Hands up all those parents whose children have recently, if ever, said to them, 'Mum, you are *so* good at giving me praise and smiles/attends/positive touches/friendly imitation/asking me what I would like to do, and ignoring my minor naughtiness! Thanks a million!' Or, 'Dad! You got the Attention Rule right *again*! Go to the top of the class!' It just doesn't happen, does it? Even if it did, you would probably be so gobsmacked that you would be momentarily speechless! And unless you are having the formal version of the Parent/Child Game (see p. 271) you are very unlikely to have immediate and positive feedback from another adult either.

Go on, spoil yourself!

Never forget that there is great power in internal self-instruction and self-praise. What I am talking about is that 'voice' inside your brain which you recognize as your own thoughts.

As mentioned already, in relation to Cognitive Behaviour Therapy, making statements about yourself 'in the head' has a very strong influence on your mood and behaviour. Just as Negative Automatic Thoughts can depress and disable you, so Positive Automatic Thoughts can lift your mood and increase your competence as an individual and as a parent. So, in the absence of my dulcet tones praising you through an earbug, as would happen with the full Parent/Child Game, I want *you* to praise *yourself* for being Child Centred rather than Child Directive in your interactions with your child. Some of the internal comments you can usefully make would include:

- 'Well done! That really *was* Child Centred.'

- 'You're doing really well at being Child Centred! Well done, Sam/Douglas/Penny/Tom.'

- 'Great! You're definitely getting there! Child Centred mothering/fathering – here I come!'

- 'Keep it up, kiddo, you're a great Child Centred success!'

- 'I'm a miracle worker! I've cracked the Child Centred bit!'

- 'I can do it! I'm being Child Centred!'

- 'I think I'm doing very well – I'm getting more Child Centred all the time!'

You can also put yourself on a diet of small (and big) treats for channelling your energies into being more Child Centred than you were. Go on, spoil yourself – you deserve it! Alternatively, should you notice yourself being too Child Directive, simply remind yourself to try harder, especially at getting the Attention Rule right.

There is no point in devaluing yourself, coming up with Negative Automatic Thoughts about how you can't manage it; nor in giving up your attempts to be Child Centred simply because you have just had a day when you couldn't control yourself, never mind your children. These are responses which will lead to your being *less* able and balanced in the future, and not the reverse as some people seem to think.

When I am using the Parent/Child Game with a family, and during the ten minutes when the parent is using the earbug they come up with a Child Directive behaviour, I don't hurl abuse at them! Indeed, I don't even say, 'You shouldn't have done that because it's Child Directive.' I simply remark, in a pleasant tone, 'Remember to stay away from Questions/ Teaching/Commands/Saying "No"/Negative Looks/Nega- tive Touches/Criticisms', or 'Remember, we agreed "No Questions/Teaching etc."', according to whichever Child Directive behaviour the parent has just shown. I strongly suggest that you take the same sort of line if you realize that, when interacting with your child, you are exceeding the ratio of only one Child Directive for every six Child Centred behaviours. You could try saying to yourself something like this:

- 'Oops! I'll *keep on* trying to be Child Centred.'

- 'Watch it! I can *still* keep on trying to be Child Centred.'

- 'Never mind! I *won't give up* on being Child Centred.'

In other words, forgive yourself for being human, and maintain your efforts to become a balanced and Child Centred parent. It is the best recipe for positive progress, believe me.

A contract with your partner

If you are sharing the task of parenting children with an adult partner, they could be a warming source of congratulations – as could you for them. As an integral element of your new-look Child Centred parenting, try drafting in a serious clause on the topic of treats and praise for mums' and dads' success, as well as for the children. You and your partner could do a lot worse than making a contract to be Adult or Parent Centred towards one another. Model your own grown-up behaviour on the principles relating to being Child Centred.

The principles of Social Learning Theory and Cognitive Behaviour Therapy definitely apply across a whole lifespan, and not just childhood. With a little imagination, the same can be said of the Parent/Child Game. When I am working with families, or adult couples alone, the kind of mutual remarks emphasized as healthy and constructive include:

- 'I *really* like the way you do that. It's great!'

- 'You're *really* clever. What a fantastic idea!'

- 'That's one of the things I *really* love about you!'

- 'Let's do that again soon. I *really* enjoyed being with you!'

The phrases stoutly advised against go something like this:

- 'You *always* do that. It's horrible!'

- 'You *never* listen, do you!'

- 'You *always* pull that nasty face when I suggest something new!'

- 'You *never* have a good word for me!'

In other words, adults thrive on praise and positive feedback, just as children do.

So why not try the same idea with your parenting efforts? Some of my own favourite accolades are:

- 'You handled that beautifully. Well done!'

- 'You were nice and firm then. Just what's needed!'

- 'The children enjoy your company so much. I can see they love being with you!'

- 'Great work – it's really good the way you are sensitive without being soppy!'

My guess is that you would feel as pleased as punch were your partner to say to you something along these lines. Whereas being told:

- *'Don't* do that!'

- 'Your usual crisis and chaos, I see!'

- 'You mess everything up!'

- 'Some mother/father, I *don't* think!'

has a much less welcome impact. Not that I am advising you to have even rewarding interchanges at full volume when your children are hanging on every word. It is surprising, though, just how much warmth and appreciation you can put into a *sotto voce* remark. I notice that my children and their partners slide quite a lot of this supportive conversation into the usual round of 'Ben, you know roller blades are only for outside!'; 'Maeve, time to put baby Heather down for a nap so that you can have your tea!'; 'Eoin, I want you to stop being Toffo the puppy dog, it's time for nursery!'; and, 'Elliott! Time for Teletubby bye-bye!' I have heard them say things like: 'Well spotted'; 'Keep going'; 'Just right'; and the ever-welcome, 'Well done!' You could also give each other Attends: 'Daddy! You're so kind!'; 'Mummy! You've been such fun today!' A good ground rule for parents in their interactions with one another regarding child rearing is to concentrate on highlighting their partner's successes, rather than homing in on their mistakes. No one is perfect, after all!

A good solid source of reward for mothers and fathers doing their Child Centred best to meet their children's needs is the responses of the children themselves. When you give your children this type of attention, they don't usually withhold the manifestations of their pleasure in your fond and firm approach to them. In fact, children often instantaneously demonstrate their gratification at being so treated. Huge smiles, sticky kisses, delighted grins, breathtaking hugs and 'I love yous' can be quite a common occurrence when you start to be Children Centred.

In my work with troubled and abused children, even though

my relationship with them may be transitory, they too quickly become relaxed and cheerful in my company now that I am so much more reliably Child Centred towards them. I often hear that one of these children has told their parent or carer: 'I like Suejenner [they all seem to think it is just one name!], she's a nice lady', or 'I hope Suejenner comes to see me again. I had fun with her!' All this enthusiasm when I am often broaching painful topics with these 'sad children', as my grandchildren call them, must signify that I am getting something very right. My own view is that it is my capacity to relate to them in a Child Centred fashion.

What I *do* know is that, by the style of your own behaviour towards any child, you can effectively alter their mood and behaviour second by second. Given that you now know about balanced and Child Centred parenting, why not guarantee yourself some heart-warming response from your child by putting it all into practice? You have nothing to lose except a grumpy, uncooperative offspring, and your reward could be a secure, affectionate and friendly child. Go for it!

A QUICK FIX ON CHAPTER 7

1. Changing to a Child Centred style of parenting has few, if any, associated risks and can bring rich rewards for each member of the family.

Example: Sonia and Clive, parents of Elspeth aged two, Benjy aged six and Ruby aged ten, felt they had lost their way in terms of a happy home atmosphere. Ruby was often sulky and could sometimes be heard to mutter, 'Nobody loves me.' Benjy, an extroverted child, had gradually become so 'bouncy' that he hardly did a thing he was told, and Elspeth seemed to be heading into the same direction. The future did not look bright, and Clive and Sonia had begun to dread the battlefield of their family life.

When the parents had been helped to become properly Child Centred in their approach and began to work hard on getting the Attention Rule right at least 50 per cent of the time, they were quite astonished by their own success. Not only did Ruby seem to feel more sure of herself, she stopped the mutterings which had so worried Sonia and Clive. Benjy's 'bounciness', though still clearly an important part of his personality, was much more under control. In fact he actually seemed relieved that this was the case. Clive and Sonia also believed they had found the answer to much of Elspeth's 'Terrible Twos' behaviour, and felt much more confident about how to relate to her so that in future she knew that she was always loved, even if her behaviour was not always acceptable. The risk of change *had* been richly rewarded.

Evidence: Studies in the USA, and clinical data from the UK, have repeatedly found that when parents adopt a Child Centred approach to their children each member of the family, including themselves, experiences a decrease in tensions and conflicts and an increase in self-confidence and cooperative friendliness.

2. You can significantly increase the amount of family fun and parent pride you experience by becoming Child Centred in your approach to your children.

Example: Though Paul was quite pleased with the way he had been coping with life as a single father of eight-year-old twins, Anthea and Andrew, he often felt completely overwhelmed by the daily challenges. The fun factor seemed to be in short supply and Paul secretly worried that he was not really up to the job of bringing up twins single-handed. When Andrew and Anthea both began to fail at school, despite being as bright as buttons, Paul sought help.

On learning that he had a very Child Directive style with his children and that this was in all likelihood linked to their problems at school, he lost no time in trying out a more Child Centred approach. After five weeks of hard work, Paul positively glowed with pride in his efforts and said that he and the twins could now actually laugh together and have fun. His attitude towards the future was also a good deal more positive.

Evidence: Extensive laboratory and clinical research trials have shown that, when human beings receive approval for their behaviour on a regular and contingent basis, their self-esteem and efficacy significantly improve, as does their mood.

3. When you are Child Centred you are being a balanced parent. Showing your love for your children in a way they can clearly understand is the best gift you could ever bestow on them.

Example: Maria and Theo simply did not know where they had 'gone wrong' with Charlie, aged four. They showered him with toys and treats. They quite often said they loved him. Still Charlie rampaged around, trashing new games and saying 'Yuk!' in response to many of his parents' treats.

It became apparent that, when Theo and Maria were with Charlie, they were managing to be neither consistent nor contingent in their parenting style. In fact, though they were undoubtedly loving towards their son, there was no clear indication of who was running the family show. After learning about being Child Centred and the Attention Rule, Maria and Theo decided to give it a 'fair trial' of six weeks. Their perseverance paid off, and as they continued to be lovingly firm and fond in their handling of Charlie he became a more relaxed, cooperative and friendly child. He was benefiting from his parents' new-found ability to speak the language of love to him by being consistently and contingently Child Centred.

Evidence: Many avenues of research and therapy show that children are very much in need of mothers and fathers who can translate their love for their child into a parenting style which is both fond and firm as appropriate.

In conclusion

I want you to know that, though my tone has often been light, the message I have tried to put across is a decidedly serious one. I do not doubt that, day to day, every parent does their best to give their children a happy and healthy experience of family life. The trouble is that parents often have little guidance on how they might best achieve their admirable goals.

My point is that information on the benefits of using a Child Centred approach to parenting should be available to all mothers and fathers, *because it works*. Not only does balanced parenting visibly reduce many conflicts to a manageable level, it also enables fathers and mothers to speak the language of love as understood by children. When you are being Child Centred and getting the Attention Rule right half the time, your love for your child is obvious to them and enormously encouraging. I believe you can give your children no better start in life than to adopt the Parent/Child Game principles and practise them in your approach to parenting your much loved children. I wish you well on your journey towards a happier family life.

Further Reading

ABC OF BEHAVIOUR: Trouble Shooting for Parents of Young Children. Getting Ready for School. Right from the Start (1998). Right from the Start Publications. SN/AT. Room 194, County Hall, Kingston-on-Thames, KT1 2DJ

THE ASSESSMENT AND TREATMENT OF PARENTING SKILLS AND DEFICITS, WITHIN THE FRAMEWORK OF CHILD PROTECTION: Sue Jenner (1992), in *Association of Child Psychology and Psychiatry Newsletter,* Vol. 14, No. 5

THE ASSESSMENT OF PARENTING IN THE CONTEXT OF CHILD PROTECTION, USING THE PARENT/CHILD GAME: Sue Jenner (1997), in *Association of Child Psychology and Psychiatry Review,* Vol. 2, No. 2

CHILD DEVELOPMENT FROM BIRTH TO EIGHT: A Practical Focus (1993). Jennie Lindon. National Children's Bureau, 8 Wakely St, London EC1V 7QE

EARLY CHILDHOOD EDUCATION, 2nd edition (1998). Tina Bruce. Hodder & Stoughton

THE FAMILY GAME. By Sue Jenner. BBC Education QED programme (1993). Available from Sue Jenner (address on p. 274)

HELPING THE NON-COMPLIANT CHILD: A Clinician's Guide to Parent Training (1981). Rex Forehand and Robert McMahon, Guildford Press, New York

HOW TO HELP YOUR CHILD: Communicating with your Teenager (1998). S. Munro. Piccadilly Press, London

IS LOVE ENOUGH. Sue Jenner. BBC Education QED programme (1994). Available from Sue Jenner (address on p. 274)

PARENTING THE STRONG-WILLED CHILD: The Clinically Proven Five-week Programme for Parents of 2–6-year-olds (1996). Rex Forehand and Nick Long. Chicago Contemporary Books

PARTNERS BECOMING PARENTS (1996). Edited by Christopher Clulow. Sheldon Press

PLEAS FROM YOUR CHILD: DO'S AND DON'TS, Positive Parenting Using Step. (1996). Norma Angeli and Janet Foster. Telephone (UK) 01932 847427

PSYCHOLOGICAL METHODS: two chapters by Sue Jenner in *Standards and Mental Handicap; Keys to Confidence* (1992). Edited by Tony Thompson and Peter Mathias. Bailliere Tindall

QUANTITATIVE ASSESSMENT OF PARENTING: chapter by Sue Jenner and Gerard McCarthy in *The Assessment of Parenting* (1995). Edited by Clare Lucy. Routledge

VOICES FROM CHILDHOOD. (1995). Susan Creighton and Neil Russell. NSPCC National Centre, Publications Unit, 42 Curtain Road, London EC2A 3NH

Useful Information

The Parent/Child Game: the Official Version

Here are the steps which would occur if you were participating in the full Parent/Child Game treatment.

- An ABC analysis of the child's major problems (see p. 188).

- Before-and-after recording of the parents' ratio of Child Centred and Child Directive behaviours.

- The child and parent playing together for ten minutes in a room wired for sound and vision.

- During this ten-minute period the parent wears an earbug through which they can hear the therapist.

- Meanwhile, the therapist is behind a one-way screen prompting and rewarding the parent for being Child Centred rather than Child Directive towards their child. It is known that one of the reasons for the technique's great effectiveness is the praise delivered to the parent via the earbug.

- Throughout the ten minutes, the child cannot hear what the therapist says, though they know that the therapist is there behind the screen.

- After ten minutes' 'parent training' the child has an hour of either play therapy or fun and games.

- During this time, the parent and the therapist work together on the daily home-based version of the ten minutes' Child Centred input for the child; on the parents' unresolved baggage; and on how best to tackle the 'problem of the week'.

HELPFUL ORGANIZATIONS

EXPLORING PARENTHOOD
4 Ivory Place, Treadgold St, London W11 4BP
Telephone (UK) 0171 221 4471
An organization whose central themes are parenting and partnership. Workshops, publications and a national advice line.

NEWPIN
National Newpin, Sutherland House, 35 Sutherland Square, London SE17 3EE
Telephone (UK) 0171 703 6326
A national UK organization with a network of local centres for parents and children in distress. Special programmes for fathers.

PARENTLINE
Rayfa House, 57 Hart Lane, Thundersley, Essex, SS7 3PD
UK enquiry line for parents 01268 757007
This organization offers support for concerned parents in times of crisis, mostly through a confidential telephone helpline. There are local groups around the UK.

PARENT NETWORK
Room 2, Winchester House, Kennington Park, 11 Cranmer Road, London SW9 6EJ
UK enquiry line for parents 0171 735 1214, fax 0171 735 4692
This organization offers preparation and education for parenting, and helps parents develop a better relationship with their child. Communication is their priority. Parent Network has local UK support groups, a newsletter and a library

THE PARENTING FORUM
National Children's Bureau, 8 Wakely St, London EC1V 7QE
Telephone (UK) 0171 843 6000
An organization for parents and professionals alike. It publishes an informative newsletter. Its major interest is promoting and developing parenting education and support. Two of their briefing sheets may be of particular interest: Briefing Sheet 3 (1996): *Men as carers for children: tackling the barriers*; and Briefing Sheet 6 (1997): *Intergenerational cycles of attachment*.

RELATE
5 Woodhouse Road, London N12 9EN
Telephone (UK) 0181 445 0888
This organization helps couples, or one partner only, where there are relationship difficulties. You may have to wait to see one of their specially trained counsellors, but it is well worth it.

TRUST FOR THE STUDY OF ADOLESCENCE
TSA, 23 New Brighton Road, BN1 1WZ

Telephone (UK) 01273 693311
Information on parenting courses for families with teenagers.

AUDIO-VISUAL AIDS

BREAKING THE CYCLE (1996)
Films of Record Ltd, 2 Elgin Avenue, London W9 3QP

DO YOU WANT A SMACK? (1997)
Three-hour video plus back-up booklet.
Fly-By-Night Film Company, 105 High St, Cheveley, newmarket, Suffolk,
CB8 9DG

IS LOVE ENOUGH ?
BBC QED TV programme video
Shows the Parent/Child Game in action with Sue Jenner, plus follow-up
footage. Obtainable from Sue Jenner (address on p. 274)

TEENAGERS – A SURVIVAL GUIDE FOR PARENTS (1997)
Thirty-minute video plus back-up booklet.
Carlton TV, PO Box 101, London WC2N 4AW

THE FAMILY GAME (1993)
BBC QED TV programme video.
Shows the Parent/Child Game in action with Sue Jenner.
Obtainable from Sue Jenner (address below)

PROFESSIONAL HELP

If you would like to contact a professional visiting, your GP should be the
first step if you need individual help. He or she can then refer you for
counselling or therapy at a local resource centre for adults. Visiting your
GP should also be your first move if you need help with family problems.
Your GP will then refer you to your local children and families services.

Should you wish to contact me professionally, my details are: Sue
Jenner BSc, M.Phil MAE, Independent Consultant Clinical Psychologist,
42 Portland Avenue, Gravesend, Kent, UK; telephone 01474 324908, fax
01474 331335.

I can provide:

- Individual Parent/Child Game sessions
- Parent/Child Game groups for parents
- Cognitive Behaviour Therapy for adults and children
- Developmental assessments for adults
- Expert Witness court reports

Index

self-worth 54, 61, 63, 216, 260
sensitivity 125
  to child's needs 55–6, 58, 238
  social 221, 222–3, 224
shaking 28
shopping 19, 40, 149–50, 151, 169, 186, 251
shouting 25, 122, 149, 158
  see also emotional flash-
    points
siblings
  arguments 208, 235, 238–40,
    242
  rivalry 144, 210
  sabotage 139
silence 95
single parent 18, 126, 148, 209, 250, 266
  and sibling rivalry 210
sleep
  catching up on 178–9
  child's routine 40, 130
  patterns 92, 130, 179
  recharging batteries 177–8
  too little 182–3
slow-to-warm-up child 130–1, 133, 156, 166
smacking 5, 25, 28, 29, 71, 83, 95–8, 158, 175, 190,
    250–1
  adult's feelings 99–100, 101
  adult's sensations 98, 100
  adult's thoughts 98–9, 100
  alternatives 102, 104–5,
    111–12, 122
  child's feelings 103–5
  guilt over 216, 235, 237
  outcomes 111
  triggers 97–8
  verbal equivalent 215
  see also emotional flash-
    points
smile 117
  Child Centred 15, 21, 25, 26
  as alternative to frown 30,
    153
smothering 64, 65
'So what!' response 115–16, 119
sociability 4, 48, 55
social development
  boys and girls 224
social events 149, 150, 227, 228, 254–6
  new 130, 131, 166
social isolation 126
Social Learning Theory 10, 73, 111, 161, 202,
    263
  and Attention Rule 22–4
  and blame/labelling 231–2
  and contingency 207
  explained 4, 259
  and protection factors
    258–9
  punishment in 170
  and sabotage 143
social sensitivity 221, 222–3, 224
socialization 55–6, 160, 201–2, 227, 229
sons, see boys
spartan parenting 68
  emergency self-help 80
  getting away from 79–80
  practical suggestions 85
speaking out 90, 106, 122
speech 17, 19
spitting 149, 174, 201–2
  Time Out programme
    196–8
Spock, Dr Benjamin 54, 183
  stability 62
stamina 168, 171, 172–3, 174, 257
  and positive outlook
    179–82
  and sleep 177–9
star chart 118
stiff upper lip 44
stimulation 54, 56, 58, 131

stress 136, 182, 186, 211, 244
strictness 71, 87
structure 125
stubbornness 95
submissiveness 77, 87
suicide attempts 243
swearing 149
Sweden 95, 97
Swindles-Carr, Joanna 259
sympathy 48

talking through 160, 105
talking to others 75, 81, 82, 238
teaching
  acceptable 28, 30
  Child Directive 27, 29, 35–7
  and developmental level 47
  as opposite of imitation 30,
    37–8, 153
teasing 239, 240, 241, 242
teenagers, see adolescents
television 149, 150, 151, 186, 220
temper tantrum 3, 19, 48, 123, 138, 250–1
  ABC analysis of 189–94
  adult response 190, 192,
    193–4
  pre-tantrum state 119–20,
    123, 157
  triggers 189–90
temperament, see personality
tension, releasing 154–5
threats 28, 164
  in facial expression 27
throwing things 95
thumb sucking 201–2
time for children 65
Time Out 169, 170, 175, 193, 206, 239
  examples 196–7
  operating 194–7
  outdoors 199
  problem aspects 198–202
  reward programme 197–8
timing 168, 169, 172, 195
toddlers, see young children
touch, see physical contact
touching objects 149, 151
tough love 170, 171
treats 150, 151
  adult's 180, 181–2, 238,
    261
  child's 79, 86, 267
trust 6, 41, 55, 56, 62, 75, 76, 77, 81, 120
  loss of 111

unhappiness 62
United Kingdom 2, 5, 96
unkindness 239, 240
USA 2, 5, 44, 96, 218
victim, attention to 128, 147, 158–60, 206
video games 149, 151
voice, calm 20

waking/sleeping patterns
  92
walking away 95
warmth, emotional 61, 69
  as basic requirement 54, 55, 58
  difficulties in showing 66,
    67
  longing for 66
warnings 28
  five-second 163–4, 194
welfare, child's 13
whining 24
working parents 66, 219, 220, 229, 230

yoga 182
young children
  as physical beings 221–2
  rewards 118
  using Attends with 16–17